BURNUM BURNUM'S
ABORIGINAL AUSTRALIA

A TRAVELLER'S GUIDE

Edited by David Stewart

ANGUS
& ROBERTSON
PUBLISHERS

PROJECT STAFF

EDITOR: David Stewart

EDITORIAL ASSISTANCE: Marji Hill, Al Grassby, Alex Barlow,
Daphne Rawlins, Dr Laila Haglund, Andrew Witton

ART DIRECTION: David Stewart and Margret Mulray

CONSULTANT ART DIRECTORS: Tony Gordon, John Stewart

CARTOGRAPHY: Margret Mulray and Marlo Campbell

ILLUSTRATION: Matt Perry, Margret Mulray

PHOTO RESEARCH: Carmen Ky

PHOTO EDITOR: Andrew Witton

RESEARCH: Australian InFo International

PROJECT COORDINATOR: Peter McGill

This book was designed, typeset and produced on MacIntosh computers,
with the kind assistance of THE ART MACHINE PTY LTD
and WALTER DEBLAERE TYPESETTING PTY LTD.

Clan maps were derived and adapted from a variety of sources
at the Australian Institute of Aboriginal Studies.

This project was produced with the assistance
of the Australian Bicentennial Authority.

ANGUS & ROBERTSON PUBLISHERS

Unit 4, Eden Park, 31 Waterloo Road,
North Ryde, NSW, Australia 2113:
94 Newton Road, Auckland 1,
New Zealand; and
16 Golden Square, London W1R 4BN,
United Kingdom

First published in Australia
by Angus & Robertson Publishers in 1988
Published by arrangement with
Dolphin Publications Pty Ltd,
44 Cowan Drive, Cottage Point,
NSW, Australia 2084

ISBN 0 207 15630 1

Printed in Singapore

Contents

FOREWORD

G'DAY, I'm Burnum Burnum, of the Wurundjeri people, who married a girl from the Yotta Yottas and had children at Wagga Wagga. My mother grew up close to Nowa Nowa, which is just near Mount Baw Baw. I've travelled to Goonoo Goonoo, Kwork Kwork, Yerri Yerri and Bulu Bulu, and once, at the Bong Bong picnic races, I backed a horse in the Melbourne Cup called Gatum Gatum.

For me this book represents a lifetime's work, a journey to find my own roots in this great country. I was born in 1936, under the family gum tree at Mosquito Point, by the side of Wallaga Lake. But, under the policies of the day I was seized by government officials and separated (at 3 months) from my family. For the next ten years I grew up on a mission near Nowra, before being moved to the Kinchela Boys Home, near South West Rocks, where I became the first Aborigine to gain a bronze medallion in surf life saving. My sister was sent to Cootamundra Aboriginal Girls Home, separated from me by more than 1600 kilometres.

In some ways these events, painful as they were (and still are), gave me opportunities I would not have had growing up at Wallaga Lake. After an education at Kempsey Boys Home and the University of Tasmania, I won a Churchill Fellowship (in 1976) and had something of a career in Rugby Union, representing Parramatta Rugby Union Club for many years and New South Wales in 1962. At that time I was known as Harry Penrith, but I changed my name to Burnum Burnum in 1976, in honour of my great grandfather (of the Wurundjeri) and as part of my search to get closer to my own Aboriginality.

This book is the expression of that mission, an attempt to give the traveller a chance to view this extraordinary country as it was seen by the original Australians. On the journey we get a glimpse of the Dreamtime through the oral traditions of many of the nations which made up this great country. The work of archaeologists is also illuminating, as they scrape through layers of history in their own search for the roots of perhaps the most successful people who ever lived on this planet. Modern ecology can learn a great deal from a people who managed and maintained their world so well for 50 000 years.

As we move through the landscape and the traditional lands of the nations who once ruled this continent, we see how they lived, the foods they ate and the traditions which kept their culture alive for so long. Much of this lives on today and Australians are gaining a new pride in their real heritage, the one which covers 2000 generations.

The story has an inevitable edge of sadness, as we understand the process and pattern of dispossession suffered after 1788. This material has been included not to provoke guilt, but to give a perception of the extraordinary differences between the original Australians and the invaders who came in 1788. In most areas of early contact, they were greeted warmly by the Australians, who had no idea that these strange white people intend-

ed to stay. The land had been under their control and guidance going back to the Dreamtime; every hill, valley, river, animal and plant had been placed in the landscape for the use of the people. The thought of somebody arriving from the edge of the ocean to simply take their lands was inconceivable and the reality of their new position was slow to dawn. When it did, resistance grew and we will look at the efforts of several individuals who stood courageously against the invasion and firepower of the Europeans.

We also see the ongoing struggle for land rights, as attempts are made to redress the imbalance of dispossession created by the doctrine of terra nullius, *which meant, literally, that there were no people on the continent. Non-Aboriginal people often find it difficult to understand the traditional relationship between the land and its people. The concept of land ownership, in the western model, was simply beyond the comprehension of the original Australians.*

In Europe, as people developed their civilisation from the caves to the cathedrals, they left clear evidence of their achievement for future generations to admire. In Australia, the land itself is the cathedral and worship is not confined to any four walls. Each step is a prayer and every form in the landscape — and everything that moves in it — were put there specifically for the people to use and manage. And the mythic beings made clear the responsibility of the people in preserving and nurturing the environment. Their success in managing their world so successfully, and sustaining their culture for so long, is now attracting the worldwide respect it deserves.

I hope the reader will find no bitterness in the story: the past cannot be turned back. The story of dispossession is a sad and moving one, but many of the Dreamtime stories are equally tragic. The challenge of the future is the important issue, and an acceptance of the past is the first step to a positive future. Australia is now a mix of many nations (though not as many as in traditional times) and the land is itself the ultimate power. No one people have a sole franchise on the ability to feel an affinity with this timeless landscape.

The reader will notice that I have often used the term Australian to describe the original inhabitants of the continent, which was originally called New Holland by the Europeans.

The 'discovery' of Australia by the Dutch, Portuguese, Spanish and finally the British, provided social darwinists with ideal opportunities to test their theories, particularly as they related to skull size and form. This subtle and academic form of racism has persisted longer than most would acknowledge, influencing the way archaeological discoveries have been interpreted and the needs and opportunites of Aboriginal people assessed. I have personally been asked by European 'scientists' whether they could measure my head size.

As recently as 1902, in the first year of the fledgling Australian parliament, it was argued that there was absolutely no evidence that the Australian Aborigine was even a human being. Thankfully, attitudes have changed since that time, but racism persisted in more subtle ways, particularly when it came to giving Aborigines educational opportunities. Many people, who claimed vehemently that they were not racist, still argued that Aborigines were wonderful, noble desert people, but were just not suited to a university education.

The success of Aboriginal sportsmen and women have given their people a better perception of their own worth. Evonne Goolagong (Cawley), Lionel Rose, Polly Farmer, Dave Sands, Pastor Doug Nicholls (later Governor of South Australia), and the Ella brothers have all won wide respect for their skills. Though even in sport the road has been a rocky one. In the nineteenth century Aboriginal athletes were so good they were excluded (by white administrators) whenever possible. In Queensland, the Amateur Athletic Association, having failed to lock them out on the grounds of being mentally deficient, finally declared all Aborigines to be 'permanent professionals', thereby excluding them from amateur athletics.

Despite the fact that the very first Australian cricket team to tour England was all-Aboriginal, Aborigines have never been given much chance to perform in what was a white man's domain. In the 1930s, an Aboriginal fast bowler called Eddie Gilbert had considerable success playing for Queensland. He once bowled Donald Bradman for a duck. But he was hounded out of the game by allegations of chucking, despite his offers to bowl with his arm in a splint.

My fondest hope is that this book can give some real insight into this wonderfully diverse and challenging land — with all its timeless imagery —and the people who understood it so completely. From the rugged peaks of the Snowy Mountains (where the people once had annual feasts on the bogong moths) to the bunya lands of Queensland; from the stunningly beautifully Katherine Gorge to the staggering Simpson Desert; from an ice age cave in the south-east corner of the continent to the rainforest culture of the north-east, we see cultures of great complexity and discipline.

The journey that unfolds in this book is one of many levels and I hope the reader will have an enriched trip because of it. Along the road you'll need to be respectful of this often harsh and unforgiving land and well prepared for the remote regions. The music of the landscape will touch you and you can choose your own music to travel by, Aboriginal, modern or classic.

Personally, I'd suggest Mozart.

Burnum Burnum

*The western MacDonnell Ranges
in Central Australia. Photo by
AusChromes.*

Introduction

HE traditional view of the Australian continent is one of a dramatic, dry centre surrounded by sunny beaches. But the continent has so much more, from the tropical north to chilly Tasmania and as one explores the subtleties and complexities of the society of the original Australians — who inhabited this continent for some 50 000 years — a growing appreciation is gained of a people totally at one with their world.

These were a people who experienced their land as a nurturing force and a home shared with everything that grew, moved and breathed within it.

Modern science has revealed a great deal about the Australian heritage. It's known that the continent of Australia, including Tasmania and New Guinea, began its process of separation from the Antarctic continent some 50 million years ago and drifted slowly north. It was at this time that the key elements of the Australian landscape were formed: the jagged north/south mountain range, which runs along the east coast, the vast plateau to its west and the shallow depression between them. In the oral traditions of the original Australians the stories which tell of the creation of these landmarks are passed from generation to generation, enshrining deep religious meaning and significance. The stories tell of the creation of the mountains, rivers and waterholes, the plants and animals, indeed all the features of this ancient land. After considerable scientific and archaeological research, scientists have come to a new appreciation of these stories.

This book encompasses a circuit of a vast continent. It's important to understand that just as the appearance of the country changes — sometimes suddenly, sometimes gradually over hundreds of kilometres — so too do the original Australians, who were a people of 600–700 separate nations, mostly with different languages and dialects, and with varying cultures and traditions. As one travels through the landscape, appreciating the art, tools, weapons, lore and lifestyle, there are dual themes of similarity and difference.

Throughout this vast continent with all its contrasts — from arid desert to tropical rainforest — the original Australians developed a workable, stable relationship to their environment. Lifestyles in the north, where monsoonal seasons bring plentiful rainfall, were adapted to that environment; in the south rainfalls and temperatures were generally lower. The summer season is hot all over the continent, except in the highest areas, and hot winds from the centre can create continuous daily temperatures of more than 40 C. The coastal regions were favoured with more moderate climates — cooling winds from the sea generally keep temperatures down along the coast — and with an abundant availability of food. However, even in the most inhospitable regions, the Aborigines managed to evolve a lifestyle which allowed them to flourish in areas considered, even today, to be uninhabitable.

Climate and terrain affect and are in turn affected by the availibility of water. Vast areas of the continent have no continuous water supply, no running rivers. The Great Western Plateau (as the area from western New South Wales and Queensland almost to the west coast of the continent is called by geologists) is typical of this climate: there are streams which flow only after heavy rains — which may come many years apart — and the water generated in them drains into salt lakes and desert country. Although there is little surface water, there are permanent waterholes and there may be water below the bed of a stream long after it has stopped flowing. The Lake Eyre basin is typical of these regions: surface water is rare, though there are periodic heavy rainfalls. This vast stretch of salt crust has streams draining into it from the west, north and east, though they bring very little water, most of it evaporating or soaking into sandy desert. The rivers from the west only flow when there

has been rainfall on the plateau and although the rivers to the north and east flow from mountains which may attract considerable rainfall, and although these rivers may carry the water a long way, it rarely reaches Lake Eyre.

The Channel country, to the north of Lake Eyre, is a maze of meandering, braided streams, which will fill suddenly and overflow the claypans for many kilometres. This spread of fresh water over salt creates a crucial renewal of the land and we see rapid plant growth and much wildlife, especially birds. In dry times the rivers become chains of shrinking waterholes, the best of them fringed with trees and regularly visited by wildlife, which made them excellent resting places for people travelling through the country. Away from streams, people had to depend on permanent waterholes such as seepages or springs in rock outcrops and mountain ridges.

To the west is a vast area of sand dunes called the Simpson Desert. These dunes stand up to 30 metres high, are some 300 kilometres long, and run parallel to each other, lying in a north-south direction. They are so old they seemed etched into the landscape as a permanent form, though modern vehicles and machinery can quickly disturb their shape by breaking the surface and allowing the sand to move. Even in these desert regions there are still plants — clumps of spinifex, shrubs and occasional small trees — as well as many small animals.

The stony desert to the south, covered with a crust of rounded quartzite pebbles, allows very little flora or fauna to survive. This country merges to the

Above *Menindee Lakes, New South Wales. Photo by Grenville Turner.*

Opposite *Sand and spinifex, Simpson Desert, Northern Territory. Photo by Mike Gillam.*

south-west into the Nullarbor Plain, a dry, riverless and almost treeless desert plateau which meets the sea in the Great Australian Bight in sweeping limestone cliffs. These areas, when viewed on a map, look flat and formless and yet when one moves through this landscape there are many undulations — ridges, dunes, channels and dry lake depressions — which can make travel for the inexperienced dangerous.

In the far south-west of the continent, a maze of small mountain ranges attract rainfall and water collects in many small streams. Many of these streams are short and dry up at times, draining into dry or salty lakes, but there are also several permanent rivers, the largest being the Swan River. Well-watered parts of this region are heavily forested — including great karri and jarrah forests — interspersed with extensive areas of scrub and bushland.

The northern part of the continent features higher mountain ranges, which form watersheds and supply a series of major rivers that wind through spectacular gorges and unforgiving deserts. Some of these, like the Murchison, drain into the Indian Ocean, others into the Timor Sea and the Gulf of Carpentaria. Some, like the Ord River, start in the drier inland as a seasonal flow before ending up as large, tidal channels, bordered by mangroves and mudflats. Of those rivers which drain into the gulf, the Roper and Gregory flow

all year round: the rest are mostly seasonal in their upper reaches, comprising chains of often beautiful waterholes. Other rivers meander across broad expanses of coastal mudflats, saltpans and mangrove swamps before reaching the sea. Monsoonal forests of paperbarks and pandanus palms fringe these waterways. During the wet season the low-lying regions become impassable, reverting to swamps during the dry season.

Inland from the coast are regions of woodland and savannah, which may be very dry for much of the year, but burst into flower with each wet season. The mountainous areas and inland slopes behind the coastal plain have sub-humid and semi-arid woodlands, grading into wide grasslands towards the dry centre.

It's only on the east and south-east coasts that perennial rivers are common. Fed by the watershed of the Great Dividing Range, these rivers are sometimes short and fast, like the Tully and the Barwon (where the Divide is close to the coast), or slow and twisting, like the Burdekin or the Nepean, meandering quietly to the coast through deep pools and basins. The rain caught in the mountains supports extensive rainforests in north Queensland. These forests become less exuberant, and poorer in species, further south.

Away from the rainforests we find a patchwork of sclerophyll forests of varying kinds and scrubby bushland, though much of this has been cleared for farming during the past two hundred years.

Top *Millaa Millaa Falls, north Queensland.*
Right *Minyon Falls rainforest, northern New South Wales.*
Photos by Tony Gordon.

The highest parts of the Great Dividing Range are in the south-east of the continent and are treeless (and snow-covered in winter), though they carry a profusion of herbs and low shrubby plants during summer. Along much of the south-eastern and south-ern part of the Divide, the dense vegetation is in the valleys, which are often steep-sided. The lower ridge tops carry open forest or woodland and offered better country for those moving through the mountains.

The longest watercourse in Australia, the Murray/Darling system, rises in the Great Divide, south-west of Brisbane, and runs south-west into the ocean, south of Adelaide. The river starts as a series of slow and silty streams, but further south, fresh, clear water comes into the system from the mountain creeks and rivers. This river system is bordered by vast areas of floodplain.

Just as modern Australians have spread around the coastline in their development of the continent, so the original Australians chose to live along the coasts and rivers. During their long, unchallenged position on the continent, they were forced to constantly move and adapt to changing coastlines, rivers and, eventually, to the arrival of the Europeans.

Above right *Simpsons Gap, Northern Territory.*
Photo by Robbi Newman.
Right *Australia's rugged north-west costline.*
Photo by Bill Bachman.
Below *Jim Jim Gorge, in Kakadu National Park, Northern Territory. Photo by Philip Green.*

The peopling of Australia

The origin and age of the original Australians has been a source of considerable academic debate, particularly since 1965, when archaeologists began to write a new prehistory for Australia.

At that time it was believed that life on the Australian continent had a timespan of some 10 000 years, but discoveries at Lake Mungo and later at Willandra Lakes have forced a significant re-evaluation of these dates. It is known that the first humans reached these shores at least 40 000 years ago, and probably around 53 000 years ago, when the water levels around the continent of Australia were at their lowest.

This was during the last of the Ice Ages, when changes in sunshine and temperature — which brought cold and snow — locked up vast amounts of water in gigantic sheets of ice covering the coldest parts of the world and all the highest mountains. As the sea receded, islands turned into hills and for a long time it was possible to walk from New Guinea to Tasmania. But once the end of the Ice Age arrived, around 25,000 years ago, and the waters began to rise again, the coastline changed once more and the hills gradually turned back into islands. It was during this time that Tasmania was cut off, and islands such as Kangaroo Island and those of the Dampier Archipelago formed.

In the Arnhem Land region, many stories have been retainded of the first people, who came from across the seas. Right across northern Australia one of the major themes of the Dreamtime legends concerns the arrival of the great Earth Mother, a symbol of fertility and the creator of life.

Among the Gagadju people of Arnhem Land, her name was Imberombera and she came from across the sea arriving on the coast of Arnhem Land with her womb full of children. According to legend, she trav-elled far and wide, forming the hills, creeks, plants and animals and leaving behind many of her spirit children, with a different language in each group.

So, if the original Australians arrived here 50 000 years ago, from where did they come? We know that they could not have walked here, because during the last 3 million years there has been no complete land bridge between Australia and Asia. For some 40 million years the Australian continent has been drifting steadily north towards Asia, a process which continues today, at the rate of five centimetres a year.

Scientists believe that for the last 3 million years there has never been much less than 100 kilometres of open water separating Australia from Asia. This is confirmed by the lack of any Asian animal species in Australia, other than the dingo, which we know arrived in Australia less than 12 000 years ago and was probably brought across in the company of humans.

It is also known that human existence in Asia goes back a million years at least, so the clear possibility exists that the narrowing barriers of water were finally breached by humans in boats, sailing south from Asia.

These first boat people would have landed on the continental shelf which is now under the sea. The rapid rise in the waters as the ice and snow melted would have been noticeable in a single lifetime. These people managed to sustain life in the coastal regions, but they also spread throughout the continent in a relatively short period and adapted with great resourcefulness to the challenge of living in drier areas.

Since the discovery of the first Pleistocene human skull in Australia in 1886 argument has raged about origins. Subsequent finds in Cohuna (1925), Keilor (1940) and Kow Swamp (1967) — all in Victoria — and

Once upon a time, at Lake Mungo

ILLUSTRATION BY MATT PERRY

Australia is the world's driest inhabited continent, but that was not always so. Before the last Ice Age, the climate was quite different. The rainfall in inland areas was greater than today, and temperatures and evaporation levels were lower. This was especially so in the semi-arid belt that fringes the dry heart of the continent, such as the area of Lake Mungo, in western New South Wales. This area once had abundant water and huge lakes teeming with fish. Now dry, Lake Mungo would have been 20 kilometres long, 10 kilometres wide and up to 15 metres deep. The lake was full of water for around 100 000 years, until 25 000 years ago when the temperature across the continent began to rise and the water to fall. There is no evidence that the area was inhabited by humans before 50 000 years ago, though it was occupied continually from then until the drying process began.

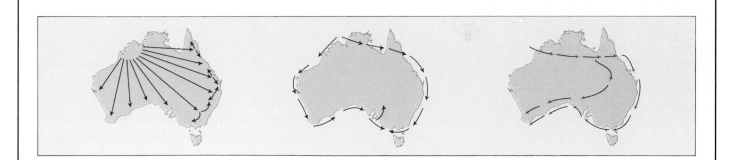

Patterns of immigration

Many theories have been offered for the pattern of occupation of the Australian continent, despite the lack of clearcut evidence in the archaeological record. The first was by an American anthropologist Joseph Birdsell (left), who proposed a radiation model for the spread of humans throughout Australia from an arrival on the north-west coast. This theory was challenged by Sandra Bowdler, whose pattern of occupation (centre) follows a coastal spread by a people adapted to living in coastal regions. The archaeological record, with a distribution of ancient sites along the coast and up major river valleys (with none in the arid inland) tend to support this viewpoint, although a lack of inland archaeological research leaves the issue open. David Horton's model of occupation (right) is based on a people with an all-purpose economy who moved into Australia through the well-watered regions on both sides of the Great Dividing Range, penetrating all but the arid centre of the continent by 25 000 years ago. Then, when the inland began to dry up, they retreated to the coastal regions, before moving back some 12 000 years ago, when the current climate was established. This theory has problems also: no sites older than 25 000 years have been found far inland, nor do inland areas appear to have been left after 25 000 years ago. Other scientists have pointed to the Cape York Peninsula as a likely entry point into Australia.

then at Lake Mungo (1974), contributed to the creation of a fascinating riddle for archaeologists.

These skulls appeared to divide into two very different groups, termed by archaeologists the 'robust' and the 'gracile'. The robust characteristics are the projecting eyebrow ridges, sloping forehead and thick bone. The gracile skulls are more 'advanced' in evolutionary terms, with finer bone, less pronounced brow ridges and an upright forehead. That these two types of skull types should be found in the archaeological record was not a surprise: the problem was that the rugged, robust and archaic skulls found at Kow Swamp and Cohuna were much younger than the gracile skulls found at Lake Mungo. This troubles archaeologists greatly as it was the reverse of what they would expect to find.

A changing continent

The ocean's water level has fluctuated widely over the last million years as a result of several glacial periods. This diagram shows the shape of the Australian and Asian continents when the water level was 100 metres below current levels. Although it was possible to walk from Burma to Bali and from New Guinea to Tasmania, there remained a clear gap between the continents of Australia and Asia. It is clear that Tasmania was populated during the Ice Age when a complete land bridge existed between Tasmania and the mainland. This bridge disappeared under water around 12 000 years ago.

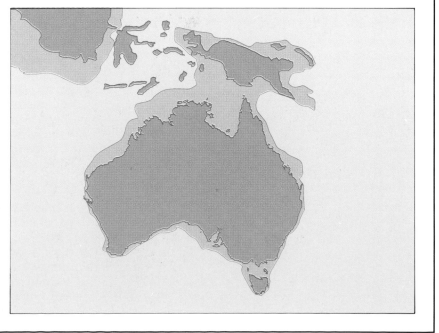

The puzzle was answered, in the view of some, by the discovery of a new skull at Willandra Lakes. This skull, called Willandra Lakes hominid 50 (the 50th skull found in the area) which had opalised (the normal phosphate had been replaced by silicates), suggested great antiquity. And the skull was far more robust and archaic than any other found in Australia.

More recent studies of a greater number of skeletons, with allowances for more variables (relating to bone size, structure and shape), have shown that, on the whole, the various fossil examples fit within the broad range of variation found in recent Aboriginal populations. Differences in shape have been found to be concentrated on the face and such variations seem to be interrelated; a large lower jaw (to hold large teeth) is matched by the upper jaw, and the muscles holding the jaw need to be attached to massive bony ridges.

Other recent studies have concentrated on biochemical traits, such as bloodgroup antigens, serum protein groups and red cells, as well as serum enzyme groups. Again, the results have proved inconclusive, with differences found often contradictory. We can conclude that there is no clear evidence of the existence of two well-defined and significantly different prehistoric groups of people.

It is worth noting that differences in bone size and morphology are known to develop over time in response to differences in diet and climate. The effects of genetic drift working on a small founding population — and, later on, splinter groups isolated by rising seas — could also account for some of the differences found. Variations in bone structure, colouring and hair can depend on quite small and limited genetic differences, while even quite complex biochemical differences may show up only through extensive tests. But early physical anthropologists had to be satisfied with studying the visible differences and so came to over emphasise these.

There have also been theories that a founding population entered Australia some 70 000 years ago, followed by a second wave 20 000 years later. Some have even proposed an initial entry at least 120 000 years ago, but both proposals remain totally speculative as no evidence has been found to support them. Indeed, several sites with sediments and charcoal from about 120 000 years ago have been explored without any clear evidence of human occupation.

Although scientists are convinced that our ancestors came from Asia, they have been unable to single out a group of Asian people who fulfil the requirements of an originating race.

Of all the facts, figures and theories, nothing contradicts Aboriginal oral traditions, which record their passage to Australia a very long time ago, before time could be counted, in the Dreamtime.

A cave painting in Kakadu National Park, showing Imberombera releasing the children from her womb, each with a different language. Photo by Carmen Ky.

Insights in Tasmania

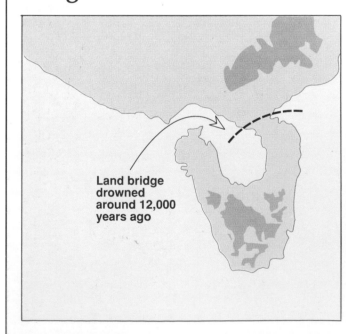

Land bridge drowned around 12,000 years ago

Until 12 000 years ago it was possible to walk from Victoria into Tasmania, via a continuous land bridge, which even today is only 100 metres below the surface of the water. Archaeological sites show human occupation as far back as 25 000 years ago. At this time the temperatures were significantly colder than today; in fact Tasmania represents the southernmost point of occupation in the world at a time when icebergs littered the waters and glaciers covered the highlands. But the people stayed and those who were still there 12 000 years ago lost the option to move as the land bridge was closed by rising waters. Tasmanian Aborigines of the nineteenth century were considered by early observers to be 'the world's most primitive people'. It has been suggested, however, that their use of a bare mimimum of different tools may be more a testimony of skill. The Tasmanians survived 15 000 years of ice and 12 000 years of isolation; 200 years of European occupation has proved a greater trauma.

Animals of the Dreamtime

Aboriginal oral traditions abound with stories of the mythical beings of the Dreamtime, stories which have been passed from generation to generation and may enshrine memories of the giant creatures which once roamed the continent.

The archaeological record documents the existence of these giant marsupials in Australia 50 000 years ago, the time when humans probably arrived here. These slow giants would have been easy prey for hunters and it's likely that the process of extinction was hastened by the arrival of man.

Those of the giant marsupials which survived the human depredations were further jeopardised with the change of climate during the last Ice Age, some 15 000 to 25 000 years ago. These animals probably needed large amounts of water and herbage, so as the waterholes and lakes dried up their habitat quickly disappeared. It appears some species of megafauna found refuge in the heavily wooded areas along the coast, as they survived there significantly longer than in the arid inland.

The first evidence of these megafauna was found in a cave west of Sydney by Sir Thomas Mitchell, then Surveyor-General of New South Wales, who discovered the tooth of a *Diprotodon optatum* — the largest marsupial known to have lived. These animals were then assumed to be still in existence and when inland journeys were undertaken, encounters with them were expected.

The largest was the *Diprotodon optatum,* a wombat-like browser of rhinoceros proportions, but the most numerous were the giant kangaroos and wallabies, the Macropodidae, which means 'big feet'. The largest was *Procoptodon goliah,* a huge kangaroo some 3 metres tall, with a broad, short face and powerful jaws.

There were at least three fossil species of giant echidna, *Zaglossus. Megalania,* a goanna which grew to at least 6 metres, with sharp teeth and claws, once roamed the continent in safety. Among the birds which have disappeared was *Genyornis,* a large and flightless bird with a heavy beak, similar to the moa of New Zealand.

Thylacoleo, a predator, was the size of a leopard, with powerful teeth and claws, but it disappeared around 15 000 years ago. Some animals survived longer in Tasmania, the best known being the Tasmanian devil, *Sarcophilus* (which survived until a few hundred years ago on the mainland and is still thriving in Tasmania), and the Tasmanian tiger (or wolf), *Thylacinus.* This animal has been the subject of 'sightings' on the mainland in recent times, though the youngest bones yet found are at least 3000 years old.

There has been considerable argument about the part that the Aborigines played in the extinction of these animals. It's clear that three factors were involved: depredations by hunters, change of climate and habitat alteration by man-made fires. There is some doubt that human intervention was a major factor. However, about one-third of the giant animals that existed 50 000 years ago, at the time humans first arrived here, had been wiped out by 15 000 years ago. In western New South Wales, most of the giant marsupials had disappeared before 25 000 years ago (and before the lakes and water-holes dried up), which indicates that human intervention was at least a contributing factor.

ILLUSTRATION BY MATT PERRY

Insights from Archaeology

The original Australians have left many traces of their presence in the landscape, but clear determinations of their meaning are difficult. There are no ruined cities of stone or pyramids which dominate the surrounding land, but there is a considerable heritage of spectacular rock art, which honours the mythology of the landscape and the spiritual relationship between the people and their land. There are also ceremonial sites, often with arrangements of rocks or earth mounds, which form an integral part of the lore and law which orders traditional Aboriginal life.

Such places of importance, or other areas which show occupation or use at some point in the past, are often called Aboriginal sites. In much of the popular press this has been simplified to 'sacred sites', which creates immediate misconceptions. Some sites are truly sacred and of great religious significance, particularly to those Aborigines bound to that site by right and responsibility. Others have great spiritual and emotional importance to Aborigines from all over the country, such as the Lake Mungo campsites. These places represent symbols of antiquity, though there are many other sites which have substantial evidence of practical, everyday living.

Most of the evidence from these sites comes from the refuse the people discarded, particularly bone and shell fragments. This shows us food sources, climate and lifestyle. Archaeologists can sometimes determine how often a site was used and at what times of the year, and guess the size of the group, how the food was prepared and what foods was eaten by a particular group. In some sites, there is clear evidence that people came to an area from far afield for one particular food. In Victoria, this was the annual bogong moth feast: in Queensland, the bunya nut festival.

The shape of tools and the indications of 'wear and tear' also give us insights to the use of these

Top *Lake Mungo today. Photo by AusChromes.*
Above *A cave in Kakadu National Park which was in use until 40 years ago. Photo by Carmen Ky.*

Sacred sites

The concept of sacred sites is difficult for non-Aboriginal people to understand. A sacred site is a place where Aboriginal people find a manifestation of divine power, a sense of contact with a creative force.

In the traditional view, all of nature is sacred, but in certain places the spirit power manifests itself more readily. These are the places where the great events of creation history took place, and the landscape itself is a network of potent locations, linked by the paths of the ancestral creators.

It was these spirits, or ancestral beings, that created the totems, which may be an insect, bird, fish, reptile or mammal. Members of a group share a common totem — in the case of my group it's Umbarra, the black duck — and these totems have been inherited since the dreaming creation. Each member of the group also has his or her individual totem. My own is the black crow, chosen for me by my grandfather.

Sacred sites also marked nation and clan areas and within these boundaries we felt safe, because our totemic ancestors were a source of constant comfort and security. Moving outside these areas was difficult.

Sacred ceremonies, social ceremonies and other rituals are events of great importance and are planned and conducted by the elders. Sometimes these events relate to local clans, at other times many clans and nations are involved. In the past, invitations were issued with message sticks or smoke signals and considerable planning was put into these events. Groups would travel great distances to attend such ceremonies as guests.

Bora grounds

In eastern Australia there are still remains of bora grounds, places for ceremony and initiation. These were areas of great significance, and traditional life was severely interrupted in the areas where such grounds were taken over by European settlers. These places are no longer made or used, though their use was documented by early white settlers.

The grounds were made up of two rings, outlined with mounds of earth and linked by a path. The larger ring was for everybody, the smaller ring — kept out of sight — was used by the initiated men and boys for the secret ceremonies. Sometimes one ring was made for ceremonies and formal fights, which were often a part of the ceremony and carried out according to strict rules.

Other ceremonial grounds, some of them like bora grounds in shape, were made with rocks. Archaeologists group all stone constructions which formed a part of traditional Aboriginal life as 'stone arrangements'. Some were clearly for practical purposes, such as stone fish traps and weirs, which made easy the harvest of fish or eels. But there are other arrangements which express religious and ceremonial aspects of life: we find stones in circles, semicircles, lines and complicated patterns. Many of these stone arrangements resulted from considerable effort and co-operation: large stones have been rearranged or set upright, others have been transported over long distances.

Earth mounds, stone cairns and carved trees sometimes mark burial sites, but the bones and ashes of the dead were buried in unmarked graves, or left in secluded caves or rock clefts. Specific areas were set aside as burial grounds in some areas, the choice being at least partly dependent on the role of the dead person within that group.

Above right *A bora ceremony. From the Tyrrell Collection, courtesy Macleay Museum.*
Right *Two boys are carried in the circle prior to initiation. From the Crooks Collection, courtesy Macleay Museum.*

tools. Even the charcoal in the fires can be helpful. It can be used for dating the fires and tells scientists what woods were burnt and what trees grew nearby. Sometimes nuts and seeds fell into the fire and were preserved, rather than being eaten or rotting away.

With archaeological study of the first Australians in its infancy, it's important to remember that these sites carry significant keys to the mysteries of Australia's antiquity and need to be preserved and respected by all those who visit them. Even scratching around in the surface can destroy the patterns and interconnections which are the only means of telling the story. Once lost, they are lost forever.

The climate which predominates through much of Australia necessitates cool, sheltered places to live, protected from the cold winds but with sun for the early and late cool of the day. Naturally occurring shelters such as caves and overhangs provide many such locations and were used by Aborigines over

thousands of years. Many of these sites are still intact, but others have been disturbed by animals and others destroyed by farming, mining and building.

So often, through rural Australia, one will find a homestead, positioned on a small hill, overlooking the river (but above flood levels), with wide views in several directions. Such sites are high enough to catch a breeze which will keep mosquitos away, yet below the ridge behind, to provide protection from storms. Many of these homesteads have probably been built on top of an Aboriginal site. In areas settled by Europeans, the old campsites which remain are probably in locations which would have been second-best or in less accessible spots.

A modern aspect of the problem facing archaeologists working on Australia's heritage is the reticence of farmers to declare evidence of Aboriginal occupation on their land for fear (due to misinformation) of facing a claim against the land as a sacred site.

The nomadic lifestyle

Archaeological sites across the country reveal insights to the lifestyles of the original Australians. Much of this supports the traditional view of the hunter/gatherer nomad, but there are also indications that these people were constantly developing new tools and food sources. Through networks of contact they traded items of use, such as good quality stone, which could only be obtained from certain quarries. They also exchanged gifts, stories and ceremonies.

The pattern of movement through the country depended on the resources and climate of each region. In arid areas, where food and water were in short supply, there was a nomadic pattern of survival; but on well-watered coasts and rivers relatively permanent settlements were possible. In areas where

bountiful fresh water and food were available all year round, a group might have a series of semi-permanent camps and move from one to another according to available animals, fish and plants. Some camps were described by early white settlers as villages of permanent huts, which were left empty at times and then re-used. Some archaeologists have observed that many Aboriginal groups were in the process of abandoning the nomadic tradition at the time of the European invasion. In Victoria many examples of sophisticated stone dwellings have been found. Moving camp was often necessitated by the 'fouling' of the surroundings by permanent settlement. It was as much a matter of hygiene as necessity, and once abandoned, the camp refuse would decay, lose its smell and become a part of the process of soil renewal. It seems they had a clear concept of recycling waste in this way and an understanding of when each camp would be ready for re-occupation.

There are many place names which are based on words which mean 'a fouled place' or something similar and probably came about through conversations between whites and Aborigines, where descriptions were misinterpreted as place names. It's likely that if the same questions had been asked at another time, the answer would have been different.

Top *Children feast on lily fronds, Groote Eylandt.*
Left *Stripping paperbark for a canoe. Photos by Thomas Dick, courtesy The Australian Museum.*
Opposite *Four portraits, with a variety of headdress. Photos by Charles Kerry, courtesy National Library of Australia (top), and The Australian Museum (bottom).*

Australian art

A priceless heritage

The extraordinary art of the original Australians is a rich tapestry of lifestyle, culture and spirituality which has only come to be fully appreciated in recent times. The originality and complexity of this artistic achievement has done much to force a worldwide re-evaluation of the first Australians, particularly by those who were eager to deny these people the imagination and skill to produce such art.

Art represents an intrinsic part of Aboriginal culture and is found throughout the continent in a wide variety of styles and techniques. While some art may have been created for the sheer pleasure of making something beautiful, the predominant motivation was a religious commitment to spiritual mythology.

It is likely that artistic expression has been a part of Aboriginal culture for a very long time. Red ochre was, after all, used in burial ceremonies at Lake Mungo 30 000 years ago. Much of the art created has perished; some because of natural weathering or vandalism, some because it was frail and never meant to last, as for example body painting or the patterns created on the floor of ceremonial grounds. Images have a better chance of surviving if they have been engraved in or applied to stable rock faces. But it takes a combination of lucky circumstance and scientific technique to provide a secure date to an example of prehistory art, and these are rare.

Prehistoric flintminers made squiggly patterns on the walls of Koonalda Cave, rubbing their fingers against the soft, damp limestone or cutting lines with sharp pieces of flint. Several kinds of circumstantial evidence suggest this happened some 20 000 years ago. And Aborigines who visited a cave in Cracroft Valley in Tasmania (sometime during the last Ice Age) left red ochre hand stencils on the walls of the cave. The stencils, some 12–20 000 years old, have become blurred and encrusted with stalactites, establishing that they are no recent addition. The treeless valley of the Ice Age has since filled with dense rainforest.

Engravings in the Early Man Shelter, near Laura (in northern Queensland) were partly buried by archaeological deposit, and this shows that some of the engravings must be at least 13 000 years old. There are several examples of art that is at least 5000 years old and, with luck (and research), more examples of ancient art are sure to be found.

It has been suggested that some early engravings and paintings depict now extinct animals, or that the images must be old because they show what are assumed to be extinct animals. The large size of some of these images, and the engravings of tracks, has been taken as evidence that these images depict some of the huge animals (for example, the Diprotodon and the gigantic bird, Genyornis) that still existed during the early period of Aboriginal settlement of the continent. But there are equally large images of human shape and also giant human footprints — often in the same locality. Traditional songs and stories describe spiritual ancestors and culture heroes (in animal and human form) as gigantic and it would be fitting to

The huge Wandjina paintings of the Kimberley have attracted world-wide interest ever since their discovery in 1838 by Sir George Grey. The figures are painted on a white background as a thick line design. The eyes and nose form one unit, but the mouth is always excluded. The body, when added, is small in proportion to the head.

In the Lake Eyre region, the Diyuri people sculptured toas as signposts. Each toa — and some 400 have been preserved — indicates a particular locality, according to topographical character and events which took place in the Dreamtime.

In the x-ray art of western Arnhem land, so-called because internal bone structure and organs are partially depicted, there is a commitment to detail and grandeur in the depiction of the kangaroos, crocodiles barramundi, tortoises, goannas, emus and other birds. Immense numbers of paintings in this style are found in the South and East Alligator Rivers and Coopers Creek areas and their watersheds.

The Laura region of north-east Queensland is the home of some of the most spectacular rock paintings found anywhere on the continent. Hundreds of painted caves have been discovered in which ther are naturalistic paintings of gigantic figures.

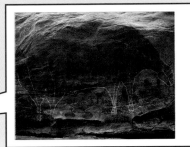

In western New South Wales, a series of rock engravings featuring linear designs and motifs have been found around waterholes and creekbeds. Similar sites have been discovered in eastern South Australia. Stencil images are also popular.

The engravings of the Sydney-Hawkesbury region are among the most varied and imaginative to be found anywhere in the world. Throughout the area, innumerable flat or gently sloping surfaces created an ideal medium and some 4000 figures have been documented. These engravings have left a record of religious and economic life and an enduring reminder of the occupation of the region.

depict that size in any images. The tradition may have been inspired by knowledge of extinct, gigantic animals, but so far no picture has been identified with any certainty as showing a particular species. The evidence for interpreting some images as thylacines (Tasmanian tigers) is much stronger — but this animal was present also on the mainland until a few thousand years ago.

Three basic methods were used for engraving: friction (pushing an implement horizontally across

the face of the stone), percussion (vertical hammering) and drilling.

The most spectacular expressions of Aboriginal art are found in rock paintings from the Kimberleys to the east coast, their appearance dictated mainly, though not exclusively, by the availability of suitable rock surfaces. Paintings are found in caves and rock shelters and on exposed walls and are used to retain knowledge, to depict achievements and express desire. Subjects include the animals of their world; kangaroos, snakes, echidna, lizards, emus and other birds, as well as fish, dolphins, whales and sharks are all popular elements and recur all over the country.

Aboriginal rock art represents a psychological and ritualistic link between the living and the dead, a binding connection between the present culture and its mythological origin. Some ceremonies are based around the repainting of the symbols of the Dreamtime spirits.

In many areas of the continent, the rock art depicts great spirit beings of the Dreamtime. These expressions vary from the spectacular Wandjina art of the Kimberleys to the haunting images of the Quinkan galleries on Cape York and the larger-than-life spirit figures, mainly engraved, found around Sydney (but also in the north). Another notable variation of this theme is found in the remarkable x-ray paintings found in western Arnhem Land.

Shelters with art occur in many different types of location. Some are hidden away and difficult to get to; others are near the base of a cliff or just below the

Top *Giant wallaroo gallery, Cape York Peninsula. Photo by Jutta Malnic.*
Left *Mythological dogs, moulded from spinifex resin, Lake Eyre, South Australia. Courtesy South Australian Museum.*

crest, within easy reach and enjoying a splendid view of the valley below. Some of these shelters have bare rock floors and it is clear that no one camped here. Other painting sites were used for many generations.

In many areas rock paintings represent the work of many generations, over thousands of years. The older works are believed to have been completed in the Dreamtime by the spirit beings. In Arnhem Land, for example, all unfamiliar art was considered to have been painted by the Mimi spirit people.

Rock art was the concern of men and so shellfish and plants, which were the domain of women, are the rarest subjects for rock art. Men chose to depict their world in these images, and so concentrated on hunting, fishing and dancing as the subjects for art. Many sites in north, central and western Australia still play an active role in the religious experience of the people. Often it was only the deepest meaning of these paintings which was kept secret from all other than those entitled and trained to understand it.

The most popular painting technique is stencilling, which is found all over the continent. The stencils are made by blowing either powdered or liquid pigment (from the mouth or from a sheet of bark) around an object held against the rock. This process creates a spotty coloration on the face of the rock which is thickest near the outline of the stencilled objects. The human hand, usually the left, is the most popular subject, along with boomerangs.

Above right *Figures at Mount Grenfell, New South Wales. Photo by Jutta Malnic.*
Right *X-ray art, Arnhem Land. Photo by AusChromes.*

Colours and Pigments

The rock paintings of the original Australians demonstrate ingenious use of available materials.The most popular colours are red, white, black and yellow, which are found throughout the continent, although different regions favour varying mixes and pigments. Mostly they used dry or raw pigments, but they also mixed paint. Some areas provided an abundant supply of natural pigments, whereas other clans had to trade with neighbours or undertake long journeys to gather painting pigments.

Black is easily obtained from charcoal, white from pipeclay, gypsum or burnt selenite. Yellow was the most difficult to obtain and occurs least often: deposits of yellow ochre in Arnhem Land were regarded as totemic centres, the ochre being deposited there by mythological beings. Purple and brown are obtained from ochres and the blue, in the Kimberleys, comes from glauconite. The blues of north Queensland derive from an ochre on the Johnstone River. It is the red ochres, which vary from pink to a deep reddish brown, that are so representative of Aboriginal painting.

The colours vary with the origin of the ochres, derived from manganese, iron oxide and ferruginous sandstone. Red was also obtained by burning

Kakadu National Park. Photo by Colin Beard.

yellow ochre, clay and rocks, and in the Adelaide district decorative reds were obtained from the bulbous roots of plants. Once obtained, the pigments were broken up into powders on a portable stone mortar, then mixed with water. In areas where water was scarce, the powder was mixed with the fat of fish, emu, possum or goanna. Coastal tribes often mixed the paint in shells. The paint was applied with a finger, a brush (made of a twig chewed and teased out at the end) or with feathers tied to the end of a stick.

Charcoal and lumps of ochre were also used as crayons for drawing on rocks and for decorating the body, possessions and sacred objects.

Tools and weapons

The original Australians, over thousands of years, developed a set of tools and implements ideally suited to their needs. A great variety of materials from land and sea were used to make these implements and a great deal of skill was required for some items. These Aborigines knew which rocks to use and how to shape them, which plants contained valuable resins and how to extract them, as well as the subtle skills required to shape the arms of a boomerang or to fashion a new spear. They extracted usable fibres from plants and made watertight containers out of porous materials. Almost everything they made was constructed to be as light as possible and preferably to be useful for more than one purpose.

Around the country, implements vary according to local materials and use. Nets and spears for hunting are usually different to those used for fishing. In most groups, women had the major role in food gathering, and most of their work was done with a simple digging stick, pointed and often hardened in the fire. Containers were also important — mainly dilly bags or baskets of bark or plaited fibres (sometimes waterproofed with gum) — to carry shellfish, berries and nuts, fruit and herbs back to the camp. Bowls and dishes were made of bark or wood, often by prising off big burls, removing the bark and scooping out the fibres from inside.

The big bowls are also used for winnowing seeds and mixing flour to a dough. Net bags may be used to soak nuts in water to leach out poison and make them edible. In the past, all cooking was done on the coals and ashes of a fire or in earth ovens.

In many areas women still do a lot of the fishing, usually with hook and line or nets. Where once they made fish hooks by filing holes in circles cut from turban shells, now the steel hook is ubiquitous. All kinds of fibre and fur, even human hair, are used for spinning cord and lines. Some of these are used for practical purposes, but some, especially spun hair, is made into belts or decorations such as necklaces and headbands, perhaps with beads and feathers added. Net bags are also decorated with colours.

Nets are used on land and in the water, by both men and women. Long nets with wide mesh were used in kangaroo and wallaby drives, while nets with finer mesh were set across rivers and streams to catch fish. These nets took a great deal of time to make and are rarely produced today, though early white explorers noted the fine nets they saw.

In the colder south of the continent, from Perth right across to Sydney, Aborigines once made elaborate possum and kangaroo skin cloaks, constructed from many skins, scraped and sewn together with the fur inwards, towards the body. The outer surface was often incised and decorated with red ochre patterns.

The men were responsible for tracking and killing larger game, so they usually carried less than the women since speed often made the difference in a hunt. Spears were manufactured with considerable care. They varied from the simple, straight stick with a fire-hardened tip, to elaborate spears with shafts of several materials and ornate or multi-pronged heads. If it is difficult to find a straight piece of suitable tough wood, a spear shaft can be straightened by careful heating and bending. Part of the shaft might

Grinding stones and chipping flakes, Port Macquarie, New South Wales. Photo by Thomas Dick, courtesy The Australian Museum.

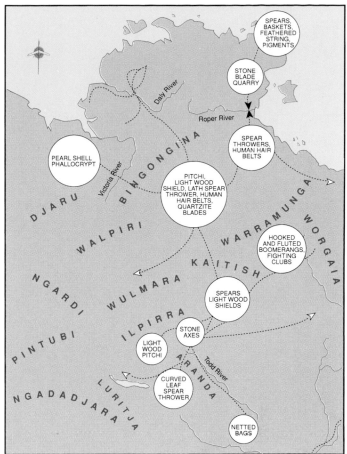

Above *Traditional patterns of trade in central Australia.*
Left *A successful hunting mission. Photos by Thomas Dick, courtesy The Australian Museum.*

be bamboo or the flower stem of a grass tree, to keep it light, and the rest hardwood. The head might be stone or bone, chipped or ground to a point (or steel when they could get it), with barbs of stone or bone, depending on the use of the spear. In the north, special spears with strong harpoon heads (fixed with twine) were made for hunting dugong. Gum (a kind of resin) or fresh kangaroo sinews can be used to bind the parts together. As the resin cools, it hardens, and as the sinews dry, they shrink, making it secure.

Spears are used for hunting, fishing, fighting and ceremonies. The heads and shafts are sometimes elaborately carved and painted and the spears can vary greatly in length, from 2 metres to 4 metres, depending on their purpose and available materials.

There is also great variation in the style of spearthrowers or woomeras. Some are narrow, like a spear; others are broad and form a shallow basin. In most areas, they were used for several purposes: for working wood, as a mixing bowl for pigment or for ash and native tobacco. The side could also be used as a shovel or broom for scraping the ground clear in camp or when preparing for ceremonies. The spearthrower was also used as the hard friction-edge rubbed against softer wood when making fire.

Boomerangs have become a famous symbol of the original Australians, but as far as is known, their use was not general at the time of the European colonisation. On the other hand, several boomerangs have been excavated from a 10 000-year-old camp site at Wyrie Swamp, in South Australia. It is normal for wood to decay, but these boomerangs have been perfectly preserved in peat.

Across the continent we find many kinds and shapes of boomerangs, but only some are made to

return. Most are used for hunting, although some are made, usually in pairs, to be used as musical instruments in ceremonies. The classic boomerang has a shape of great beauty, and they were often elaborately decorated with engraved or painted patterns.

Clubs vary in design and use. Some are flat, almost like a boomerang, with one broad tip; others have a thick heavy head. Simple clubs are a part of the hunt, for killing wounded game or small animals. Elaborate and elegantly carved clubs are used for ceremonies.

Stone was ground or chipped to make tools for scraping skins, working wood and cutting meat. Shell and bone were used a great deal, but fewer have survived the passage of time than stone implements. One can only marvel at some examples of the fine stone spearheads which have been found in the Kimberleys and applaud the skill involved in such fine work.

When it came to a fight, spears, clubs and boomerangs were used, but shields were important for warding off blows or turning spears away. Shields can be broad, often of softwood and designed to take a blow (or stop a spear), or narrow, often in harder wood, a design for parrying. They are usually decorated, often with totemic designs, and are not usually carried all the time. Depending on the type of shield and wood used, they could also be used for music and making fire. In north-east Queensland, big 'swords' — hard and heavy — were used in formal fights.

Lifeways

Western society holds, and has held, several remarkably different views of Aboriginal lifestyles, past and present. They range from describing traditional lifestyles as bleak, wretched and brutish and the people themselves as ugly, mean, cowardly and weak-witted, to painting a romantic picture of a proud, free, harmonious people living in complete balance with nature in some earthly paradise, devoid of care or strife. The image of present-day Aboriginal society tends more towards the bleak and brutish. What the images have in common is the lumping together of all Aborigines and their lifestyles.

Aborigines are not a group of clones — they are people with personalities as varied as you would find in any other society. With so many different personalities in such vast and varied environment, over such a long time, it is only to be expected that many and varied patterns were developed for all aspects of social and economic life. We can say that a major difference between the broad pattern of Aboriginal life and those of the Europeans showed in the contrasting ways they balanced their social and economic organisation.

The great complexity of Aboriginal social organisation, with its networks of contacts, rights and obligations (relevant to the landscape as well as to persons), balanced life when times became difficult because of drought, floods and similar disaster. This made a complex economy — in terms of production, storage and distribution techniques — unnecessary. And this pattern is a complete reverse to that of the invading British, with their wide commercial and industrial motivations and patchy interest in the social welfare of the citizens.

However, the traditional Aboriginal economy was much more complex and varied than most textbooks have described it. Some white explorers and early administrators described villages of finely constructed huts, methods of harvesting and storing grass seeds to prolong the season by many months, as well as complicated fish and game traps. Some of the fish traps, as at Brewarrina, still exist, though damaged by time and vandals. In Victoria, a vast network of canals and ponds, which brought eels across a mountain range to be stored and harvested at will, has been discovered and partly excavated. Gradually it is dawning on the outside world that life in the traditional Aboriginal way involved a great deal of knowledge and skill.

So why has this been completely forgotten? There are probably many reasons. The most obvious is that the areas grabbed first by the new settlers were those richest in water and food resources, where a group needed a fairly small territory to get a reasonable living and could stick to a few semi-permanent villages as base camps. The traditional economic base was removed in the quick swoop of new residents and the old ones displaced and reduced in numbers by disease and violence.

Few of the new settlers had the ability, time or inclination to record Aboriginal ways of managing the land. Most of them could not consider them as forms of land management. Rare individuals, right through the last two centuries, observed the Aboriginal ways and some even wrote about it. But society in general was simply not interested and blocked its ears. As violence was needed to ensure a 'hold' over the land — and create the kind of society the British were used to — it became necessary for the policy makers (the few who thought about it at all) to justify their way of dealing with the land by putting down the former owners, denying them any form of title or right to the land.

When professional ethnographers and anthropologists came on the scene, to study the lifestyles of traditional Aboriginal groups, they had to head for the drier centre of the continent to find any of the original people. What was happening to the tribal groups was of little scientific interest to them, though some cared a great deal about the maltreatment and misfortunes they witnessed. The history of humanity was seen as an orderly progression through savagery and barbarism to the pinnacle of western civilisation. Their scientific purpose was to document what they saw as examples of an early stage of human history, somehow left unchanged in this isolated continent. There was good reason to study the most nomadic groups, which seemed to be the purest, most ideal examples. Examples of economic complexity would only muddy the picture. Such examples, if recognised, were often brushed aside as later irrelevant additions.

In the wide variety of lifestyles and economic strategies of traditional society some two hundred years ago, and probably for many thousands of years before that, we can discover common aspects: Aboriginal ways of looking at life and society. The details vary from group to group over time, but there is something more, call it a special style or feeling, most clearly seen in the mutual relations of the original

Killing a snake. Photo by Thomas Dick, courtesy The Australian Museum.

Spearing fish near Port Macquarie. Photo by Thomas Dick, courtesy The Australian Museum.

Australians to their land. These form the basis for religion, law and other aspects of social and economic organisation, which in turn justify and support this close relationship. There is no disentangling one from the other. And so you will find that a source of food or water, and the way you may use it, has been shown by one of the spirits of the creation period and has been remembered and taught to successive generation through stories and ceremonies.

Nevertheless it is possible to look at much of this from a typically western point of view, trying to see the good practical sense of the rules and methods. If we start with the division of labour and the food quest we can work details into patterns. But in discussions of economy and good sense it is too easy to forget how much time there is for excitement and fun. Cheerful banter abounds, even when things seem pretty bad.

Women do most of the collecting and carrying. As babies and toddlers need carrying and feeding — and they are weaned quite late, as mother's milk is easier to get and eat (and more reliable) than many other foodstuffs — women are tied to moving fairly slowly. They collect shellfish, fruit and berries, fish (usually with hook and line) and dig for roots during the day, and hunt small game such as lizards, snakes and turtles or they may stay mainly in one spot, depending on the type of country and on what sort of food they have in mind that day. Small children and young girls come along too, helping to carry the smallest items and learning what is good to eat or good medicine, what materials to use, where to find them and how to prepare them. It is important to know how much you can take and how much should be left, so that the supply will be replenished. Some of the food is eaten during the day, but some is saved and shared with the men in the evening at the camp.

The men hunt and fish, and have to move fast and far. They may also collect plant food and shellfish to eat during the day, and sometimes cook some of the small game as well, but the bigger catch is usually brought back to camp. Sometimes (in some areas at most times) there is plenty of food, and a big meal of meat and fish is appreciated. But in many areas, or during a bad season, the family depends on the women's contribution which is more reliable and gives a range of things that are important to good health, such as vitamins.

Men and women sometimes work together, and perhaps in fairly big groups, for example when catching fish with nets, or arranging hunting drives or perhaps a big ceremony.

In the drier parts of Australia, where a group moved over a wide area, children were usually spaced several years apart, giving each child a better chance of food and attention. The tradition of keeping young men waiting for a wife (but allowing older men more than one, often quite young) may seem hard on the young ones, but it does mean that old people — an old husband and perhaps the older wife — have some family members who can support them. The wives have company and help each other while they spend the day getting food and caring for the children. A wife would normally leave her own group and area to join a husband, and moving into the husband's family as a very young girl gives her a chance to learn from the older wives about the resources of her new country and how to move through the land in safety. The older wives are often close relatives and friends and she, in time, gets another husband closer to her age.

People also gain support and security through having relations, blood relations as well as a great many who count as relations. Blood relationship to certain persons, and the individual's place within the sequence of generations, makes everyone some kind of relative of other members of the wider group, according to systems much more elaborate and far-reaching than in white society, where only close relationship by blood or marriage seem to count for much.

A view of the heads at the entrance to Port Jackson, New South Wales, October 1st, 1824. Aquatint by Joseph Lycett, in his Views of Australia. *From the Rex Nan Kivell Collection, courtesy National Library of Australia.*

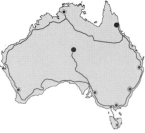

Sydney

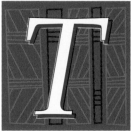HE selection of Sydney Harbour as the birthplace for European settlement on this continent was an admission of the beauty of this unique waterway. The reasons it was selected by the British — climate, topography, shelter and availability of food — were the same reasons it had been chosen by the original Australians.

Sydney has retained much of its rich tradition of rock art, with many fine engraved images preserved, mainly in bushland to the north and west of the city. This one is at West Head, in the Ku-ring-gai Chase National Park. Photo by Carmen Ky.

Within that landscape they lived and moved in harmony with a world which had sustained them for many thousands of years. And throughout the region, the rock art remains a living tribute to Sydney's original inhabitants. When Captain Arthur Phillip established the colony at Sydney Cove in 1788, he had no idea that he had chosen an art gallery as a backdrop to the Sydney settlement. This art extends throughout the area known as the Sydney sandstone region and stretches from Bundeena in the south, where the stranding of a whale has been etched into a flat rocky ledge, to a secluded cave north of Gosford where the haunting image of the omnipotent being Baiame has been painted on the walls.

The people of Sydney, lords of their land for 2000 generations prior to the arrival of Europeans, were the Eora. Their boundaries encompassed the greater city area and extended from Port Jackson to Botany Bay and inland to Parramatta. The Eora warriors earned the admiration of early English and French expeditions, and became increasingly hostile once they realised that the British had come to stay.

The Eora people, with their long, elegant possum skin cloaks (which they wore during the colder months) looked larger than life to the Europeans. During the summer they put their cloaks aside, just as the sunseekers on Bondi and Coogee do today.

On ceremonial occasions, the men presented a regal sight to the newcomers, their bushy beards combed and flowing, a bone through the cartilage of the nose, patterns scarred on their arms and breasts and hair adorned with ornaments made from animal teeth, lobster claws and small bones secured with gum. During these dance ceremonies, they used white clay and red ochre to paint their faces and bodies in traditional designs.

The Eora, it was noted, were not tall, but strongly built, exuding good health and vitality (until the onset of disease within their community). The European custom of shaving fascinated the Eora: it quickly caught on among the locals and in early Sydney town many of the Eora men went clean shaven. They quickly perceived the difference between the French and the British and showed a great aptitude for foreign languages. Fond of singing, the Eora would often surprise the British by singing English songs they had picked up.

The dwellings of the Eora dotted the Sydney landscape. Constructed from the bark of several trees, these shelters were put together in an oval form with a single entrance, at which a fire was kept burning. The women worked hard at food gathering and cooking, while the men concentrated on fishing and taking game.

The Sydney region is characterised by massive sandstone outcrops. Along the coastline, after years of wind and wave action, they weather, forming dramatic shapes and bands of colour. This sandstone — especially on the rock faces away from the coast — created an ideal medium for the Eora artists who developed their engraving skills in the receptive sandstone all around them. Photo by Phillip Quirk/Wildlight.

Their main weapon was the spear, which was observed in three varieties. The simple pointed spear was the most common, but there was also a barbed design (used for fishing) and a jagged-edge spear, which was used mainly in war. The Eora also used war clubs and woomeras (spearthrowers), which were often carved and painted with elaborate designs. They also made stone hatchets and firehardened wooden shields.

The pattern of their life and customs was shared by the Eora with their neighbours, the Dharuk people, who lived along the Hawkesbury River. There has been considerable debate among scholars and linguists concerning the tribal breakdown of the Sydney area. The area considered by most authorities to be the lands of the Eora was occupied by many clans and groups — including the Ku-ring-gai, Kameragal, Bidjigal, Borogegal, Buramedigal and Kadigal — and there is considerable disagreement about the relative importance of each. Spelling also varies greatly as the Aborigines employed no written language: Dharuk also is spelled Dharug and Daruk.

West of Sydney, towards the Blue Mountains were the Darkinjung; south-west, the Gundungurra; and south, the Tharawal.

This coastal area — and the abundance of ocean resources it offered — sustained a significant Aboriginal population. They speared fish from rocks and canoes, chipped oysters off rocks, dived for crayfish and used fibre fishing lines and shell hooks. From a watercolour painting by Joseph Lycett, 1774-1841. Courtesy National Library of Australia.

Kangaroos were once plentiful in the Sydney area, particularly the open, swampy grounds which became Centennial Park. They were encouraged by regular burnoffs which create new growth and sustained open areas in the bushland. Photo by Gary Steer.

Aborigines were observed to use a variety of means for hunting kangaroos, and trade took place to give the fledgling colony access to fresh meat, though the flesh was not popular with Europeans. From a watercolour painting by Joseph Lycett, courtesy National Library of Australia.

The region surrounding Sydney remains something of a mystery, in terms of any meaningful study of the original inhabitants. They were the first to be wiped out in the wave of settlement which followed 1788, and they were gone so quickly that their culture had sunk without trace almost before anyone noticed, let alone cared.

The precise number of clans and bands in the Sydney region will never be known, but observations at the time of the fleet's arrival indicated that the Eora and Dharuk people were far more numerous than had been first estimated — probably around 3000 in the Sydney area, with half in the coastal regions from Botany Bay to Broken Bay. These estimates are cross-checked by anthropologists in many ways; on one day, for example, diarists with the fleet counted 67 canoes on Sydney Harbour. Another time, 49 canoes were noted in Botany Bay and the very next day a war party of some 212 armed warriors was observed on the shores of Botany Bay. 'The Natives...', wrote Phillip, 'are far more numerous than I expected to find them.'

Now known as The Three Sisters, this stark landform in the Blue Mountains west of Sydney once lay in the lands of the Darkinjung people. These mountains proved to be a considerable barrier to exploration and development of the interior. Photo by AusChromes.

Numerous they may have been at the arrival of the fleet but the English firepower and diseases soon reduced their numbers to tattered remnants. The Kadigal band, which lived around the area of the settlement in Sydney Cove, was reduced from about 50 in 1788 to 3 in 1790. Smallpox spread so rapidly through the Aborigines that by the time the English expeditions reached the Nepean River, 50 kilometres west of the colony, many of the Aborigines there were already dead from the virulent disease. Within 55 years only 300 were left alive.

So great was the death rate that traditional burial ceremonies were forgone and bodies were found floating in the harbour or piled in rock shelters. Thus decimated, the traditional clans forged new alliances for sheer survival: cultures mixed and blended, and much of the original structure of the Sydney peoples was lost.

Sydney retains many place names of Aboriginal origin. Some — like Ku-ring-gai, Cammeray and Maroubra — relate to the clan which lived there. Others come from Aboriginal expressions: Bondi(from boondi, the sound of tumbling water), Coogee (from Koocha, meaning bad smell), Taronga (a beautiful view) and Warringah, a sign of rain.

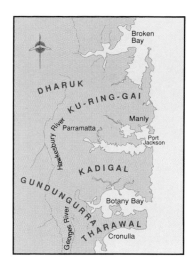

This map shows traditional territories of the Sydney region in 1788, though there is little agreement among 'experts' about what constitutes boundaries. It seems that within the lands broadly called those of the Eora people, there were many clans, some with as few as fifty people.
Left *Kanangra Wall, in the Megalong Valley, west of Sydney. Photo by Trevern Dawes.*

Below *Aborigines spearing eels, from a watercolour painting by Jospeh Lycett. Courtesy National Library of Australia.*

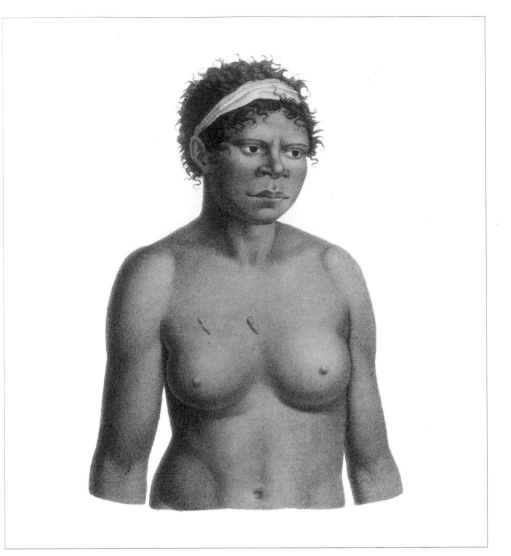

Above *Many of the early observations of Sydney's Aborigines were made by the French, who arrived at Botany Bay shortly after the British. This copper engraving of a man advancing for combat was made by B. Roger from a drawing by N. Petit and published in Peron's* Cartes et Planches. *Courtesy National Library of Australia.*

Right *A young woman of the Cam-mer-ray-gal clan. Copper engraving by N. Petit from a drawing by B. Roger. Courtesy Mitchell Library.*

Below *Corroborees were a regular event around Sydney and attracted the interest of artists such as Joseph Lycett. Courtesy National Library of Australia.*

ILLUSTRATION BY MATT PERRY

The legend of the red waratah

One of the plants common around Sydney is the red waratah, which was adopted as the official emblem of New South Wales. In the creation legends of the Eora there is an explanation of how the red waratah was created.

Long ago, in the Dreamtime, all waratahs were white. At that time, the first wonga pigeon camped in the bush with her mate and they grew fat on the abundant food to be found at ground level. They never flew above the trees, because they were afraid of their enemy, the hawk.

One day the wonga pigeon's mate went searching for food and failed to return. She searched a long time for him without success and finally resolved to fly above the treetops to see if she could see him from above. As she left the shelter of the trees she heard her mate call from down in the bush and, with a glad heart, she turned to fly down to him. But the circling hawk had seen her and swooped down, grasping her in his sharp claws and tearing open her breast.

Wrenching herself free from the hawk, she hid among the blossoms of the waratahs. The hawk couldn't find her and flew away, and again she heard her mate calling. Weak from loss of blood she tried desperately to reach him, but she could only fly short distances and every time she rested on a white waratah, her blood stained the blossom, turning it red.

As her life ebbed away, she changed the white waratahs to red and today it is rare to find a waratah that is not tainted with the blood of the brave and loyal wonga pigeon who lost her life searching for her mate.

(Adapted from C. P. Mountford, The First Sunrise: Australian Aboriginal Myths, *RIGBY, 1971.)*

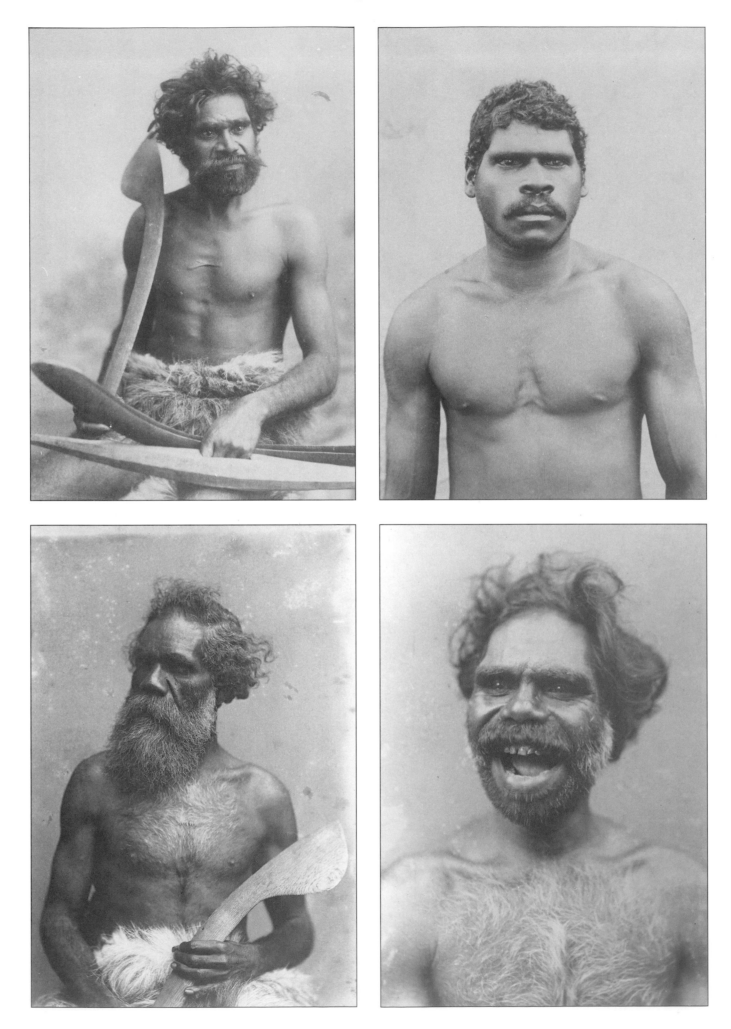

War comes to Sydney

EFORE the tragic conflict which began with the arrival of European settlement, Sydney Harbour's blue and unpolluted waters had sustained the Eora fishermen for thousands of years. In the small bays and sheltered, sandy coves, children played in the waters of the Eora lands unaware of the dramatic changes which lay ahead.

The enduring peace of 2000 generations of Eora changed dramatically with the arrival of the First Fleet in 1788, with nearly 1000 soldiers and prisoners, to take possession of their lands. At first, the Eora were friendly to their guests, believing that, like James Cook before them, they would sail away again. But as it became increasingly clear that the British were planning to stay, relations quickly soured. This was accelerated by continual attacks on Eora women and the spread of diseases, brought with the fleet, which began to affect significant numbers of the Eora.

By 1790 the lines had been set for a ten-year guerilla war. For the Eora, and their compatriots, the Dharuk, it was a war they could never win: but their struggle and commitment to save their traditional homelands from the invading settlers is a heroic story, one little known in Australian history.

After several skirmishes, the first major battle took place in June 1795. The administrator of the time, William Paterson, advised his London superiors that he planned a major military operation to kill or drive back the Dharuk people from their traditional lands along the Hawkesbury.

The English soldiers of the New South Wales Corps marched out from Sydney, along what is now Parramatta Road, resplendent in tight pantaloons and heavy, red wool greatcoats, complete with tails and lacy cuffs. They marched the 24 kilometres to Parramatta, then mainly open country, passing only a handful of dwellings along the way: a striking contast to the unbroken rows of shops, factories and houses that line Parramatta Road today.

From Parramatta, already a military outpost of some strength, the troopers marched north, past Toongabbie, to the Hawkesbury. The following day, in an open area near Richmond Hill, the English force drew its battle lines and moved on the Dharuk war party that had assembled to meet them.

The spears of the Dharuk were no match for the muskets of the English troopers and they were cut down before retreating into the bush. Although they rallied for a further attack, the conflict ended in complete victory for the redcoats, and an end to the Dharuk people's unchallenged ownership of the lands along the Hawkesbury.

Above *After several skirmishes around the Sydney Cove settlement, the first real conflict came west of Sydney, on the banks of the Hawkesbury River, in 1895. Courtesy Mitchell Library.*

Opposite *A selection of portraits taken by Henry King in Sydney around 1890, courtesy The Australian Museum.*

Etching of an unknown New South Wales Aborigine by an unknown French artist, based on illustrations made during the French voyages of 1810. Courtesy National Library of Australia.

The process of dispossession left children orphaned, alienated and alone. Photo by Henry King, courtesy The Australian Museum.

The tragedy of Bennelong

So much of the change presented by the arrival of European settlement can seen in the tragic life of Bennelong, the best remembered (and most scorned) Aborigine of the modern era. Along with his friend Colbee, Bennelong was captured by British soldiers in 1789, when he was around 26 years old. Governor Arthur Phillip decided to kidnap young men and women of the Eora in an attempt to introduce them to English ways and habits. In Bennelong, he found a perfect student.

After six months of captivity, Bennelong had learned to speak English well, though his captors hadn't been able to learn any of the Eora language. After rejecting liquor initially, he developed a liking for the strong spirits readily available in the colony. He later boasted of his 'kissing encounters' with the wives of his captors.

On 3 May 1790, Bennelong escaped and rejoined his people. Phillip led the search parties in person, which resulted in his being speared through the right shoulder at Manly, in September of that year. Bennelong met Phillip ten days later, explaining that he had beaten an Eora warrior, Wil-ee-ma-rin, for this unprovoked attack on the governor. Bennelong and a group of friends accepted Phillip's invitation to visit Sydney, where they were given blankets and urged to stay.

Yemmerrawanie, who sailed to England with Captain Phillip and Bennelong — only to become a novelty to British people eager to see a living example of the 'noble savage' — never returned to his homelands. The author visited his grave in London during his 1988 visit. Photos by Carmen Ky.

The rise and fall of Pemulwuy

In contrast to Bennelong and Colbee stands the uncompromising figure of Pemulwuy, the inspired and devious resistance leader of the Eora nation in its war with the colony, which lasted from 1790 until 1802. A legend in his own lifetime, Pemulwuy was held in such reverence by his own people that they came to believe that the English muskets could never kill him.

Even his English enemies paid tribute to his courage and daring and his name began to dominate dispatches to London. His co-ordinated attacks on the fledgling colony inspired awe and fear in the British and limited the expansion of the settlement.

Pemulwuy grew up with his family at Botany Bay and is thought to have been born in 1760. During his twelve-year war of attrition with the colony he moved around the outskirts of Sydney, appearing at Castle Hill, Toongabbie, Parramatta and Botany Bay. He may well have fought with the Dharuk in the Battle of the Hawkesbury in 1795, although it was considered doubtful at the time because he had been seen at Brickfield Hill a month previously.

Pemulwuy's Eora forces developed the first true guerilla tactics of waging a war against overwhelming firepower. They raided settlements, taking food and provisions before levelling the buildings and driving off the stock. The British regularly sent redcoats after his forces, but they were easily avoided, or attacked when the terrain suited. In several of these clashes Pemulwuy

Early portrait of an Eora youth, befriended by Governor Macquarie and painted by an unknown artist. Courtesy Mitchell Library.

During the following year, Bennelong, Colbee and friends stayed in Sydney town itself; they sometimes performed corroborees for the English. Phillip sought Bennelong's assistance with the emerging problem of Pemulwuy, an Eora warrior who had begun to co-ordinate resistance against the colony and had succeeded in pinning the settlement down to the fortified area of Sydney Cove.

Bennelong was encouraged to act as an intermediary between the English and Eora and he proudly wore the red coat of the British military around the colony. Phillip built him a brick hut on the eastern point of Sydney Cove, which still bears his name, Bennelong Point. The Sydney Opera House today sits on the site of Bennelong's home.

Late in 1792, Bennelong and a fellow Eora, Yemmerrawanie, sailed for England with Phillip, where Bennelong enjoyed a high profile as the 'noble savage' rescued by Britain. He even met King George III, before returning to Australia with the new governor, John Hunter, in 1795.

His absence had created a gap between him and his people which would never be bridged. His wife had taken a new husband, whom he challenged to a duel. Though he beat the young lover, his wife refused to return to him. Bennelong had won the fight but lost his woman and his self-esteem never recovered. Although he stowed his English clothes and went back to the bush, he was shunned by everyone.

A lonely and isolated figure, Bennelong even tried to steal his old friend Colbee's wife, Boo-ree-a. A bitter conflict ensued, in which Bennelong was badly beaten, suffering severe face and head wounds which disfigured his face and impaired his speech.

The once-handsome, would-be ambassador, who had travelled around the world and dined with a king, was reduced to drunken days alone. In his final years he wandered the colony alone, mostly drunk, accepting handouts from the British. He died at Kissing Point on 3 January 1813.

Colbee, who had refused to go to England, maintained his family traditions, yet retained the respect of the British and was granted land by two separate governors in recognition of his efforts to bring about peace.

Early engravings of Bennelong (top) and Yemmerrawanie, the first of their people ever to venture away across the seas. One never returned, the other never recovered. Courtesy Mitchell Library.

One of the better known characters of early colonial life was Bungaree, an elder of the Karigal clan centred in the West Head area near Broken Bay. Bungaree picked up English quickly and proved himself an important ally to Phillip and the Sydney Cove colony. He accompanied Matthew Flinders and Phillip King in their explorations of the coastline, becoming the first Aborigine to circumnavigate the continent. Eventually granted land with other families at Georges Head, north of Sydney, Bungaree developed an impressive garden before falling victim to alcohol. He died in 1830 and was buried at Rose Bay. Courtesy Mitchell Library.

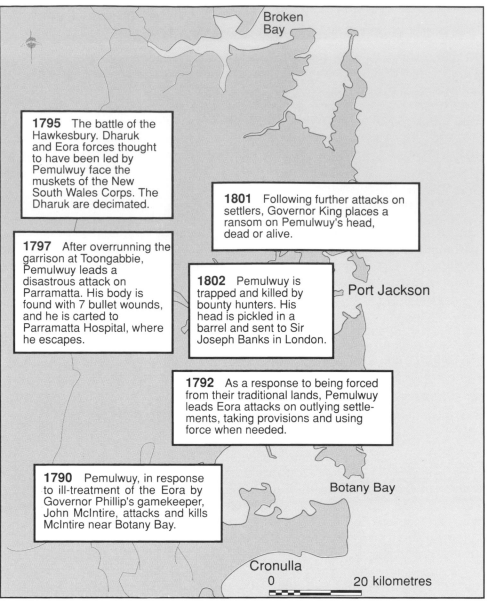

1795 The battle of the Hawkesbury. Dharuk and Eora forces thought to have been led by Pemulwuy face the muskets of the New South Wales Corps. The Dharuk are decimated.

1801 Following further attacks on settlers, Governor King places a ransom on Pemulwuy's head, dead or alive.

1797 After overrunning the garrison at Toongabbie, Pemulwuy leads a disastrous attack on Parramatta. His body is found with 7 bullet wounds, and he is carted to Parramatta Hospital, where he escapes.

1802 Pemulwuy is trapped and killed by bounty hunters. His head is pickled in a barrel and sent to Sir Joseph Banks in London.

1792 As a response to being forced from their traditional lands, Pemulwuy leads Eora attacks on outlying settlements, taking provisions and using force when needed.

1790 Pemulwuy, in response to ill-treatment of the Eora by Governor Phillip's gamekeeper, John McIntire, attacks and kills McIntire near Botany Bay.

was wounded but survived, adding to his reputation (which had also grown within the ranks of the troopers) that they could not kill him.

After a fight with a Madagascan black, John Caesar, in which he was badly injured, Pemulwuy withdrew to the bush and word began to circulate the colony that he was dead. Much as the English wanted to believe the rumours, it wasn't long before Pemulwuy had led renewed attacks, despite the considerable price on his head (dead or alive) and the increased military operations. His commitment was intensified by the rape and torture of a young woman of his family, and he stepped up his campaign of surprise attacks, travelling throughout the expanding colony to coerce support from neighbouring clans.

The battle of Parramatta

It was in March 1797 that the second battle of Australia took place. It was the day of Pemulwuy's greatest triumph and worst disaster. It began with the overrunning of the English outpost at Toongabbie, when Pemulwuy charged at the head of more than 100 warriors. The remaining soldiers retreated to Parramatta, where they had time to warn of Pemulwuy's impending attack and prepare the garrison for the coming assault. The redcoats were lined up with muskets as Pemulwuy and his warriors attacked across open ground near the Parramatta River.

Pemulwuy led the charge and was wounded seven times before being brought down by a massive head wound. His warriors fought on against the steady fire of the disciplined militia, but soon had to retreat to the bush. Pemulwuy was found, barely living, among the dead and dying, and, in a rare sign of respect, his body was carried to Parramatta Hospital where he was given nominal medical assistance and left chained.

Much to the shock of the British, Pemulwuy managed not only to survive his wounds, but escape, still with one leg iron in place.

After another period of recuperation, Pemulwuy was again leading attacks on the settlements at Lane Cove and Kissing Point. Despite his crushing defeat at Parramatta, his reputation for invincibility had survived intact, even enhanced, and Governor Philip Gidley King increased the reward for his capture or death. With the colony expanding, the governor worked desperately to isolate the 'outlaw' Pemulwuy, though the attacks continued until 1802, when he led his last war party against the colony.

Finally the financial inducements offered for his assassination paid off and Pemulwuy was surprised and murdered by two unnamed English settlers, who cut his head off and delivered it to the governor. The head was then pickled in a barrel and dispatched to Sir Joseph Banks in London, along with a report that the Eora people had been 'pacified'.

Thus perished the first resistance hero of the Aborigines. In a land of cenotaphs, there is not a single memorial to either Pemulwuy or his people, the Eora. Not even a place name.

The Russians at Port Jackson

One of the many nations to show an early interest in the Pacific was Russia. From the time of the documented visits to 'New Holland' by William Dampier in the seventeeth century, Russian scholars had been keenly interested in the ethnography of the original Australians.

The Russian navy, still in its infancy, had already acquired considerable knowledge of the region early in the eighteenth century. This was to be reinforced by the discoveries of James Cook. The first Russian naval venture to the Pacific was mounted in 1803 and although they did not call at Sydney, the fledgling colony had played host to ten visits by Russian ships by 1825. These visits averaged one each year over the following fifty years.

In contrast to the British, the Russians showed great interest in the Eora people and collected implements and artefacts which they took back to Russia. This collection, perhaps the most important single collection of artefacts from the Port Jackson area anywhere in the world, is now housed in Leningrad as part of the N.N. Miklukho-Maklay Institute of Ethnography of the Academy of Sciences of the USSR.

Two illustrations by the Russian artist, P. Mikhaylov, during the Russian explorations of the South Pacific. At left, Sydney Cove around 1820. At right, a group of Aborigines prepare fish in a domestic setting. The girl to the left of centre with lighter skin was Bungaree's daughter, the result of a union between a European and one of Bungaree's five wives. Bungaree often laughed about the colour of his daughter's skin: 'My gin eat too much white bread,' he would say when asked. Courtesy Mitchell Library.

Sydney's rock art . . .

T HE Eora left behind them a legacy of quite extraordinary rock art. The Sydney region may well have had the densest population of Aborigines on the continent: they certainly left the most extraordinary art gallery as a permanent tribute to their life on the Sydney sandstone.

In an area of some 2 million hectares, over 2000 Eora art galleries have been identified, featuring exquisite rock carving. They are located on horizontal sandstone surfaces from Gibbon Point, at Bundeena, to Brisbane Water, north of Broken Bay: some are small, finely detailed figures; some are huge animals and spirit beings.

The Sydney region is unique for its large sandstone rocks and the Eora found these surfaces ideal for their art, which creates intriguing insights into their lifestyle, lore and legend. The images include fish, animals and reptiles but they also engraved many human forms, mostly in outline. The engravings vary in age and size, many thought to be at least 1000 years old. Some even record the arrival of the square-rigged ships. The new colonists, however, took very little interest in the art of the Eora. Perhaps now, 200 years later, an appreciation of this extraordinary achievement is dawning.

Most of Sydney's rock carvings are on horizontal rock faces, many overhung by trees and

The favourite subjects for the Eora rock artists were their creative beings, Baiame and Daramulun, though the animals of their world — especially fish, whales, kangaroos, birds and dolphins — feature regularly in their images. Photo by Carmen Ky.

Hand stencils were also popular and are still to be found in bushland and national parks around the city. These images were created by blowing ochre from the mouth across the outspread hand. Photo by David Hart.

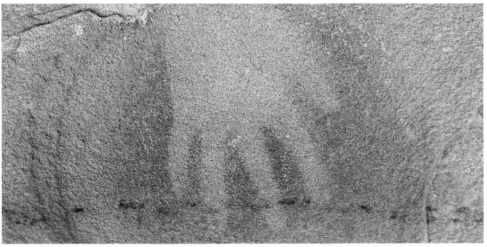

a silent legacy

overgrown with moss and weeds. Photography often fails to capture the power and simplicity of these images. John Clegg is one of Australia's foremost authorities on rock art and he has spent many years accurately recording these extraordinary carvings. The selection of images above are all from the Sydney area, just a few of the dozens of images painstakingly recorded by Clegg over the past two decades.

Clockwise from top left *A striped echidna in the Ku-ring-gai Chase National Park; emu hatching eggs, Wisemans Ferry; a sea bird in flight, Brisbane Waters; a man-fish being, in a suburban Sydney garden. Drawings by John Clegg.*

The Ku-ring-gai Chase National Park

Ku-ring-gai Chase National Park offers a visitors' centre on the road between Bobbin Head and Mount Colah, where many animals can be seen in their habitats and displays provide information to the visiting public. At West Head there is an exhibition centre, which also houses displays of art and wildlife.

JUST 30 kilometres north of Sydney — and within easy reach by car — is one of the continent's most spectacular national parks, a vast expanse of sandstone headlands, gorges and drowned river valleys, bordered to the north by Pittwater, Broken Bay, the Hawkesbury River and the Cowan Creek system.

These waterways — over 100 kilometres of them navigable — thread through the valleys of the park (an area of some 15,000 hectares) and offer some of the best recreational boating found anywhere in the world.

Cowan Creek and Smiths Creek offer a real glimpse of the Australia of yesteryear, though sadly without the land's traditional owners. From the water, one gets a clear view of the sharply rising hills and the massive sandstone outcrops, interspersed with casuarinas and some most resourceful angophoras, which squeeze between rocks, around rocks and even through them as they reach upward for their place in the sun. At the waterline, the bottom falls away quickly — in many places reaching depths over 15 metres just a few metres off shore — and the shoreline is dotted with massive boulders. At high tide these boulders make ideal spearing platforms, from which a hunter could get well above his prey and easily spear many fish. At low tide, shellfish and oysters were plentiful.

The hillsides are dominated by the massive sandstone outcrops, which, in the weathering process of millions of years, have formed caves and sheltering overhangs. These outcrops — some of which are cathedral-like in their domination of the hillside — provided ideal cover for hunting the mammals which inhabited the area, as well as offering shelter. The caves and rock shelters were the homes of the Ku-ring-gai clan, who fished the rivers, hunted on the hillsides of a world created in the Dreamtime.

The park has hundreds of excellent carvings, several of which can be seen from the water in a small boat. Most drawings feature marine animals: whales, sharks, fish and eels. Kangaroos occur frequently, as do representations of the great ancestral being, Baiame.

Still rich in wildlife, the park boasts many species alive and well, including the black-tailed swamp wallaby, several varieties of possum, koalas, echidna, goannas, snakes, lyrebirds, rosellas, wrens and sea birds.

A waterfall on the America Bay track. Photo by Trevern Dawes.

West Head offers a spectacular view of Barrenjoey Headland, Broken Bay and the mouth of the Hawkesbury River. Around West Head and elsewhere within the park there a variety of walkways that offer an insight into Sydney's sandstone-based landscape. Many of the exposed sandstone faces have angophora gums clinging determinedly to their faces. There are many excellent examples of rock carvings to be seen on clearly marked walking trails within the park. Photos by Tony Gordon.

PHOTO BY GEORGE GITTOES

How the world was born

In a society without the written word, pictorial art takes on immense importance as it becomes a way of documenting history. In the paintings and engravings of the Aborigines, animals and birds represent totems of clans and individuals. These are intimately connected with the Dreamtime, which not only explains the past but provides guidance for the present and the future. Dreamtime beliefs give meaning to the universe and provide a set of laws and guidelines which discipline all aspects of life.

The Dreamtime represents the drama of creation, when the mythic beings emerged from the heavens or the underworld and moved across the land. The arrival and departure points of these beings became the rivers, rocks, hills, mountains and billabongs. According to the legends, it was these beings who created all the animals, birds, fish, plants and people. All living things were linked to the beings of the Dreamtime, who could be in human or animal form, or could change from one to the other.

The landscape having been shaped, the creation beings left human children and laws for them to live by. Although they disappeared into the sea or the heavens, the Dreamtime creators, in the belief of the Aborigines, never really left the land. They remained in the landscape, creating a life force for human kind, with the right to intervene when needed by the animals of their creation.

The art represents the constant link between the people and their creators, and the artists constantly sought to re-establish links with the mythical beings of the Dreamtime. In the art, the great events of the Dreamtime are re-enacted, as the artist captures those images which relate in a spiritual way, recording his own relationship with the totemic designs and living things of his world. The great spirit beings dominate the rock engravings of the Eora, although there are also many carvings which were associated with ritual practices to promote more successful fishing and hunting.

The Dreamtime stories of the Eora were 'veiled' and visitors from outside Eora lands were only allowed to relate the stories with the permission of Eora elders. In other areas, only one person in a clan had the authority to create sacred designs, explain their meaning and pass on the lore of the people to succeeding generations.

Aboriginal Sydney today

YDNEY today is a truly multicultural city, with an extensive Aboriginal population comprising an enormous mix of people from country areas, most of whom have come to the city in search of employment opportunities.

The metropolitan area of Sydney, once the homelands to so many of the Eora people, has very few of its traditional people left. Around La Perouse a few, like the Williams, Stewart, Timbery and Ella families, have maintained their presence. They deserve great admiration, having survived the European invasion longer than anywhere else in Australia. Yet despite their continued occupation of this last bastion of Aboriginal culture in Sydney, they have been forced away from direct access to their beloved coastline by escalating land prices. The Aboriginal reserve at La Perouse has became a tiny enclave, surrounded by high density housing.

Apart from La Perouse, other areas — at Llandilo and Salt Pan Creek — were gazetted as Aboriginal reserves. The Llandilo land, on the Penrith–Richmond road, remains under Aboriginal control.

In the inner city, Redfern has become an area with a high Aboriginal population, offering emotional security for people from vastly different areas. The Aboriginal housing estate is serviced by a retail food outlet called 'The Black Market', the Aboriginal Legal Service offers a vital support base for people caught in the web of modern urban life and the Aboriginal Medical Service provides health support systems. Bennelongs Haven is a facility geared to helping alcohol-based problems and Father Ted Kennedy's manse offers overnight refuge for the homeless. Christian services, operated by caring andf well-meaning people, have made strong inroads into Aboriginal culture, at the expense of traditional rituals and methods of worship.

Redfern has seen a steady build-up in its Aboriginal population over the past twenty years, and with the increasing numbers has come a new-found

The arrival of the First Fleet re-enactment fleet in Sydney Harbour on 26 January 1988 heightened a new awareness of Aboriginal rights and led to a considerable though orderly protest on the harbour's fore-shores. Photo by Oliver Strewe/Wildlight.

sense of being. Redfern is also headquarters to offices of the local, regional and state Aboriginal land councils, as well as the Eora Educational Centre and preschool kindergarten.

Sydney's re-emerging Aboriginal identity includes the widely acclaimed Aboriginal and Islander Dance Group, which teaches modern and traditional dance to people from all over the country. Their end-of-year performances are fixed as clearly in my annual calendar as September's brown boronia season.

At Glebe, the Tranby Aboriginal training college helps mature students with the development of co-operative ventures and other enterprises. The college offers training in management procedures, book-keeping and other practical skills crucial to the development of Aboriginal enterprises. Recently, some 22 trainees underwent an intensive course to equip them as rangers with the National Parks and Wildlife Service.

The Aboriginal Training and Cultural Foundation in Balmain, directed by two highly motivated and qualified people in Margaret Valadian and Natasha McNamara, provides a similar service to Tranby.

Government housing policies have resulted in most Aboriginal families residing in outer metrolopitan areas of Sydney, such as Campbelltown and Parramatta and of the 30,000 Aboriginal people resident in Sydney, very few live on the north side of the harbour. Even fewer have the chance to live along the harbour and ocean foreshores which had been theirs since the beginning of time.

Despite situations of real urban hardship and endemic alcohol addiction, there remains a deep pride in the people, and you'll never see an Aborigine fossicking in garbage bins for food, nor find grafitti on the walls of Aboriginal public toilets.

Over the past twenty years, as Aboriginal people have begun to move back to Sydney in significant numbers it has been the contributions of individuals such as 'Mum Shirl' (Shirley Smith) who have worked tirelessly to give us a sense of belonging in a big and often unfriendly city. Mum Shirl has personally 'mothered' hundreds of Aboriginal children in need. Her face has also become a familiar sight at Sydney's law courts defending and winning

Radio Redfern operates a community access radio station run by Aborigines and developed as an Aboriginal voice in Sydney. Here, announcers Gavin Duncan and Mick Bayles prepare a programme. Photo by Oliver Strewe/Wildlight.

Ernie Dingo is just one of many new Aboriginal faces appearing on cinema screens around the world. Photo by Caroline Jones/Wildlight.

leniency for Aboriginal people on the wrong side of often confusing laws. She also travels widely to prisons, offering encouragement and comfort to Aboriginal inmates, repeating the same pattern year after year with her important message of hope. Karakumba, established at St Albans near Wisemans Ferry after extensive lobbying by Mum Shirl has become a staging point in the rehabilitation of Aboriginal people suffering from the effects of alcohol.

Another saintly figure in Aboriginal Sydney is Val Bryant, who has worked tirelessly to create alcohol rehabilitation centres throughout the state which offer environments suitable and inspiring to Aboriginal sobriety.

The Aboriginal Development Commission has provided land in New South Wales amounting to more than 30 000 hectares for the establishment of farming and rehabilitation enterprises.

Each year an annual Aboriginal rugby league carnival is conducted over the October long weekend in a friendly but highly competitive atmosphere. This competition represents much more than an exciting football carnival, as it provides a rare opportunity for players and spectators to come together in festive atmosphere with singing, dancing and other celebrations which allows the group soul of Aboriginality to dominate the weekend.

Most of Sydney's rugby league clubs have Aboriginal players and the expansion of the Sydney competition to include Illawarra, Canberra, Newcastle, the Gold Coast and Brisbane gives more Aboriginal players the chance to excel in this, the toughest football competition in the world. The talents of players such as Ricky Walford, John Ferguson, Cliff Lyons, Mal Meninga, Mal Cochrane, Scott Gale, Wilfred Williams, Bruce Longbottom, Dale Shearer and Colin Scott continue a great Aboriginal tradition in the game. Rugby Union in Australia tends to draw less on the football skills of Aboriginal Australians, unlike New Zealand where Maories form the heart of All Black rugby, although the era of domination by the Ella brothers, Gary, Glen and Mark and the extraordinary talents they displayed all over the world will never be forgotten by those who witnessed it.

The Aboriginal Arts Board is headquartered in Sydney and a number of Aboriginal art and craft retail outlets are now found in The Rocks, the Royal Arcade, the Queen Victoria Building, Darlinghurst and Redfern. The city has also seen an appearance of Aboriginal fabric designers, such the Designer Aboriginals in Rozelle. A casting agency, Abart Productions, is located in Redfern and Sydney is home to many respected Aboriginal actors, such as Bob Maza and Ernie Dingo.

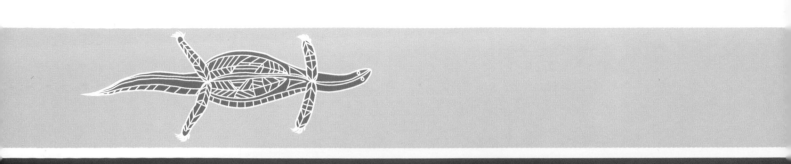

*Broken Head, just one of many
distinctive headlands on the New
South Wales north coast. Photo
by Grenville Turner/Wildlight.*

North to the Tweed

HE north coast of New South Wales is one of the greatest surfing, sailing and swimming coastlines to be found anywhere in the world, with long sandy beaches cut by rocky headlands and stretching up the coast between a succession of rivermouths.

When travelling north from Sydney the sun and wind are of little importance and have little impact on travelling times, unlike east-west travel, when the position of the sun in the sky can have a significant impact on visability and driver comfort. Leaving Sydney we see the full impact of modern technology on the landscape as we pass through massive cuttings in the hillside and across the Mooney Mooney Bridge, which dramatically spans the Hawkesbury River.

Although there is little visible evidence of Aboriginal occupation from the highway, the area is rich with tradition and art. There are significant rock art sites near Maroota and Wiseman's Ferry. The freeway to Newcastle is so fast that much of the landscape is missed.

The lands of the Eora and the Dharuk are left behind with the Hawkesbury River as we enter the lands of the Darkinjung people, who shared much of the culture of their two great neighbours. Like them, they were overwhelmed by the expansion of the Sydney-based settlement. The Hawkesbury River system, flowing out to sea at Broken Bay, represented a major cultural and linguistic barrier, its tributaries and waterways a rich and bountiful support system. Muogummara Reserve, near Brisbane Waters, another of the waterways flowing into Broken Bay, is maintained by the National Parks and Wildlife Service and has some exquisite rock art. Among many images is a complex engraving of a whale feast, with many people queued up for a ceremonial portion.

The town of Wyong stands near a glittering group of lakes and represents the southern border of the Awabakal nation.

As a part of the British strategy, Aborigines were set up in small farms along the Hawkesbury River, where they were encouraged to cultivate wheat and maize. Courtesy The Australian Museum.

The world of Awaba

The area surrounding modern day Newcastle was once the traditional homelands of the Awabakal. Observations made by explorers, surveyors and settlers during the early years of contact provide us with an insight to these people, although the smallpox outbreak of 1789 had an immediate and devastating effect on the local populations of the entire central coast.

One of the most authorative sources of information relating to the Awabakal people comes from the observations of L. E. Threlkeld, who established a mission at Lake Macquarie in 1825 at a location now known as Toronto. During the mission's 17 years in the area Threlkeld studied Awabakal customs and traditions and documented the language. He observed patterns of land ownership, cultural variation between clans, patterns of

Above *An early aquatint of Newcastle by Joseph Lycett, courtesy National Library of Australia.*
Right *In a sheltered cave to the west of Mount Sugarloaf is a painting believed to represent the great ancestral being Baiame. Photo by Carmen Ky.*

movement during summer and winter, marriage and burial customs, sacred sites and interclan rivalries. Threlkeld's painstaking documentation of the Awabakal people gives us a chance to understand something of their lifestyle prior to European settlement.

Although precise delineations of clan areas are uncertain, it seems the the southern margins of Lake Macquarie, or Awaba, as it was known, represented the southern boundary of the Awabakal language. There were also many dialects spoken within the broad area defined as Awabakal country. South of Awaba were the lands of the Kuringgai, to the west, the Darkingung, and to the north, the Worimi. Threlkeld observed and commented on interclan relations: 'The natives here are connected in a kind of circle extending to the Hawkesbury and Port Stephens.' He also noted that people from far afield would regularly visit Lake Macquarie.

Among the Awabakal, clan territories were passed on from generation to generation along patrineal (male) lines, and women were required to marry outside their own group. Marriage ties often gave clan members access to the resources of other groups or clans. Often, husbands and wives spoke different languages and the children would be taught both, further cementing inter-

The feasts that followed whale strandings are well recorded in Aboriginal rock art. Here, a European artist, Joseph Lycett, captures a whale stranding scene at Nobbys Beach, Newcastle. Courtesy National Library of Australia.

In the world of the Awabakal many features of the landscape had meanings known only to elders and deep totemic symbolism was attached to these places by the people. Below are two rock outcrops in the area believed by living Aborigines to embody a lizard and frog. Photo by Carmen Ky.

clan bonds. These marriage alliances generated contact between widely differing groups who came together for important ceremonial occasions, such as initiation ceremonies and corroborees.

Linguistic studies have placed the Awabakal language within a group of related languages with includes the Darkingung, to the west of Awaba, and the Worimi, centred around Port Stephens. Research in the Hunter Valley indicates a high level of interaction with coastal peoples, despite some language differences. Threlkeld observed that: 'Although tribes within 100 miles do not, at first interview, understand each other . . . after a very short space of time they were able to converse freely . . .' He also describes co-operative enterprises between neighbouring clans, such as the clearing of land or hunting.

Like most coastal peoples the Awabakal utilised caves and overhanging rocks for shelter, though Threlkeld noted that, during wet weather, they often constructed temporary shelters, usually bark (from stringy bark or box trees) stretched across stakes. Their tool kit included a *kul-ta-ra*, a fishing spear about 2 metres in length, usually made from the spent flower stalks of the *Xanthorrhoea preisii,* and hunting spears, which were longer and fixed with a hardwood or stone point, secured with resin. Battle spears, or *wa-rai*, were similar to hunting spears, but often had additional pieces of sharp quartz glued along one side of the hardwood tip. Later, glass was substituted for the quartz. The spearthrower, or *womera*, was also employed, as well as stone hatchets, nets and fishing lines with simple hooks. Other implements included the boomerang, or *tur-rur-ma* and club, or *nullah nullah*. Shields, called *ko-reil*, cut from the buttress of the nettle tree or great fig tree, were carved and decorated with red ochre and pipe clay.

The Awabakal manufactured canoes from river gum or kurrajong bark, which they removed with hatchets and secured at each end with vines. Struts were inserted at each end for strength and a vine cord, tied across the middle of the canoe, held it together. Heavy stones, tied to vines, were used as anchors. These simple canoes could carry up to 8 people.

Mount Sugarloaf offered a spiritual centre to the Awabakal people and in many areas the true spirit of this bush can still be found. The distinctive forms of the Xanthorrhoea preisii *— also known as the blackboy, grass tree and kangaroo tail — are a reminder of times past. There are some 23 varieties of* Xanthorrhoea *found around Australia and all were put to great use by the Aborigines. Stems made excellent spear shafts, grubs were collected from the hollow trunk and the sap was used to make an adhesive for attaching spear heads. Photo by Carmen Ky.*

Every individual of each clan had a totem, obtained by descent, which reflected the connection between that person and a particular animal in their enviornment. Along the coastline totems included fish, sharks and dolphins, whereas further inland kangaroos or emus were more likely to be the totemic symbols. Threlkeld observed an intimate relationship between each individual and his or her totem and noted that two people of the same totem were not permitted to marry. Within the territories of each clan there were sites specific to particular totems.

Threlkeld observed a strict code of behaviour when the area was visited by other clans. A visitor would wait at a respectful distance until the elders of the host clan invited him to their fire. Trespass across boundaries without permission was a common cause of dispute, usually settled with a formal gathering and fight. Abductions of women and elopements were another common cause of dispute. The area had a vibrant trading pattern, *Xanthorrhoea* shafts from the coastal areas often being traded for possum skin rugs and cloaks from the interior.

Young men passed through several stages of initiation as they were taught the responsibilities of clan and totem membership, the set codes of behaviour and reponsibilities of adulthood. Initiation ceremonies involved tooth avulsion or removal for men and young girls usually had the top of the second finger of the left hand removed.

The food resources of the Awabakal included shellfish and marine fish species from the ocean and estuaries, as well as a wide variety of bird life in the marshlands. The undulating coastal plain, dissected by several freshwater creeks, offered a wide variety of habitats and wildlife, and fire was a vital part of hunting technique and land management. Firestick farming, as it has often been called, offered short and long term benefits. Firstly, fires made the nests and holes of prey more obvious and animals could be caught in the fire or driven towards the spears and nets of waiting hunters. In the longer term, fires provided breaks in the forest cover, which would attract the herbivorous animals to the grass, and early indications depicted the area as being abundant with kangaroos.

Two reminders of Paradise Lost. At left, a canoe tree, still showing the scars of bark removal for a traditional bark canoe. At right, a natural ravine in the hillside, through which the cold wind whistles at night. Local people believe this natural 'prison' was used to punish offenders against tribal law, who would be forced to spend cold nights inside. Photos by Carmen Ky.

Traditional clan areas in the Newcastle region.

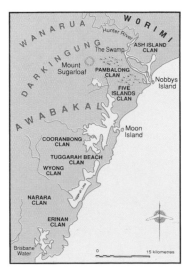

The Myall Lakes, a chain of three linked lakes, are famous world-wide for their spectacular beauty. The lakes should not be confused with the Myall Creek massacres, which took place on the table-lands between Glen Innes and Moree. Photo by Robbi Newman.

Opposite *The red waratah, a member of the Proteaceae family, is generally accepted as the floral emblem of New South Wales. The name comes from an Aboriginal word meaning 'seen from afar' and the generic name,* Telopea, *is based on Greek words of the same meaning. Photo by Philip Green.*

After the impact of the European diseases in 1789, which were spread from Sydney along traditional communication routes, a further outbreak hit the lower Hunter River area in 1810. Exploitation of the area, initially for coal and cedar, began in 1797 and quickly led to clashes over resources and the abuse of Aboriginal women. Veneral diseases also decimated the population, with a parallel decline in female fertility. The surviving males had, by now, been reduced to alcoholism. By 1840, observed Threlkeld, the Aborigines had deserted their precious lake for employment and rum in Newcastle.

West of Newcastle city is the Hunter Valley, an area rich in the traditions of the original people of the area. In 1981, the National Parks and Wildlife Service listed 1000 Aboriginal sites in the valley. Further research over the following six years increased the number to 1650, which is 12 per cent of the known sites in New South Wales.

North of Newcastle and across the Hunter River the traveller begins to get a feel for the bushland setting. The small town of Karuah is host to a large Aboriginal population. North of the town on the west bank of the river is a reserve, its site typifying the government policy of locating Aboriginal people far enough away from town to prevent their participation in civic affairs and their enjoyment of facilities like the local school. North of the Karuah a right turn takes you on an alternate route out to Hawkes Nest then through Mungo Brush and past the Myall Lakes, to Forster and Tuncurry.

Around Buladelah, the highway winds through dense, verdant forests of stringybark and bangalow palms. Photo by Philip Green.

Travelling up Highway One from Karuah to Taree through Bulahdelah, Coolongolook and Nabiac is spiritually breathtaking as the highway winds through forested hills with an umbrella covering of tall, straight stringybarks and tree ferns which exude an atmosphere of tranquility as well as rejuvenating oxygen. The roadside stop at the base of O'Sullivans Gap is highly recommended for its freshness and bush setting. Sapling Creek, with its tall trees and bare white trunks, set against a green mosaic of leaves and undergrowth, exudes harmony for the traveller to appreciate. Along the older road to the left through Stroud and Gloucester, nearer the mountains, the landscape is exquisite. Around Stringybark Creek the tall, majestic forest offers emotional support for the traveller about to tackle the curved hazards of the highway between Nabiac and Taree.

South of Taree the highway passes adjacent to the Purfleet Aboriginal Reserve, situated just far enough from town to create seperate delivery of education to black and white children in the area. This now-abandoned government policy of restricting Aborigines to fenced reserves, thus restricting their access to traditional lands, caused bitter resentment and racial tension in towns like Taree. In fact it was in a Taree hotel that I was once refused a lemon squash on the basis of my Aboriginality. After the Transport Workers Union cut off the supply of alcohol to the entire town the pubs quickly decided that they didn't discriminate against Aborigines. A small victory, but one that created the idea for the now-famous tent embassy, established on the lawns of Parliament House in Canberra in 1971, where it remained until 1976.

In recent years many Aboriginal families have moved into town to be closer to facilities such as shopping, hospital and education opportunities for their children. In such towns, Aboriginal Land Councils, Aboriginal Legal and Medical Services and Local Aboriginal Educational Consultative Committees operate under self-management, evolving self-determination programs, aided by government services such as the Department of Aboriginal Affairs.

A campfire scene at the mouth of the Hunter River, Newcastle. From a watercolour painting by Joseph Lycett, courtesy National Library of Australia.

The land of the three rivers

TAREE marks our entry into the land of the three rivers — the Manning, Hastings and Macleay — and is the land of three nations, the Birpai, Ngamba and Ngaku.

The tributaries of the rivers almost meet at their common watershed on the eastern edge of the New England Tableland. From this plateau of open country, some 1300 metres above sea level, the rivers fall into a maze of deep gorges and mountain ranges before crossing a narrow coastal plain to the sea.

The area is known as the Falls Country and its kaleidoscope of forests, mountains and rivers is still only accessible in some areas on foot or on horseback. This impenetrable barrier of rainforest — featuring great trees of hardwood and wattles, as well as vines, ferns and myrtle — became the final fortress for the three nations as they retreated before the English invasion.

These nations had initially shown a peaceful front to the invaders, but the relentless push to take over their land, water and food supplies drove them to war with the settlers in a final act of despair. Starving and outcast in their own country, they fought back from the green fortress in the Falls Country, to raid settlements for sheep and cattle and challenge the muskets of the invaders.

The river valleys of the Manning, Hastings and Macleay Rivers, with regular and abundant water supplies, represented a rich and plentiful homeland for the people of the three rivers. They proved immediately attractive to European settlers for just the same reasons. Photo by Lee Pearce.

With only a need for the most basic of shelter, and an abundance of available food, the people of the three rivers enjoyed a rich and sustaining lifestyle. Photos by Thomas Dick, courtesy The Australian Museum.

Eventually, orders were given to break the resistance of these three nations and a series of horrific massacres followed. More than twenty have been documented, of which the best known is the Myall Creek Massacre, near Inverell in 1838, when men, women and children — some still at the breast — were murdered without mercy.

Despite the superior firepower and tactics of genocide used against them, these nations maintained a stubborn resistance for more than 25 years. They were supported in their struggle by the Dainggati people, whose lands were around Bellbrook (between Kempsey and Armidale), but were reduced, in one generation, from a proud and numerous people to a pitiful remnant.

North of Taree heading for Kempsey, the narrow, hazardous road winds through a somewhat uninviting forest requiring considerable caution before the landscape opens out around the turn-off to Port Macquarie and Blackmans Point. These areas are very popular in traditional times for the spearing and netting of fish and the gathering of shellfish and they remain favourite holiday areas today for keen anglers.

Above *Aboriginal woman with child, Macleay River district. Courtesy National Library of Australia.*
Right *The sand dunes of the New South Wales coastline. Photo by Trevern Dawes.*
Below *Blue-tongue lizards are common throughout eastern Australia, and often grow to around 75 centimetres in length. A member of the skink family, blue-tongue lizards were an important food source for Aborigines. Photo by Philip Green.*

The Macleay River Valley

The Macleay River Valley, of which Kempsey is the main town, edges up to the New England escarpment. The scene downstream from Kempsey is very different from the days when the three nations ruled. The river has built up a huge, delta-shaped flood plain, and, in the lower reaches, large sand banks and mud flats show at low tide. Towards the sea there are sand dunes, swamps and lagoons.

Along the coast a dual system of dunes has developed, with marshes and swamps between. Areas of open grassland have been overrun with lantana, banksia and species of heath. In traditional times, the land would have been kept open through the practice of regular firing.

Kempsey is the town of my teenage triumphs. It was at Kinchela Boys Home that I spent my teenage years, as we were trained to become farm labourers for the rich landowners. Apart from the pain of being separated from my beloved sister — some 1500 kilometres away in an Aboriginal girls home at Cootamundra — like all the boys at Kinchela I felt the devastation caused by the absence of any female role model in my life. Denied any perception of the influence of a sister, mother, aunt or grandmother, we all suffered significant problems in later life coping with society in general and women in particular. Our substitute parent at Kinchela was a homosexual sadist. One time, when I accidently broke a window while playing cricket, I was forced to drop my pants and bend over to receive ten lashes with a stock whip, the scars of which are still in my mind and on my buttocks.

Our annual pocket money allocation of 25 cents hardly gave us a basis to deal with money management.

By the time I left school I had already experienced racism at its worst, being banned from access to the local swimming pool and being relegated to the black-only front three rows downstairs at the local picture theatre. When I was hospitalised after a football injury I found myself in the black ward at Kempsey Hospital. Over the years I saw many of my friends and family turn

After rising in the rugged hills to the south of Armidale, the Macleay River winds its way through lush farmlands — once bushland rich with game and other natural resources — before entering the ocean at South West Rocks. Photo by Lee Pearce.

65

Right *Collecting pippies on the shore near Port Macquarie. Photo by Thomas Dick, courtesy The Australian Museum.*
Below *Early group photo by J. W. Linolt. From the Ferguson Collection, courtesy National Library of Australia.*
Bottom *The Aboriginal hunter almost blends with his background as he silently waits to spear a fish. Photo by Thomas Dick, courtesy The Australian Museum.*

to alcohol as an escape from the pain of their existence and, at the age of 15, I made the decision never to drink alcohol or smoke cigarettes — both major agents of genocide — a golden rule I have followed throughout my life.

On the credit side, I grew up healthy and developed athletic prowess in rugby, cricket, running and surf lifesaving. My sporting abilities enabled me to continue at school and gain my matriculation as well as the respect of my peers. This gave me the chance to break the farm hand cycle and so my path took a different route to the others. I was the oldest of 45 boys at Kinchela, yet today only 5 are still alive.

The period at Kempsey gave me a great appreciation of the surf and I had the thrill of surfing at Hat Head with the dolphins beside me on the waves. Once I saw a small wallaby surfing and I'll never forget the time I caught a wave to escape a large shark that was after a group of us.

Above Stone technology was an important aspect of Aboriginal life. Stone flakes were used as cutting implements and as a vital part of the making of tools and weapons and they remain signs for archaeologists peering back through the mists of time. Photo by Thomas Dick, courtesy The Australian Museum.

Left Collecting stalks of the Xanthorrhoea, or grass tree, which provided ideal lightweight shafts for spears. Photo by Thomas Dick, courtesy The Australian Museum.

Chipping flakes from larger stones created effective cutting implements needed for a variety of functions. Photo by Thomas Dick, courtesy The Australian Museum.

Opposite *Portrait of a New South Wales Aborigine by Henry King, courtesy The Australian Museum.*

A selection of Thomas Dick's photos of Aborigines in the Port Macquarie area. The two photos on the right show alternate methods for climbing trees. Photos by Thomas Dick, courtesy The Australian Museum.

Many years later I had the chance to create the beaurocratic machinery necessary to turn Kinchela Boys Home into Benelongs Haven, an alcoholic treatment centre. Tragically, some of the boys who spent their youth here found themselves at the same place for treatment of alcoholism in their adult life. Benelongs Haven stands today as a monument to the commitment and dedication of Val Bryant and James Caroll, who have been responsible for bringing hundreds of Aboriginal people back to sobriety.

The Macleay River area was rich in food resources; black bream, flathead, jewfish, leatherjacket and blackfish were all caught in the river, and mullet, snapper and other ocean fish and pipis were taken on the surf beaches. On the sand banks and mud flats, shellfish were plentiful and the mangrove swamps provided crabs and oysters. The seafood diet was supplemented with birds and game such as kangaroo and wallaby.

In traditional times the locals enjoyed a rich and inexhaustible larder, which included flying fox, emu, brush turkey, eggs, platypus, echidna, bandicoot and possums. The possum skins also provided material for rugs and cloaks, which were worn during the winter months.

Their range of vegetables included the *towwack,* a small, potato-like vegetable, wild spinach, cabbage palm hearts, burrawang nut kernels, cunjevoi roots and a variety of other delicacies which are today widely sought after. Many of these foods required elaborate preparation. The cunjevoi had to be beaten and pounded for several days and then soaked in running water before being baked. Fern roots were beaten until reduced to a paste and then cooked on hot embers.

The last of the Dainggati

The region of the three rivers is rich with stories of the downfall of the three nations. A Mrs M. Quinlan, one of the last remaining Dainggati people, provided testimony which covered her life in a changing world in *Aboriginal Child at School* (1983). Born on the banks of the Macleay at Bellbrook, in a family of nine, she was a part of a people whose land was centred around Walcha.

She remembered the time of the killing:

> *They were killing everywhere, all through the area*
> *. . . I lost one grandmother over the bluffs near*
> *Armidale. They killed a lot of our people, pushing*
> *them over the bluffs . . . The other grandmother I*
> *lost on the Macleay on Pee Dee Creek. They used to*
> *herd them up and shoot them.*

She recalled how the family walked from Armidale, which was too cold for the Dainggati people in winter, to Bellbrook, where a camp was established. Her father went on to fence 60 acres and established a farm, raising fowls and growing corn and vegetables. She remembered how her father had to give his European landlords half of everything he owned, so he could stay on the land — his own traditional land.

Mrs Quinlan recalled how her father, following the bloody defeat of the Dainggati people, banned the old language and forbade his sons to take part in ceremonies. And she documented the kidnapping of her sister and cousin by the government as Aboriginal wards and their departure for Sydney.

Stone fish weirs were built across rivers to harvest fish. Some of these traps were complex arrangements covering up to 20 000 square metres, with thousands of stones making curved walls which were functional at all tides. Traps constructed from woven nets and baskets were used also. Considerable time was spent maintaining these traps as they played an important part in supplying food. From the Tyrrell Collection, courtesy Macleay Museum.

The bora

Highway One skirts the territory of the great Kamilaroi, whose lands stretched westwards from the Great Dividing Range. The Kamilaroi were one of the most populous and extensive nations of eastern Australia and their language was so widely known that strangers would often greet each other with the words: 'Do you speak Kamilaroi?' It is the language influence of the Kamilaroi which has given eastern Australia the word *bora,* derived from 'bor' or 'boor', the fur string belt worn by the initiated men of the Kamilaroi.

The bora ceremony was the institution for the admission of young men into the privileges and duties of manhood, as well as an instruction in the social and religious duties which would bind them for the rest of their lives. Among other things, these codes governed precisely who each individual was allowed to marry and what responsibilities resulted for the wife, children and relatives.

This law was taught as coming from creation itself, timeless and immutable. The bora ceremonies were designed to reinforce the civil and religious law and those who administered it. It was a rite characteristic of eastern Australia and brought every clan together for the ceremonies on full moon summer nights. On those occasions,

large nations — such as the Kamilaroi, Wiradjuri and Bundjalung — could assemble as many as 6000 people for the ceremonies.

The bora ground itself is a circular cleared area, some 10 to 15 metres in diameter, edged with low banks of earth. Sometimes there are two circles joined by a walkway flanked with images of totemic human and animal figures.

These photos by Charles Kerry show something of traditional Aboriginal ceremonies.
Right *'Arrival of the king'.*
Below *'Death of the wild boar'.*
Below right *'Lying in wait'. From the Tyrrell Collection, courtesy Macleay Museum.*

Above *Carved trees, or dendroglyphs, can still be found at various places around New South Wales. Usually they indicated important graves. This tree marks the grave of Yurinigh, near Molong. Photo by Jennifer Isaacs.*

Above right *Nambucca Heads offers long beaches, clean sand and excellent fishing. Photo by Lee Pearce.*

Moving north past the dramatic setting of Mount Yarrahapinni and on through the towns of Macksville, Nambucca Heads, the Belligen region, and Sawtell, north to Coffs Harbour, Aboriginal faces become more prominant in public places. Along the way there are large reserves. One in particular stands as a monument to the treatment of Aboriginal people in earlier times. At Bowraville, a reserve — which still exists — was built on the town's sewer and rubbish dump, whilst the black population was exploited on the banana plantations and diary farms which dominate the district. The majestic eucalypts which once gave such nourishment are mostly gone.

Nambucca Heads marks the southern frontier of the Kumbainggiri people, who once occupied the rich coastal belt north to Coffs Harbour. The heritage of these people lives on in the carved trees (or dendroglyphs) at Nambucca Heads. The complex carvings depict animals and include geometric and linear designs.

There is little information available about the carved trees at Nambucca, but they do seem to have been associated with the bora ceremonies and the initiation of the young males into the lore of the tribe.

The north-east corner of New South Wales has a rock art tradition with various regional styles. In the Clarence Valley there are numerous engravings and drawings, mostly in rock shelters and on vertical rock faces.

On the northern tablelands, the style favours red ochre paintings, which are found on the protected surfaces under gigantic granite boulders. On the western slopes of the tablelands, both paintings and engravings are numerous.

The Clarence Valley is proving rich in art, though interpretations have been difficult: many sites feature designs with a maze of intersecting lines

Stuart Island

Stuart Island is located south of the township of Nambucca Heads, on the Nambucca River, just before the northern bypass.

It was declared an Aboriginal reserve at the beginning of this century and contains generations of Kumbainggiri remains in a burial site right at the sixth hole of the Nambucca Golf Course. It represents a sad chapter in Kumbainggiri history, that the occupants were forcibly removed (to nearby Bellwood Reserve) to make way for the pursuit of white man's leisure, on such a choice piece of real estate. In fact most of the great river systems on the New South Wales coastline empty into estuaries containing small islands to which Aboriginal people were removed once the potential for dairy farming on the fertile river flats they naturally occupied was realised.

and curves. South-west of Grafton, five shelters containing art have been found at Blaxlands Flat, featuring excellent hand stencils, goannas and fish, although much of the imagery has been vandalised in recent times. Other galleries have been discovered in the Sandy Creek valley and at Chambigne, as well as in several other areas. Many paintings feature white stencilled hands, which have attracted considerable interest and speculation, and a variety of goanna designs, which dominate the art of the entire Clarence Valley area. It is thought that the goanna had special totemic significance for these people.

The engravings of the Clarence River Valley (together with a site north of Kyogle) are the only engraved sites east of the Dividing Range in northern New South Wales. They differ considerably from the engravings of the Hawkesbury region, but have much in common with those found in the Carnarvon Range in Queensland.

Left, below *The Clarence River. Photos by Lee Pearce.*

Above *The defiance dance of the Yarra-Bandine clan. Reproduced in Clement Hodgkinson, Australia, from Port Macquarie to Moreton Bay (1845). Courtesy National Library of Australia.*

Right *Despite being slow to grow, many huge Xanthorrhoeas could once be found along this coastline and offered coastal clans a major trading item with clans from further inland. Few such specimens can be found today. Photo by Thomas Dick, courtesy The Australian Museum.*

Three stages in the construction of a bark canoe. Above, the donor tree — usually a river gum — is selected and a section of bark carefully removed. The bark is then smoked (above left) to give it flexibility and to increase its resistence to water penetration. Once the ends were tied off with fibre or vine, the canoe was ready for action (left). Sometimes props were used to hold the centre section open. Despite their simplicity these craft were most effective for stillwater fishing. Photos by Thomas Dick, courtesy The Australian Museum.

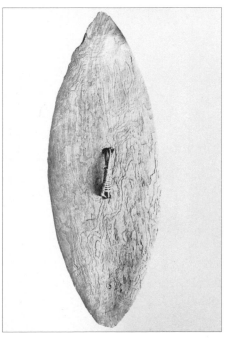

Shields were made from solid sections of tree truck or from the buttressed roots of fig trees. The wood needed to be light in weight and complex enough in its grain not to split or break under assault. The selected section of wood was removed with stone wedges, carved and then painted into clan designs. Photos by Thomas Dick, courtesy The Australian Museum.

Below *North coast rainforest. Photo by Grenville Turner/Wildlight.*

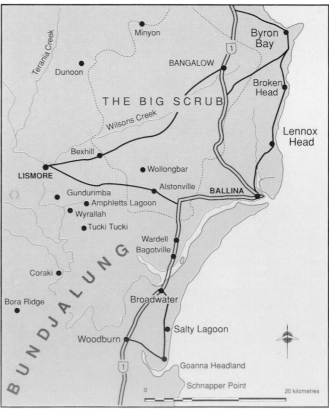

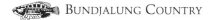

Bundjalung country

THE crossing of the Clarence River marks our entry into Bundjalung country. One of the most important nations in eastern Australia, the Bundjalung have reunited in this generation and their language and culture are now taught at the Northern Rivers College of Advanced Education at Lismore.

Another tribute to the enduring culture of the Bundjalung is the adoption of their language by Victorian Aborigines, whose own languages are almost lost. The Bundjalung language is now being taught to Victorian children and also at Monash University, to which the Bundjalung people send language teachers each year.

Bundjalung National Park, between the Clarence River and Evans Head, is named for the people who dominated the area in traditional times. There is dispute about the full extent of their territory, some authorities believing their lands stretched north as far as the Beaudesert area of Queensland.

In pre-colonial times, Bundjalung country encompassed some of the richest hunting and fishing grounds anywhere on the continent. Today, those same lands represent some of Australia's most expensive and striking realestate. According to the oral traditions of the Bundjalung, these areas were first settled by the Three Brothers and their descendants. The first landing was made at Yamba, at the mouth of the Clarence, and another at Evans Head. While two of the brothers remained on the coast, the third went inland towards the Lismore region.

Bundjalung country at ground level. The buttresses of these fig trees were used extensively in the manufacture of shields. Photo by Mark Lang/Wildlight.

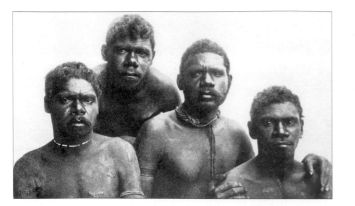

Above *A group of blacktrackers. Photo donated by Mrs N. Brown, courtesy National Library of Australia.*
Above right *Aborigines who resisted the invasion of their lands were dealt with in a similar way all over the continent. Reproduced from* The Lone Hand *(1911), courtesy National Library of Australia.*

The area was heavily populated prior to the arrival of European settlers and numerous shell middens have been found along the coast. Mining, agricultural and urban developments in the Yamba area, which marks the southern boundary of Bundjalung country, have left few remaining traces of the original settlements. However, from Wombah, north of Yamba, to Woody Head, there is an almost endless belt of middens, indicating continuous and extensive use of this land.

When excavated, these middens provide archaeologists with an extraordinary volume of information about the past, shedding valuable light on aspects of lifestyle, ecology, diet, technology, material culture, population size and age. Stone and bone artefacts, and the presence of dingo and shellfish remains provide added insights to settlement patterns. Middens are essentially rubbish dumps associated with old campsites.

Contraception and fertility

Modern science has committed considerable resources to the development of contraceptive pills, but Bundjalung women discovered their own hundreds, if not thousands, of years ago. Now, researchers from California are examining the seed of the *Cymbidium madidum,* in an attempt to discover how Bundjalung women managed to use the seeds so successfully as a contraceptive.

Totemic sites throughout the country were used for fertility rituals, where young girls wanting children could be entered by the birth spirits. One of these sites is at Tatham (derived from the Bundjalung word for baby), another is on the small island known as Goong and Water Island, near Cabbage Tree Island.

The story of the three brothers

In the very beginning, three brothers — together with their wives and mother — travelled from far across the sea, arriving on the Australian coast at the mouth of the Clarence River. Their boat, however, was blown out to sea in a storm, so the brothers decided to build canoes in order to return to their homeland.

They completed building the canoes but could find no sign of their mother anywhere so they set off without her. On returning to find she had been left behind, the mother climbed to the top of a hill and cursed them for abandoning her. She called the ocean to anger and the wild seas forced the brothers back to land at Chinamans Beach, near Evans Head. Once the seas had abated one of the brothers returned south to find their mother. The others settled near Evans Head, developed families and a thriving community.

One of the families moved north, another west and the third to the south, forming the three branches of the Bundjalung people.

Baryulgil

Baryulgil is a small town about 100 kilometres from Grafton, on a country road linking Grafton and Tabulam, near Casino. It is off the highway, but well worth a visit. The Baryulgil people, who represent an important component of the Bundjalung nation, have recorded in their Dreamtime stories the creation of the Clarence River.

Long ago, among the forests of tall trees, high in the mountains near Tooloom, an old woman called Dirrangun kept a hidden spring. She did not want anyone to know about her secret spring, but one day she fell ill and when a handsome young man called Bulagaan called by, she asked him to bring her water. Arriving at the spring to collect water in his coolamon, he discovered it was dammed. Bulagaan broke the dam and the water began to flow. Dirrangun rose in panic and tried to dam the water again, in the process creating the mountains we see today, but she failed to stop the flow of water, which became the Clarence River.

Mount Ogilvie was one of the mountains she created in her attempts to dam the water, but it broke through and flowed down to Yamba. Dirrangun realised she couldn't stop the water, so she cursed it and turned it into salt. And, as she stood at the mouth of the river, she continued to curse until she was turned into stone.

This story, told by a Bundjalung woman, Lucy Daly, to Roland Robinson and documented in his book *The Man Who Sold His Dreaming,* has intriguing parallels with the Biblical story of Lot and his wife, fleeing from Sodom and Gomorrah. Lot's wife defied the injunction not to look back and was turned into a pillar of salt. The story of Dirrangun has a similar theme, and the standing stone remains at the mouth of the Clarence.

The Baryulgil people trace their prosperity to the great river created in the Dreamtime by Dirrangun. The small turtles that the people easily caught by hand in the river are still plentiful. Cooking them became a special tradition for the Baryulgil. Cleaned and washed, the turtle was placed, shell down, on the hot coals and cooked slowly, without burning a hole in the shell, which became the serving plate for a great delicacy.

After the defeat of neighbouring peoples by the advance of European settlement, the Baryulgil were herded into a mission near the town which bears their name. But their suffering was not yet at an end. In 1944, white asbestos was discovered in the area and mining commenced. The Baryulgil people worked in the mines, and brought home sacks, which were used for wall cladding and bedspreads.

Over the 35 years that the mine operated, 350 Baryulgil people worked in the mine. Eighty are already dead (an average age of 49), with the cause of death linked directly to the asbestos.

Colonial authorities were fond of handing out brass name plates to leaders of surviving clans, on whom they bestowed the title of 'King'. Photo taken by Henry King around 1900, courtesy National Library of Australia.

The rivers of northern New South Wales offer a rich diet, especially turtles, which formed a vital part of Baryulgil lifestyles. Photo by Lee Pearce.

Goanna Head

Rejoining Highway One at the Bundjalung National Park, the next major reminder of the tradional times is at Evans Head. The headland (*djurebil,* or 'sacred place') is believed to be inhabited by a totemic being, a goanna who is responsible for bringing rain. The headland certainly looks like a goanna with its tail stretched out.

The whole area has a lot to tell us about the past. In the sand dunes west of Snapper Point for example, archaeologists have found a site used by local people to make tools more than 6000 years ago. On the south side of the river investigation of a midden about 9 metres deep showed it was in use 500 years ago.

Goanna Headland was the scene of a major massacre of the Bundjalung during the 1840s after the people had taken action against the intrusion of Europeans on their traditional lands. Over a hundred warriors died in a final defence of their beloved headland and for years after their skulls could be picked from the rocks by white souvenir hunters as evidence of their conquest.

Salty Lagoon, north of the Broadwater National Park, is a place in Bundjalung mythology, that tells about Gaungan, a female ancestral being. Flying from Woodenbong she landed on a beach close to the lagoon and turned into a black rock. J. G. Steele, in *Aboriginal Pathways in Southeast Queensland,* describes her as 'tall and slim, with long flowing hair, beautiful hands and long fingernails'. This was a considerable attribute in pre-colonial times, when a woman who wanted to catch a man would place nail parings in his drink and then whisper a spell as he drank it. According to the story, when this female being moved between Salty Lagoon and Wardell on the Richmond River she often appeared as a shining light. In her travels around the coast she would try to seduce men into coming into the sea or the lagoon.

Goanna Head. Photo by Lee Pearce.

PHOTO BY LEE PEARCE

The creation of Goanna Headland

Way back in the Dreamtime, Nimbin, a wise man of the Bundjalung, elicited the help of a goanna to stop the snake from tormenting a bird. The goanna chased the snake from a hill near Bungwalbin, down towards Newesly, and across to Woodburn. Failing to find the snake at Woodburn, the goanna pushed on to Evans Head, where it caught the snake and bit it on the tail. The snake, however, managed to bite the goanna on the head, which forced it to retreat upstream for special grasses to counteract the venom.

The goanna recovered quickly and again took up pursuit of the snake, which headed seawards before doubling back to create Snake Island. Then it escaped into the sea. When the goanna reached the shore it lay down to rest and await the snake's possible return, where it waits to this day as Goanna Headland. The head of the goanna is to the north of the headland, closest to the coast at Red Hill. The front right foot is formed by the rocks to the south of Red Hill beach. Chinamans Beach forms the right side of its chest and belly and Snapper Rock its tail.

This headland holds great significance for contemporary Bundjalung people and is still used as a meeting place to carry on the cultural responsibility of their traditions. The goanna is closely associated with rain, and Rain Cave, on the headland, was used by tribal elders to sing for rain. This cave was regarded as taboo for anyone other than local tribes and, it was believed, floods would result from entry by others.

At Snapper Point there is an unusual ceremonial ground which is a place of special significance, its precise location being known only to a few elders.

At sea level on the cliff, Snake Cave is one place where the snake can be heard to hiss (and the goanna to thump its tail) during strong winds and swell. The high incidence of rock fishing accidents in this area is seen by the Bundjalung as evidence of the ongoing power of this place.

Ballina

Heading north, Highway One follows the coast to a major centre of the Bundjalung people, Ballina, situated at the mouth of the Richmond River. Archaeological research on oyster shell middens in the area reveal an age of at least 1650 years.

The Dreamtime stories of Ballina tell of a young hero who left his home to test his prowess in battle and of the visits by the beautiful daughters of the Three Brothers, who came from across the mountains to visit once a year.

By the middle of the last century, perhaps 500 Bundjalung people still fished and hunted in the region from Broken Head in the north, inland to the Big Scrub. They would move to the beach each September to fish for salmon, then on to Chickiaba on North Creek for the oyster season. They had strong and finely woven nets, made from the inside fibre of the stinging tree and from the bark of the kurrajong, which they used for fishing and hunting. Local game included wallabies, bandicoots and goanna, as well as flying foxes, which gather seasonally in huge numbers and were easily brought down with boomerang or hunting stick.

In the Broadwater area between Ballina and Coraki two bora grounds were recorded. One was near Bagotville; the other, now ruined, was close to the village of Broadwater, and was reportedly last in use in 1922. The people who once used it now live on Cabbage Tree Island not far away.

About 10 kilometres south-west of Coraki is Bora Ridge, which, according to J. G. Steele was named after the bora ring that once stood there. It was first encroached on by the local school and then destroyed. In contrast, the bora ring now a part of Tucki General Cemetery has been well maintained. Located on a ridge which commands panoramic views of the valley, it is looked after by the National Parks and Wildlife Service and fenced against the vandalism which has seen so many other bora grounds destroyed.

This great bora is on the route used in ancient times by people travelling to Lismore and the north. Trade took Bundjalung people far into Queensland, bartering for new spears and implements, as well as bunya nuts. Such trips

King Benalong, from Urunga. From the Tyrrell Collection, courtesy Macleay Museum.

Traditional contests were conducted throughout Australia. Ballina was a centre for such events on the north coast of New South Wales. From a watercolour painting by Joseph Lycett, courtesy National Library of Australia.

North of the Broadwater National Park, Salty Lagoon is a place where, according to Bundjalung tradition, Gaungan, a female ancestral being, would try to seduce men into the water. Photo by Lee Pearce.

were important events and the people sang special songs to welcome the travellers on their return. These visits became annual pilgrimages, the Queenslanders coming south on reciprocal visits from the bunya country. Seeds brought south on these visits probably gave birth to the bunya pines now growing in the Lismore, Woodburn and Wyrallah districts.

The Wilsons River, in the Wyrallah area, runs through flat plains with tea tree and she-oak, while the banks are lined with rainforest trees. Wyrallah was the name given to the local Bundjalung people and it is believed to come from *wyaroo*, meaning hungry.

Amphletts Lagoon, near Wyrallah, is a place to be avoided at night because an evil spirit lives there. On the top of a hill known as Parrots Nest (*goorambil*, meaning pine trees in Bundjalung) — some 6 kilometres northwest of Wyrallah — is a stone arrangement of great religious significance, marking the place and the clan totem, the hoop pine. Annual ceremonies were once held here to restore the stone arrangements with solemn singing and dances.

A clump of hoop pines on a small knoll beside the river marks the main settlement of the Wyrallah clan. At nearby Pelican Creek was a famous ceremonial ground where traditional cermonies were recorded up to 1899. An account written in the 1860s described a mortuary ceremony in detail.

Agra, a young wife, was bitten by a snake and died. At the funeral her body was placed in a circle of fire: the men marched around with their spears — to keep out the evil spirits — while the women wailed. The next day, Agra's body was carried 5 kilometres to the burial ground in a solemn procession, led by the grieving husband, who carried Agra's infant son. Her body was placed in the fork of a tree, about 4 metres above ground, under a canopy

Below *An emu takes an early morning drink.*

Below left *The distinctive black rocks of Bundjalung National Park, formed by continual wave and wind action on the peaty rock. Photos by Lee Pearce.*

of branches. A circle was drawn around the tree and, after songs were sung, the husband stood and made his proclamations of love and loss.

An observer in the Lismore region in the 1870s recorded the story of a ritual battle in which disputes were settled when young blood ran hot. A young warrior from the Tweed had eloped with a Lismore girl and 500 warriors from each clan assembled to settle the dispute, each armed with two spears, two boomerangs, a nulla nulla and a shield. The warriors were gaily painted, their hair adorned with parrot feathers to mark a ceremonial occasion.

The chosen battlefield was Currys Creek and when the two armies clashed, the peace of the bush was broken by the cries of battle and the clash of weapons. The lawmakers of the clans permitted the fight to continue for several hours before they declared a draw, honour satisfied.

Some 2 kilometres south of Nimbin, in a rainforest on the western side of Goolmangar Creek, is an impressive outcrop of rhyolite obsidian rock, known as Nimbin Rocks. The rocks have an unusual and dramatic profile, reaching into the air like giant stalagmites, and are a site of considerable importance to the Bundjalung. These rocks are considered to have special powers, which go back to a little man of great power, called Nyimbunja, who was, it is said, buried on the south-eastern slopes near Nimbin Rocks. The rocks are considered a reminder of the powers of this little man and a place of great sacred spirits. Local Bundjalung who still respect the traditional ways will not go there, because they respect the powers of Nyimbunja. The site has been declared an Aboriginal site of significance and is controlled by the local land council.

Right *The site of a famous bora ground at Tucki Tucki. Marked, but hardly preserved. Photo by Lee Pearce.*
Opposite *Desmond, a clan leader from New South Wales. From a watercolour painting by Augustus Earle, courtesy National Library of Australia.*

Lennox Head

Lennox Head. Photo by Lee Pearce.

Just 8 kilometres north of Ballina is Lennox Head, now a small township with a number of motels near the beach. It was here at Lennox, according to Bundjalung legend, that the founding Three Brothers made one of their famous landings, said to be near today a group of black rocks on the beach.

When one of the brothers, Yarbirri, thrust a spear into the sand, fresh water ran, and when the tide is low you can still see a rusty stain.

After their landing at Lennox Head, the Three Brothers moved north to Brunswick Heads, where they created the first bora ground. Thousands of years later, a bora ground remains at Lennox, protected by the National Parks and Wildlife Service and open to the public. It is on sandy ground one block back from the beach, on the west side of Gibbon Street (about 300 metres north of the school), and can be entered through a fenced pathway. The land has been cleared but originally banksia, cypress and many heath plants grew there.

The early morning profile of Mount Warning, known to the Aborigines as Wollumbin, or fighting leader. Photo by Lee Pearce.

The pelican was an important totemic symbol for the people of the Tweed Valley. Fossil remains of these birds, which are found all over the country, date back some 30 and 40 million years. Photo by Lee Pearce.

The Tweed valley

LEAVING Lismore and the Richmond River behind to the south, the Tweed Valley — one of the jewels of Bundjalung country — unfolds before us. The McPherson, Tweed and Nightcap Ranges form a backdrop to the coastal strip which extends from Byron Bay and Brunswick Heads to Tweed Heads. Local legends acknowledge the role of the Three Brothers in their creation and settlement of the area, and the bringing of law, religion and language.

John Oxley was the first European to venture into these lands. In 1823, he travelled up the Tweed, 7 kilometres from Fingal, where he and his companion, John Uniacke, encountered the Bundjalung people for the first time. Uniacke recorded about 200 on the banks of the river, gathered to watch his strange vessel. He also noted the vegetation, climate and topography for the first time.

Just across the Tweed River from Fingal is an important bora ring, under the care of the National Parks and Wildlife Service. It is open to visitors, from an entrance in Duffy Street.

Razorback Lookout, on Observatory Hill in Tweed Heads, was known as *Choongurra-bannarin de-arn,* the pelican ceremonial ground. The word comes from *djungar* (pelican), *ngari* (dance) and *djagun* (ground). A traditional story says that on this hill in the Dreaming all the birds of the forest painted themselves and held a ceremony. They have kept those colours to this day.

A cave on Point Danger was called *Mog-nogumbo* (black dog) because of the roaring and howling of the sea there in bad weather. Point Danger's Aboriginal name is *Booningba*, from the word for echidna.

Above *Photo portrait of an Aboriginal 'chief' by Charles Kerry. Courtesy Macleay Museum.*
Opposite *A northern Australian Aborigine. Photo by Henry King, courtesy The Australian Museum.*
Below *An Aboriginal mia mia on the Tweed River. Photo by Charles Kerry. From the Tyrrell Collection, courtesy Macleay Museum.*

Mount Warning, or *Wollumbin* (fighting leader), dominates the Tweed Valley and is now surrounded by national park. There were numerous stone arrangements in this area but Europeans and their livestock have combined to destroy most of them. One of the most significant, known as the 'grave of the giantess' comprised up to 30 standing stones, each about 5 metres in diameter, which had been brought from a creek about 6 kilometres away. The monument was on a forest ridge of yellow clay soil on the southern side of the mountain near Terragon. According to oral tradition, the giantess was 3 metres tall and the tallest man of the clan could walk under her armpits.

It was customary for the senior clan leader to be called Wollumbin, and one of the last of such men was known to the Europeans as Wollumbin Johnnie. He inherited the title in 1870. He was buried on a hill about 2 kilometres from the Tyalgum turnoff, on the Murwillumbah–Uki road. His grave was marked by three cairns forming the points of a triangle but these were destroyed by a bulldozer.

Another great leader was Durranbah. His grave, on a ridge to the west of Limpinwood, between the Tweed and Beaudesert, stood for generations until vandalised. His presence is still felt by the local surfers who appreciate the fine waves on the beach named after him.

A path north to Beaudesert followed a spur across Mount Durigan, crossed the McPherson Range and descended to the head of the Albert River and on to Kerry. It could be seen until the 1920s, and was an important route linking people on both sides of what is now the New South Wales--Queensland border.

The route was established in the Dreamtime, when two dingoes chased a giant kangaroo from what is now the Lamington Plateau all the way to Beaudesert. There, they were caught and killed. Later, the people who owned the dingoes found their bodies and took them back to the Lamington Plateau, where they became the stone dogs on the top of Widgee Falls. Another legend suggests they became the two small peaks east of Mount Warning.

An art gallery still exists in the Doon Doon area, south-east of Terragon, which features ochre paintings of birds, emu tracks, a shark and a woman. Bora rings have survived near Tyalgum.

As we move north across the border, to the Gold Coast, we again find the stories of the Three Brothers and rivalries similar to those which exist today between the two states. The Bundjalung people were regarded here as *birin*, meaning southerners, by the people of the Brisbane River, although Bundjalung country extended all the way to the edge of that river system.

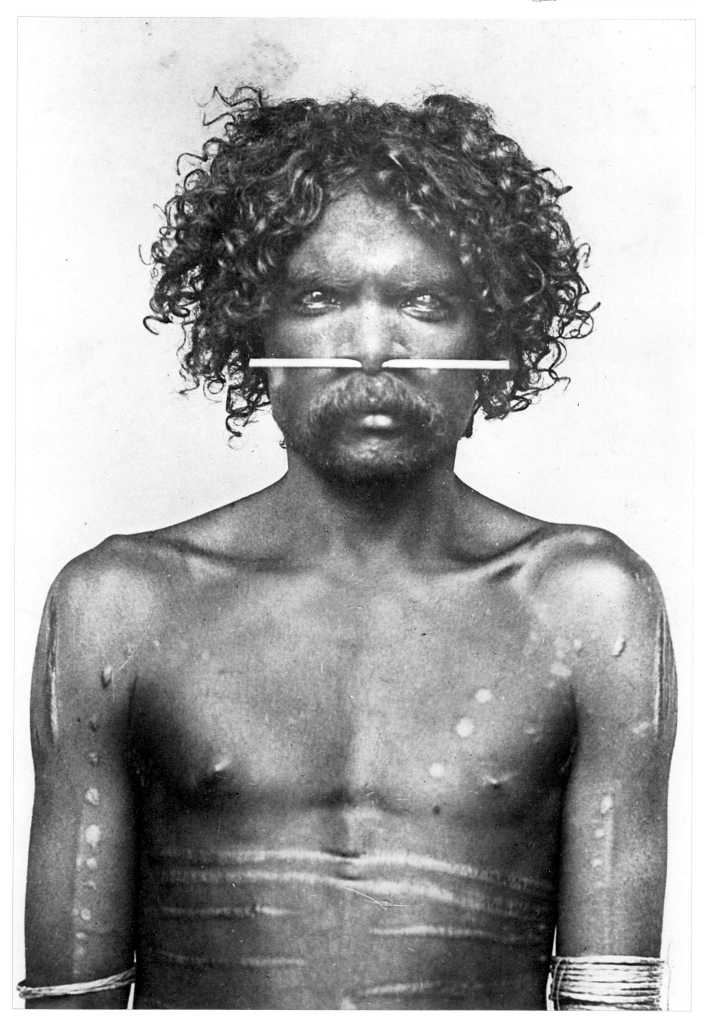

Minjungbal Cultural Reserve

Located just 5 kilometres south of Tweed Heads is an Aboriginal Educational Resource Centre operated by a local Aboriginal co-operative and staffed by Aboriginal people.

There you will find a fine display of photographs, artwork, craft and videos on Aboriginal culture, and friendly warm people. Provision is made for lectures and school children are frequent, almost daily, visitors. The central attraction and feature of the centre is the bora ring.

The centre takes its name from the Minjungbal people whose territory encompassed the estuarine lands of the lower Tweed River. The museum presents visitors with a fascinating display of cultural material. A trained Aboriginal guide explains in detail how the Aboriginal people lived, what food they ate, how they hunted and fished and what tools they made and used. Visitors can also catch a glimpse of the mythological and ceremonial practices of the Tweed Valley.

The museum displays contain a diverse range of artefacts such as dilly bags, ceremonial dishes, stone tools, palm leaf water carriers, seed head ornaments and earth ochres. As well as artefacts of the north coast of New South Wales, there are also a variety of items from Arnhem Land, Kakadu, Torres Strait Islands and Central Australia.

The Minjungbal bora ring, used as a sacred ceremonial ground for the initiation of young boys, is considered to be one of the best examples in the state and represents an irreplaceable link between Aboriginal people and their religious and cultural heritage. This bora ring was entrusted to the care of an Aboriginal woman, Margaret Kay, until her death in 1972. In 1980, the eight hectares of natural bushland which protect the bora ring were declared an historic site under the National Parks and Wildlife Act. At the same time the nearby Ukerebagh Nature Reserve was dedicated. The site is leased to the Tweed Aboriginal Co-operative Society under a special agreement with the National Parks and Wildlife Service.

Visitors are invited to take a walk around the track, to perhaps spot a koala, or watch the ibis and kingfishers feeding in the tidal zone among the mangroves. The track traverses a number of vegetation types or habitats. Eucalyptus forest, with the tall pink bloodwood and forest red gum, intermingles with the cheese tree, red ash and coastal banksia, with their yellow blooms that entice the many honeyeaters that frequent the area.

Above *Minjungbal Cultural Reserve. Photo by Lee Pearce.*
Right *The sacred kingfisher is often seen in the Minjungbal Cultural Reserve. The most widely distributed of all the kingfishers in Australia, the sacred kingfisher is found all over mainland Australia, excluding the arid centre, and Tasmania. Photo by Philip Green.*
Below *Rainbow lorikeets are just one of many bird species attracted to the reserve. Photo by Jonathon Chester/Wildlight.*

Small lizards, and the occasional goanna, can be seen in the trees or sitting on the ground basking in the sun.

A few rainforest species can be seen among the eucalypts, species which belong to littoral rainforest, which is sometimes found in association with eucalypt forests near the coast. Covering small areas of ground like a green carpet is the native violet. It you look closer you may see their delicate mauve and white flowers reaching up to catch some sun. Numerous types of orb weavers and other spiders can be seen around the track. Draped over trees are the orange-coloured devils twine and the three leaved cissus vine.

As you get closer to the levee bank, the vegetation changes to include melaleuca trees, with their thin papery bark; native ginger, which grows in clumps and has white and gold flowers; swamp she-oak; and, along the ground, the hibertia vine with its flat yellow flowers.

As you walk along the levee bank look at the mangrove. The ones that look as if they are on stilts are called spider mangroves. The other species are the grey mangroves, whose leaf has a lighter underside, and the river mangrove which has a dark green leaf covered in salt. Their roots are the spikes you see protuding from the mud. The mangroves colonise the intertidal zone and become the breeding grounds of fish, prawns and other aquatic creatures.

Feeding on the mud flats at low tide are crabs, whelks, ibis, herons and egrets; in the trees are willy wagtails, flycatchers and kingfishers to name a few. You may see kites or sea eagles in the air.

A struggle for acknowledgement

A warrior. Photo by Charles Kerry, courtesy Macleay Museum.

Aboriginal people in New South Wales bore the brunt of British settlement and have never recovered from the intensity of that onslaught.

Soon after the establishment of the convict settlement at Sydney, the Europeans caught a glimpse of the Aboriginal personality. Governor Phillip had decided to set an example by punishing a convict thief who stole some fishing implements belonging to an Aboriginal person. In the presence of both the British and Aboriginal people the thief was bound and flogged. So distressed were the Aborigines that they attacked the flogger, took the whip from him and cried for the thief.

The invaders took advantage of a people unprepared for the European approach to land ownership. In the absence of man-made boundaries like fences, settlement began in earnest. Within a few short years all the prized coastal land had been usurped.

As towns mushroomed, the Aborigines came to be seen as a nuisance, which led the government to create ghetto-type areas which were fenced off and called Aboriginal Reserves. These reserves were often on the outskirts of country towns, and some Aborigines became 'fringe dwellers', with all the accompanying ramifications of degradation for each succeeding generation. Reserves were also created on islands towards the mouths of coastal rivers in New South Wales. As Australia was 'taken up' Aboriginal reserves themselves became targets for white acquisition until the final area left for Aboriginal occupation in New South Wales had dwindled to 3000 acres (1215 hectares).

Reserves were located, by statute, at a specific distance from the local post office. Three miles (4.8 kilometres) and more away from white towns required the establishment of schools, and each reserve had its own primary school. For a long time Aboriginal 'fringe dwellers' could be refused permission to attend town schools and resentment from both sides became the breeding ground for racism.

Between Sydney and the Queensland border there are reserves at Karuah, Forster, Purfleet (Taree), Telegraph Point, Burnt Bridge, Greenhills (Kempsey), Bellwood (Nambucca Heads), Bowraville, Coffs Harbour, Glenreagh, Nymboida (Grafton), Maclean, Yamba, Coraki, Cabbage Tree Island, Evans Head and Lutitia Spit (Tweed Heads). Island reserves were located on the Macleay, Nambucca, Clarence and Richmond Rivers. The former reserve

Billy, King of the Macquarie, in ceremonial paint, with wife and dog. Having been real kings of their lands without the title, the original Australians found themselves without land or title, other than a brass plaque. Courtesy Macleay Museum.

on Stuart Island, south of Nambucca Heads, is now the site of the local golf course.

When the New South Wales government finally legislated, in 1983, the only land to actually come back to Aboriginal people was the reserves. The 1983 Land Rights Act provided no acknowledgment of communal native title, which had been employed successfully in other British countries with indigenous minority populations. It denied Aborigines any right to vast tracts of land on which Aboriginal communities could demonstrate a Dreamtime occupation, because most of that land was already under white freehold title, especially the eastern coastline and central farming belt, the choicest pieces of real estate. The same Act provided for Aborigines a three-tier structure of 115 Local Aboriginal Land Councils, 13 Regional Aboriginal Land Councils and one State Land Council. The government also decreed that 7.5 per cent of land tax revenue, over a period of 15 years (from 1983), totalling at least $300 000 000, be paid to the Land Councils. On a yearly basis $22 000 000 is provided to the Land Councils and half of this is invested so that the fund could be self-perpetuating. The other half is equally divided for Land Councils to administer and to purchase properties on the open market. The Local Land Councils get about $60 000 each, per annum, which means that they have to pool their resources to buy properties of any worthwhile size.

The 1983 New South Wales Aboriginal Land Rights Act introduced a new concept in Australian land laws in that it bestowed title to all lands owned by Aboriginal Land Councils. Aboriginal title ensures that land acquired under the Land Rights Act can never be sold, and therefore is valueless in financial terms as real estate. There can be no land speculation, because no acquired lands can ever be sold once it comes into Aboriginal title. Clearly the government sought to enshrine Aboriginal spirituality of land title in legislative form. In so doing the Act eliminated land as a commercial commodity for Aborigines in New South Wales, where no Aboriginal Land Council can use its land as collateral in a bank loan or overdraft, because the land has no real financial value.

Many are also critical of the Act, arguing that it actively discriminates against non-Aboriginal Australians. At the time of writing this act is under review by the recently elected Liberal government in New South Wales.

From the earliest days of the colony Aborigines have been offered welfare in exchange for their land. Handing out blankets in the early days. Photo by Charles Kerry, courtesy Macleay Museum.

Queensland's coast offers a
wealth of offshore islands. Photo
by Oliver Strewe/Wildlight.

The Gold Coast to Cairns

OUR journey north from the Gold Coast to Cairns covers some 3000 kilometres of Queensland's coastline. As far as Fraser Island we have constant surf beaches to the east of the highway, before we travel the sheltered coast inside the Great Barrier Reef. And all the way, the climate gets warmer and the people friendlier.

The Lamington National Park, west of the Gold Coast, offers travellers the chance to see the real wonder of this landscape. Photo by Robbi Newman.

Right *The dolphin was an important totemic symbol for this stretch of coastline long before it was formerly adopted by the Gold Coast Tourism Authority. Photo by Bryce Douglas.*
Below *The Gold Coast from Mount Tambourine. The modern view of a coastline that has always been a playground area. Photo by Philip Green.*

In a fascinating paradox of history, the glittering tourist centre known as the Gold Coast was once the playground of Black Australia. Many thousands of years before this stretch of idyllic coastline became the most popular holiday area of Australia — attracting some two million visitors annually — it was a 'recreation' centre for all the peoples of the region.

As we travel north towards Brisbane from the New South Wales–Queensland border, into the heart of the Gold Coast, we are still in Bundjalung country. The coastline north from the border offers a series of sandy beaches, warm water and perfect surf. Since my early days at Kempsey, when I learned to bodysurf the waves around Smoky Cape and Hat Head, I always take the

opportunity to surf the ocean's natural energy of this area of coastal Australia, which was such a playground during traditional times, and retains that spirit today, though somewhat inhibited by the nature of the Gold Coast's development.

The heart of the old Gold Coast was Bundall, immediately across the Nerang River from Surfers Paradise, near today's Civic Centre and the race-course. Here the clans of the spreading Bundjalung nation, who spoke four different dialects, would come together. From all over the Bundjalung country, as far south as the Clarence River, they came. These great gatherings were a time for religious rituals at the bora grounds, initiations, the settlement of disputes, arranging marriages and trade.

The region is rich in the heritage of the Dreamtime and the creation. Burleigh Heads features in of the saga of the Three Brothers. Yarbirri, the brother who travelled north from their original landing place in northern New South Wales, was known at Burleigh as Jabreen, while Little Burleigh, a headland just north of Burleigh Heads, was called Jebbribillum.

The bora ring at the corner of Gold Coast Highway and Sixth Avenue in Burleigh Heads was once part of a sacred complex.

Just north of Burleigh at Broadbeach, a burial ground which covers centuries of history, was accidentally discovered in June 1963 by a group of local soil contractors. An Australian archaeologist, Dr Laila Hagland, excavated the site, which has attracted considerable archaeological interest.

In the Gold Coast hinterland steep escarpments lead up to the high, rain-forested ranges, Beechmont, Darlington and Sarabah, and the popular Tambourine Mountain. A traditional story from the ridge near Binna Burra tells of a cantankerous old widow named Koonimbagowgunn who took to rolling rocks down the escarpment to kill children who dared to play at the bottom.

A more attractive story comes from Southport, one of the first developed areas of the Gold Coast. Gowonda was an ancestral hero known for his skill as a hunter and remembered for his physical appearance, especially his shock of white hair. One day, leaving the people of the Nerang Valley, he turned himself into a white-finned dolphin. He is still the hunter, driving fish into the nets of his people.

It is interesting to note that the dolphin is today the symbol of the Gold Coast. The choice is coincidental and probably has something to do with the performing dolphins at 'Sea World' rather than with any attempt to honour local Aboriginal traditions

South Stradbroke Island, always an important place for Aboriginal people, and recently the subject of a High Court challenge over land rights. A local resident, Dennis Walker, has claimed the island on the basis that the British claim to Australia, made by Captain Arthur Phillip on behalf of the British Crown and confirmed by Judge Blackburn in his 1971 judgement, only ever mentions the mainland. Photo by Lee Pearce.

The plaque reads 'Richard Buttong, Coolangatta, 1888'. Photo by Henry King, courtesy The Australian Museum.

J. G. Steele has collected many of the original names in the Southport region. Some remain almost the same — coombabah, or home of turtles, for Combabah Lake, and coomera, meaning a species of wattle, for the Coomera River — but many others have been replaced by English names.

Off the coast between Southport and Brisbane lie many islands. The twin islands of North and South Stradbroke were major centres for the provision of stone in the manufacture of implements of both war and peace. Even the sandy ironstone was used by the ancient craftsmen.

North Stradbroke is rich in Aboriginal heritage sites — a total of 121 have been recorded, while South Stradbroke boasts 28. For thousands of years these were the regular dwelling places of the people, who hunted and fished in these rich and abundant waterways. Further sites have been recorded on the neighbouring islands of Moreton (72 sites), Macleay (11), Russell (7), Peel (7), Lamb (3), Coochiedmudlo (1) and Perulpa Island (1).

The distinguished poet and artist, Oodgeroo Noonuccal (Kath Walker), lives on the traditional land of her people on Stradbroke Island. In her book *Stradbroke Dreamtime*, she relates the tales of the Dreamtime and recalls her days growing up as the European presence developed. Every year she welcomes young black and white Australians to learn the rich heritage of their civilisation, particularly the way it relates the land to the Dreamtime.

It is worth the effort to spend a day on Stradbroke Island and visit Oodgeroo Noonuccal's community, an educational institution with emphasis on nature through Aboriginal eyes.

Bones at Broadbeach

This Aboriginal burial ground was uncovered, well before the existence of legal protection for such sites, by a soil contractor who was selling the rich soil, full of bones and shell, as top dressing for lawns on the Gold Coast. Concerned Kombumerri locals tracked down his source, but could not stop the vandalism, as the burial ground was out of sight in quiet bushland. It was decided that the remaining skeletons should be carefully excavated and removed for safe-keeping. They are still awaiting re-burial, which will be arranged by the Kombumerri, once safeguards have been arranged, close to the original site.

This painstaking excavation showed that the site was a significant cemetery, used for at least a thousand years. About a quarter of the site had been wrecked and it was estimated that some two hundred people had been buried there. There was no suggestion that the site was ever used as anything else, nor of any period of neglect or disuse. All the evidence pointed to continued use by one group of people whose traditions changed very little over the millenium. The last four graves had been dug with metal shovels or spades, probably borrowed from a cedar cutter known to have had a hut nearby and to have been friendly with the Kombumerri people.

The burial rituals were varied, often quite complicated and some must have taken a long time to complete. The ritual chosen probably depended on the age and sex of the dead person. Early accounts by white observers suggest that the most complicated rituals were performed for people of the greatest status in the clan — the mature men. But a complicated ritual had been employed for one little baby who died shortly after birth.

Red ochre was used in most burials, and a fire was lit as part of the ceremonies. Food may have been left for the dead, but clumps of opened pipi shells (stacked inside each other, and mixed with bits of charred bone from food animals) seem to indicate that a ceremonial meal was left by the side of the grave. Almost all the dead had been tightly wrapped at the time of the burial, perhaps in sheets of bark or skins, and some were buried with bone or stone artefacts (sometimes of pretty green or orange chert, brought from west of the mountains), perhaps a prized possession of the deceased.

Shell or stone had been placed in semicircles or on the skull (or upper arm) of some bodies inside the pit. There were no gravestones to mark the burial pits, and no post holes to mark the graves. But there was clear evidence that great care was taken to avoid interfering with earlier burials when a new pit had to be dug. On one occasion, two leg bones of an earlier burial were accidentally dislodged in the digging of a new pit. But these were then rubbed with red ochre and carefully wrapped with the new body. Only when the more clumsy metal spades were used for the most recent graves were earlier burials actually cut into and damaged.

Brisbane

The Brisbane River and today's capital city of Queensland mark the borders of distinctive nations. The site of Brisbane may well have been an economic centre, as it was the meeting place of three nations, Undangi, Jagaro and Jukambe.

Today's Brisbane metropolitan area, on the north side of the river, was occupied by a clan which the early English arrivals called the Duke of York clan. The Coorpooroo clan occupied the south bank of the river. The North Pine or Petrie clan, the Chepara clan at Eight Mile Plains and the Yerongpan clan at Oxley Creek, completed the five clans of the region identified by J. G. Steele.

It was in 1825 that the colonial governor in Sydney, who had jurisdiction over the whole of eastern Australia on behalf of the British Crown, decided to establish a penal settlement at Moreton Bay. A detachment of redcoats and prisoners was dispatched for the venture under the command of Captain Patrick Logan, to establish a settlement which was later described as the worst concentration camp on the continent.

The Australian folk song 'Moreton Bay' recounts the demise of Captain Logan:

The modern face of Brisbane.
Photo by Lee Pearce.

One Sunday morning as I went walking,
By Brisbane waters I chanced to stray;
I heard a convict his fate bewailing,
As on a sunny river bank I lay:
'I am a native of Erin's Island,
But banished now from my ancient shore,
They stole me from my aged parents,
And from the maiden whom I do adore.

'I've been a prisoner at Port Macquarie,
At Norfolk Island and Emu Plains,
At Castle Hill and at cursed Toongabbie,
At all these settlements I've been in chains;
But of all places of condemnation
And penal stations in New South Wales,
At Moreton Bay I have found no equal,
Excessive tyranny each day prevails.

'For three long years I was beastly treated,
And heavy irons on my legs I wore,
My back with flogging was lacerated,
And oft-times painted with my crimson gore.
And many a man from down-right starvation
Lies mouldering now underneath the clay;
And Captain Logan he had us mangled
All on the triangles of Moreton Bay.

'Like the Egyptians and ancient Hebrews,
We were oppressed under Logan's yoke,
Till a native black lying there in ambush
Did deal this tyrant his mortal stroke.
My fellow-prisoners be exhilarated
That all such monsters like death may find,
And when from bondage we are liberated
Our former suffering will fade from mind.'

A Queensland Aborigine. Photo by Henry King, courtesy The Australian Museum.

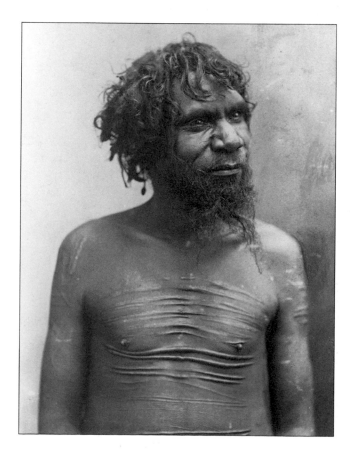

(*From Will Lawson's* Australian Bush Songs and Ballads, *Sydney, 1944.*)

Children with a catch of lung-fish. Originally these fish were found only in the Mary and Burnett Rivers of south-east Queensland. Growing to some 2 metres in length, the lungfish was called a barrumundi *by Aboriginal people, a name which has since been applied to a different fish from northern rivers. Courtesy The Australian Museum.*

It is likely that it was a member of the Moreton Bay people who struck down Logan, to the cheers of the prisoners and the relief of the troops.

The heart of today's Brisbane was once a jousting ground, where warriors came together in ritual engagements to resolve disputes. One of the most memorable in recorded history took place in 1853, at Norman Creek, in the vicinity of Cornwall and Juliette Streets, on the south side of the river.

The Ningy-Ningy and Bribie Island clans and the Amity Point and Logan clans were the participants in this ritual joust. The dispute, as was often the case, was over the elopement of a young girl with a Logan man. The contest began with the opposing clans drawn up in long lines of warriors.

At a given signal, the father of the girl challenged her lover to personal combat, while the feathered and painted warriors stood by. They were both armed with knives, and, according to reports, both fought bravely, inflicting wounds which eventually brought both of them to the ground.

This was the signal for combat to begin with spears and throwing sticks all along the line, although skilful use of shields prevented any serious injury. The combat continued until the less numerous Amity Point and Logan clans withdrew. One man from the Bribie Island clan was killed.

War against the white invaders, however, was a more bloody affair. Once it became obvious that Captain Logan, his troops and prisoners were planning not only to stay but to take over land, food resources and water supplies, then war was inevitable. The Kangaroo Point area became a front line as the expropriated land was rapidly turned into farms.

The Coorpooroo people used economic warfare, attacking and destroying the maize fields. Convict gossip had it that Logan hung up the stuffed skin of a dead Aborigine as a deterrent.

Once a large country town, Brisbane has become a concrete jungle over the past twenty years and the change from a slow, easy-going rural atmosphere to the aggressive, modern commercial centre it is today has been apparent to anyone travelling through on a regular basis. By the late 1970s the remaining riverside land enjoyed by blacks in South Brisbane had become a part of the Expo 88 site, making Aborigines less visible in the area, though many of them continue to see the inside of Boggo Road Gaol, in nearby Annersley, on a regular basis.

All the Aboriginal facilities found in other capital cities are present in Brisbane. During my time with Aboriginal Hostels Limited in Canberra, where I served as the first Aboriginal executive, I was able to secure the old Baptist Theological College for use as an Aboriginal hostel.

Temporary accommodation in all catogories of need for Aboriginal people are now well established to serve employment, transient, educational, medical and psychological needs. Aboriginal Hostels Limited is now the largest accommodation company in Australia with over 300 properties accommodating 3000 people daily, all around the country.

I felt very honoured to know old 'Uncle' Willie McKenzie at the end of his life in Brisbane 20 years ago. He was a most regal model for me and every time I pass through Brisbane he spiritually escorts me. I also held Pastor Don Brady in high esteem, almost as an Australian version of Martin Luther King, for the manner in which he conducted himself in the Aboriginal strugggle for equality.

Cheryl Buchanan, Donnie Davidson, Oodgeroo Noonuccal (Kath Walker), Norman Brown, Lyn Kirk and Michael Williams are Aboriginal contempories from this area who always remain close to my heart.

Unfortunately for the Australian landscape, hills close to major population centres have become prime targets for media communication and transmitter towers, which limits access by local residents who, for tens of thousands of years, sought high places for communication with the Creators. Mount Coot-tha in Brisbane is a prime example and because the landscape itself is believed by us to be a living thing, we feel the pain on her behalf. Booster towers run parallel to Highway One north of Brisbane and, in long lonely stretches, they become a strangely welcome sight.

Dundalli

The hero of the resistance in the Brisbane area was the charismatic Ningy-Ningy warrior, Dundalli, who, in 1845, brought the people of Moreton Bay and Wide Bay together in an alliance which fought for nine years in a vain attempt to drive the redcoats from their traditional lands.

Dundalli's strategy was to isolate Brisbane by cutting all communication through guerilla attacks on the dray roads to the capital. His brilliant career came to an end when, at the very height of his success, one of his lieutenants, Make-i-light, was captured. Dundalli staged a valiant but futile one-man raid into Brisbane to rescue him. He failed, and was captured and sentenced to death.

Despite a desperate attempt by Ningy-Ningy warriors to rescue Dundalli, he was hanged publicly not far from the General Post Office. Today local groups have petitioned for a plaque to be erected there in memory of a courageous leader who tried to preserve the traditions of his people against an unrelenting enemy.

A Queensland Aborigine in tribal decoration. From an oil painting by M. Jilt, Rex Nan Kivell Collection. Courtesy National Library of Australia.

The former beauty of Brisbane can still be seen from the banks of the Brisbane River, especially at places like Chelmer, and also from the top of Mount Coot-tha, which stands like a powerful sentinel, despite competition from television facilities there.

Today, Brisbane is a city transformed. This concrete jungle is perhaps an appropriate setting for the autocratic, opinionated people who have administered Aboriginal affairs in Queensland. Perhaps they know, by instinct, that the place and its new peoples were cursed by Dundalli when they strung him up in front of the post office in 1845.

Moreton Bay

The Moreton Bay environment, which the people fought so hard to preserve, was rich indeed. The waters of the bay abounded in mullet, silver bream, whiting, tailor and dugong, while along the shore were turtles, turtle eggs, mud crabs, whelks, cockles and oysters. Game included kangaroos, koalas, short-nosed bandicoots, carpet snakes, lizards, possums, echidnas, flying fox and marsupial mice. Feathered game ranged from emu to ducks, parrots, cockatoos, scrub turkeys, swamp hens, black swans, quails and bush hens, while delicacies such as honey and moth larvae added garnish to the diet.

Fruit and vegetables included wild yams, honeysuckle nectar, fern roots, pandanus, cunjevoi, climbing maidenhair, berries, Moreton Bay chestnuts, figs, bunya nuts and cabbage tree palms.

A hallmark of all the hunting and fishing operations was their co-operative nature. A team was formed and a chief appointed for the season to oversee operations. Parties of up to twenty men would work the shoals of fish in the bay. Lookouts in the trees identified the presence and direction of the fish. Sticks were then used to drive them in to the shore where waiting men rushed in with nets. One man was usually appointed leader for the season and instead of working the nets he carried a notched staff of office.

The Moreton Bay people also enlisted the aid of dolphins to catch fish. The attention of the dolphins was attracted by beating the water with spears and clubs or stabbing spears into the ground in shallow water. The dolphins would then chase the fish towards the shore where they could be netted. In a gesture of solidarity, some of the catch was given back to the dolphins. This co-operation between humans and dolphins recurs at several places around the Australian coastline, although such interspecies co-operation has rarely been documented anywhere else in the world.

Moreton Bay offered its original inhabitants an environment rich with food resources. From the Jean Chayet Collection, courtesy National Library of Australia.

A multi-pronged fish spear was used for fish such as tailor, whose sharp teeth enabled them to bite their way out of the nets. Fishing in rivers and streams was a different proposition. Shallow and narrow parts of the creeks were partially blocked by small dams built from rocks, with openings wide enough for a man to stand with a hand net. In coastal regions fish move downstream as the tide turns and they were easily netted as they passed through the narrow openings.

Fishing in holes in creeks was a combined operations, where the women pushed the fish out with sticks and the men caught them in nets. Perhaps the most sophisticated method employed for catching fish was poisoning the water, using a plant called *tanggul* (*Polygonum hydropiper*) which was crushed, wrapped up in tree bark and spread in the water. The fish simply rose to the surface upside down where they could be collected by hand. Fishing was not a recreational pastime, but a necessity of life.

Co-operative ventures also extended to fishing for dugong and bêche-de-mer (sea slugs), which were, and still are, prized across Asia as a great delicacy. Eels were caught in creeks with hand nets. Crabs were taken by teams of men and women using a long, hooked stick to extract them from holes in creek banks at low water, or by foraging on the beach. The women collected oysters, which were prised from rocks with digging sticks. Pipis and cockles were collected from the sand at low tide.

When hunting kangaroos the team used nets 1.2 metres high tied to trees. The hunting parties advanced in line, sometimes using fire, and drove the game towards the nets. Bandicoots and kangaroo rats were smoked out of hollow logs.

A special delicacy, prized on the menus of all the indigenous people of the South Pacific (although not yet accepted by modern Australians), was flying foxes, which were either speared or knocked down with clubs or boomerangs from the trees and collected as they fell to the ground.

Nets were placed across one end of a lagoon and ducks were driven into them with boomerangs. Other hunters hid in the water holding small branches over their heads; when a duck came close enough, the hunter simply pulled it under water by the legs. Nets were also used to trap flocks of parrots and cockatoos. Boomerangs and sounds like hawks were made to direct them into the nets.

Vegetable harvesting was mainly the responsibility of the women. They used digging tools to obtain roots up to a metre underground. Beans and yams were roasted. Many delicacies of Black Australia were poisonous unless properly prepared. Cunjevoi, with its starchy stems, needed to be repeatedly soaked and pounded before being made into cakes and roasted. Moreton Bay chestnuts, poisonous when raw, were cracked and soaked, then pounded and made into cakes and roasted. The cakes were often served with honey, which was extracted from tree hives. Zamia nuts have to be cracked and the pith soaked to extract the poison before they can be roasted and eaten.

Some nuts, such as bunya nuts, were buried for several weeks in mud to mature. They were harvested by collectors who climbed the trees with belts of vine around the trunk.

The kitchens of Black Australia offered feasts fit for kings. Sadly today few Australians know of the exotic larder which awaits them, let alone where to look and how to cook.

The Brisbane area today is a treasure trove of historic and sacred sites and many of the names of the people have been retained as place names: Banyo (believed to mean a ridge), Indooroopilly (from *yinduru-pilli*, leach gully) and Nundah (from *nanda*, a chain of waterholes).

Leaving Brisbane and the land of the three nations, we head north to Redcliffe. Bribie Island is just offshore.

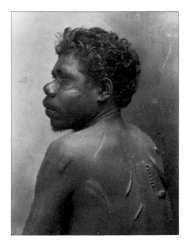

Note the scarification on this man's back. These scars, or cicatrices, were created by cutting open the flesh and inserting hot ash and ochre into the wound. Photo by Henry King, courtesy The Australian Museum.

Cumjam, arrested for the murder of a man called Ferguson in 1894. Courtesy National Library of Australia.

The evocative and easily recognised profile of a pelican in the sunset. Photo by Robbi Newman.

Long before any English names appeared on the map, Toorbul Point was the centre of religious and social occasions. A bora ground with two rings and a connecting path on the south side of Bestman Road, about 800 metres from its junction with the main road to Bribie Island, was declared a government reserve in 1970.

This is truly a cathedral of bora rings and its importance is testified to by two missionaries, Nique and Hartenstein, who in 1841 watched more than 2000 people who had gathered for the sacred ceremonies.

The people of Bribie Island (Yarun) Jindoobarrie clan, were reportedly friendly, even if they did throw a spear at Matthew Flinders, the first Englishman to visit the island, in 1801. Oxley's companion, John Uniacke, saw about 60 people on the island in 1823, but the first people Oxley and Uniacke encountered in Moreton Bay were two white castaways, Pamphlett and Finnegan, who had lived with the Redcliffe and Bribie Island clans for several years.

An impressive bora ground on Bribie Island, not far from the beach at White Patch, was destroyed by a bulldozer in 1971, but another survives at Bellara.

Highway One (the Bruce Highway north from Brisbane) begins its long trek through some of the most dramatic landscape in Australia. Dramatic not only for the mystic nature of the Glasshouse Mountains but also the powerful earth energies of its subtropical lushness and the strong black and red soils at Gympie.

The coastal road from Brisbane to Noosa reveals that Brisbane people are flanked on either side by attractive surfing beaches and a wide range of weekend venues. The Sunshine Coast, as it has been named by tourist developers, has become a popular winter retreat for people from the colder southern climates, just as it was in traditional times.

The hot, humid climate has always contributed to the easy-going, laid-back approach of the local people, a feeling that continues today. The further north one goes the friendlier the people become, the slower the movement and the broader the accent.

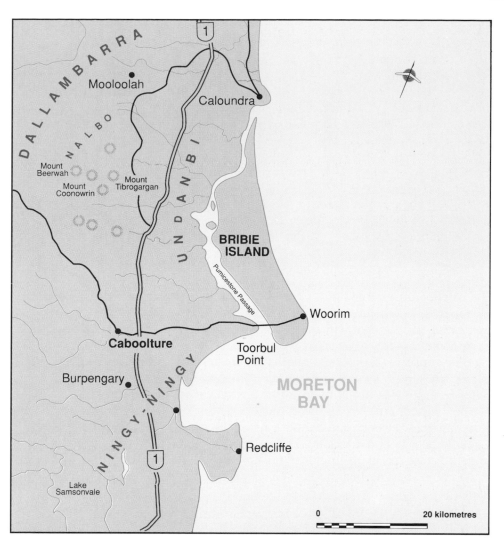

Traditional clan areas in the Bribie Island region.

The male core of the burrawang palm contains zamia nuts which require special preparation to extract poisons. These nuts were cracked and the pith soaked, then eaten raw or roasted. Photo by Densey Clyne.

Spearing fish. Photo by Thomas Dick, courtesy The Australian Museum.

Opposite *A Henry King portrait of a young girl from northern Australia. Courtesy The Australian Museum.*

At the northern end of the Sunshine Coast, Noosa Heads offers good surf, although sea lice are abundant. Clans from the south, with longstanding approvals, migrated in winter to the Noosa region which hosted annual ceremonial events.

For centuries the people of this region observed the Cape Barren Island geese, the appearance of the odd albatross, the regular visits of whales and daily frolicking of dolphins in a place where time just stood still. North of Noosa the dolphins have to wait until just south of Cairns, at Yarrabah Back Beach, before they can catch a wave again due to the calming influence of the Great Barrier Reef. Surfing freaks like me think Noosa is the end of the world and the absence of rolling surf makes the whole of the north Australian coastline somehow incomplete. Give me the Great Ocean.Road in Victoria anytime.

Before the highway was diverted travellers could see the Glasshouse Mountains from it, but we need to venture off the highway to obtain some real appreciation of the mythology of this area.

The scars on this man's back and shoulders could be ritual or battle scars. Photo by Henry King, courtesy The Australian Museum.

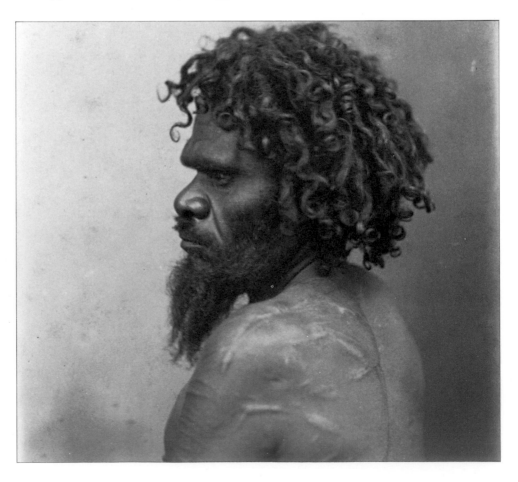

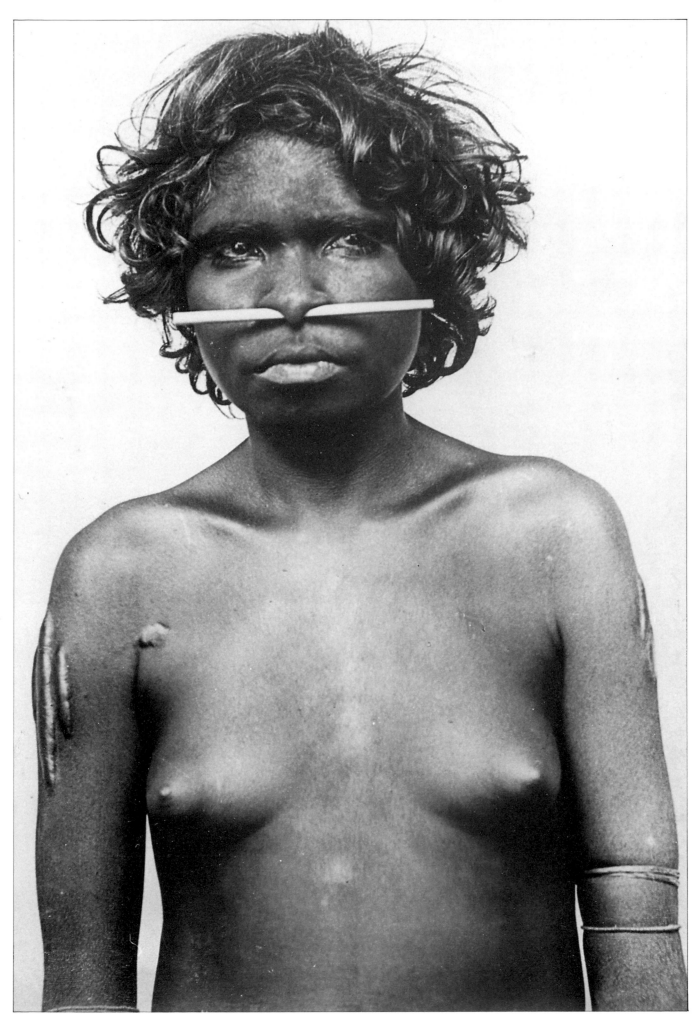

The father and son who never face each other. In the foreground, Coonowrin, the son, stands in shame, unable to straighten his neck since being struck with a club by his father Tibrogargan (in background) for deserting his mother Beerwah during the rising of the oceans many years ago. Photo by Philip Green.

The pretty-faced or whiptail wallaby is found from northern New South Wales up to the north of Queensland. Distinctive because of the colourful face markings, these wallabies were slaughtered in huge numbers for the manufacture of stuffed koalas after the koala itself was protected. Photo by Lee Pearce.

The Glasshouse Mountains

he country of the Nalbo people is centred on the region around the Glasshouse Mountains. As could be expected with such spectacular hills, tradition accounts for their shape and position. Tibrogargan stands looking out to see as he did in the ancient past with his children around him. Once he saw the seas disturbed and swelling. He collected the younger children and led them away to the mountains. He sent Coonowrin to help his mother, Beerwah, who was heavy with child. But Coonowrin ran to safety without her. So angry was Tibrogargan that he chased Coonowrin and when he caught him smashed him so hard on the head with his club that he dislocated his neck. So Coonowrin stands today with his crooked neck and Beerwah still awaits the birth of her child.

A strong spirit broods over Beerwah and for centuries it was a no-go place for the people of the area. When the Scot, Andrew Petrie, climbed the mountain and went blind, he was told the spirit was to blame.

The centre for the Nalbo-speaking people was located between the Glasshouse Mountains and the coast, where a complex of bora rings and ceremonial grounds testified to their social and religious life. Not all are accessible, but a well-preserved bora lies in the state forest just south-east of the village of Glasshouse Mountains.

A wallaby hunt in Queensland. From Among Cannibals, *by Carl Lumholtz, London (1890), courtesy National Library of Australia.*

The Sunshine Coast

Queensland's Sunshine Coast demands exploration because the area personifies the spirit of the land. Winter coldness is relative and Melbourne visitors (who seem to have made the Sunshine Coast their escape during winter) feel a very great difference.

Nambour, today a well-known holiday town, was such a popular gathering centre in pre-colonial times that many of the newcomers thought it meant 'place of corroborees'. In fact, it means 'red-flowered tea tree'. Reports from the first Europeans to visit this area, Thomas Pamphlett in 1823 and Tom Petrie in 1862, described gatherings of up to 500 for sport and religious observances. One of the ceremonial grounds was at the creek to which Petrie gave his name.

There is a bora ring, which was in use until 1900, near Yandina Creek, about 3 kilometres north-east of Mount Ninderry.

Noosa (ghost) is in the lands of the Undanbi people, who called the Noosa headland *Wantima,* meaning climbing up. At the top of the hill there is a stone arrangement within which nothing will grow. It is believed to be connected with the Uwen Mundi clan which occupied the area at the time of the coming of the English. Like the plants, the people have all gone and the bare ground in the circle testifies to their banishment from their ancient homeland. Names such as Nambour, Maroochydore, Caloundra and Buderim are believed to be derived from words in the Nalbo and Undanbi languages.

The twin lakes of Cootharaba and Cooroibah and the coloured sands of Teewah are explained in local traditions. Teewah, for example, was a warrior, who fell in love with a woman named Cooroibah, but she was stolen by a warrior called Cootharaba. Teewah pursued them. Blinded by his passion and pain, he crashed into the sandy cliffs at Cooloola and broke into many pieces. These pieces of the lovesick Teewah are now the famous coloured sands.

Mudjimba Island

Maroochy was the home of the Toombra clan, whose lands included the beach near the mouth of the river. The area was formed in the Dreamtime when a beautiful girl of that name was betrothed to Coolum in accordance with the law of the people.

One day a fierce warrior named Ninderry came from many miles away and saw Maroochy. He waited until Coolum was out hunting and then, with the help of a group of companions, kidnapped her.

On his return, Coolum found Maroochy gone and, gathering his kinsmen, set off in pursuit. Custom dictated that when he caught up with Ninderry he should formally challenge him for the return of his betrothed. Knowing the reputation of Ninderry and his companions as fierce fighting men, Coolum decided to sneak into their camp at night, free Maroochy from her bonds and flee home with her.

Next day, when Ninderry discovered she was missing, he went in pursuit. When he caught up with Coolum, Ninderry used his huge club to knock Coolum's head right off his shoulders. It rolled across the land and into the sea to became Mudjimba Island.

The great ancestral being of the sky, angered by such conduct, turned Ninderry into stone. Maroochy, bereft of both her suitors, ran to the Blackall Range where she wept so much that her tears formed the Maroochy River.

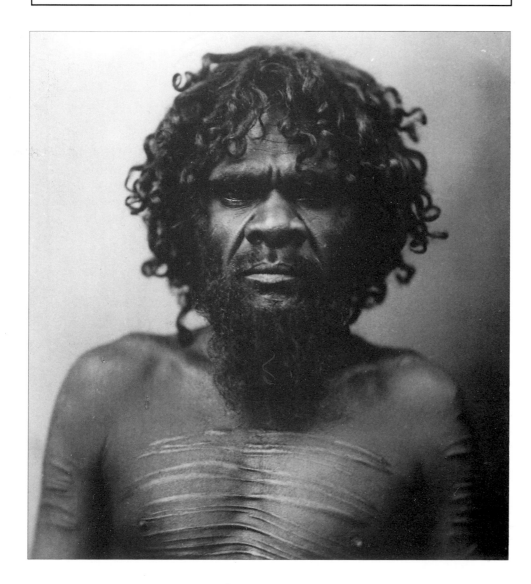

Left *A photo portrait of a Queensland Aborigine by Henry King, courtesy The Australian Museum.*
Following page *The Glasshouse Mountains. Photo by AusChromes.*

Eliza Fraser

Waddy Point on Fraser Island, where Eliza Fraser's party came ashore after the wreck of the Stirling Castle *in 1836. Photo by Dick Hoole.*

Leaving the lands of the Nalbo and Undanbi peoples we cross the border into Dulingbara country. These lands comprise the Cooloola area, extending along the coast north from Noosa in a long crescent to Double Island Point, then west and north around the shores of Wide Bay where the Sandy Strait separates Cooloola from Fraser Island, and the southern part of Fraser Island.

The Dulingbara people became widely known after the shipwreck of the *Stirling Castle* in 1836, which left Eliza Fraser living with them. They told her of an earlier wreck, the *Madeira Packet,* which ran aground on Brampton Reef in December 1831, one of a series of wrecks from 1820 on, as ships were driven in from the Coral Sea. Eliza Fraser made up many tales about her life with the Dulingbara people, all of them contradictory.

The Dulingbara people recall the Europeans being received in a friendly manner. It seems that Captain James Fraser and his party emerged like ghosts from the sea and a great crowd assembled to see them. The white party bartered clothes for food and later they were drafted into the life of the people and expected to share the workload.

Relations with their hosts were poisoned from the beginning, however, as some of the people had heard of the fighting in the settlement of Brisbane. The whites were not trusted and were kept out of their homes. Their lack of skill in hunting and foraging attracted derision and resentment.

Eliza Fraser did have a terrible time. She gave birth to a child in the open longboat, which drowned in the water-logged bottom of the boat. With the others, she suffered prolonged exposure, thirst and starvation. Her husband died within two weeks of reaching land and she found herself working with the Dulingbara women, without their skills and stamina.

Eventually, she was rescued and embarked on a career as a tent show lecturer telling tall tales to those who paid sixpence admission.

The stark and unforgettable colours of Fraser Island. The island acts as a repository for sands moving north up the coast, from as far away as central New South Wales. So much sand has accumulated over the years that Fraser Island is the largest sand island in the world. Photo by Robbi Newman.

Fraser Island

raser Island, the largest sand island in the world, is 123 kilometres long and varies in width from 5 to 25 kilometres. The sand which forms the island was deposited over millions of years, and there are only three rocky outcrops, Waddy Point, Middle Rocks and Indian Head.

For such a small area, the environment is surprisingly complex. A quarter of the island is covered in rainforest and freshwater lakes, and there are low and high dunes, heath, extensive mangrove swamps, lagoons and open woodland. The sea has abundant fish and marine life which added to the diversity of the local diet, although constant hard work was required to keep the larders adequately stocked.

Fraser Island got its present name after the shipwreck of Captain Fraser. It had been known as Great Sandy Island since Captain James Cook sailed past in 1770. Three original names have been attributed to the island — Carrina, Thoorgine and Garee.

Three groups, all Kabi speakers, laid claim to territory on Fraser Island — the Dulingbara from Cooloola in the south, the Badjala the centre and the Ngulungbara in the north. It is estimated that the permanent population of the island at the time of the white invasion was around 3000, though at times of ceremonial gatherings thousands more attended from the mainland. The population was at its highest during winter, when seafood was at its best; summer was a time of festivals and many moved to the mainland.

Every three years a major festival marked the harvest of the popular bunya nuts. Many thousands of people from faraway clans came together in a national gathering, involving weeks of ceremonies, trade and feasting.

Both men and women had elaborate and distinctive cicatrises, or raised scars, but on ceremonial occasions they *coocheed* themselves (that is, applied ochre to the body) with their clan colours.

Rigid laws governed life and marriage and the early Europeans found aspects of their law vastly amusing, especially the avoidance rule, by which

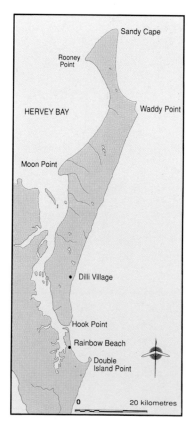

Sandy Cape

Rooney
Point

HERVEY BAY

Waddy Point

Moon Point

Dilli Village

Hook Point

Rainbow Beach

Double
Island Point

0   20 kilometres

mothers-in-law were prohibited from looking at their sons-in-law. The educational and instructional initiations associated with manhood followed the national pattern, involving secret ceremonies, but without circumcision, which was practised elsewhere.

One of the key members of the traditional way of life was the clan healer, who was called upon to minister to the sick, encourage rain and interpret a host of natural phenemona. Being a mixture of general practitioner and parish priest, the healers built great reputations on their ability to extract the source of an illness from the body. Some were even credited with being able to fly, disappear into the ground and then reappear elsewhere.

When the healing rituals were unsuccesssful, funerals were conducted according to strict tradition. In one form the corpse was laid on the ground surrounded by mourning women. The healer sat at the foot of the body. The men drew together nearby and, as the women began wailing songs, came forward, each with a green branch, forming a circle around the women. Then, waving the branches to and fro, they began to dance. The women would suddenly stop singing and the men would form a half circle at the feet of the corpse, to begin the final requiem.

At intervals they fell silent, as the healer, who had been rubbing the soles of the deceased's feet, looked into his eyes and called his name thirteen times, pausing each time to wait for a reply. Then, regrouping six paces from the body, the men would end the song as the healer announced that the spirit did not want to return. Amid loud lamentations, the deceased was then buried.

Badjala ritual prescribed that bodies should be laid straight out, feet towards the west and arms alongside the body. The grave was a metre deep with a log on each side at the bottom across which branches were laid to form a platform for the body. The hole was filled in with earth, and other logs were placed on top to mark the grave. Trees in the vicinity were blazed to form tombstones. It was believed by some clans that the spirit of the departed left the body on the third day after death, when it leaped into the sky.

Fraser Island attracts some 50 000 tourists a year, mostly in four-wheel drive vehicles, who are drawn to the island for its unique environment. Photo by Robbi Newman.

Fraser Island athletes

In the 1860s, when amateur athletics was in its infancy in Australia, Aboriginal athletes earned a fearsome reputation for their skills. In particular, the Fraser Island blacks became famous for arriving unheralded for the main running races and taking home all the major trophies. White athletes attempted to have them excluded from competition on the basis of lack of intelligence and substandard 'moral character', before they finally solved the problem. In 1872 the Queensland Amateur Athletic Association declared all Aboriginal athletes to be permanent professionals, ineligible for amateur events. This attitude remained prevalent throughout the century, denying Aborigines the opportunity to compete in any amateur sports.

Pockets of rainforest can still be found on Fraser Island, despite the logging for hoop pine, kauri and white beech, which were floated across to Maryborough for more than 40 years. Photo by Dick Hoole.

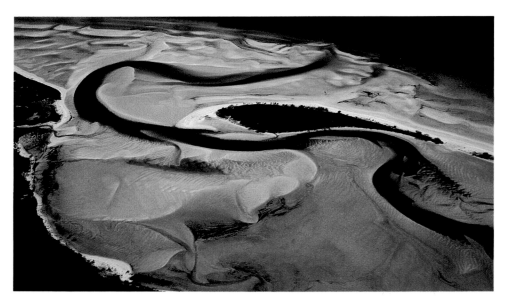

Fraser Island has been accumulating sand for millions of years. Photo by Robbi Newman.

Bunya nuts were a highly sought after delicacy and their harvesting required considerable ingenuity as the trees were often up to 80 metres tall. Photo by Philip Green.

Bunya lands

THE bunya festival was held at the time of harvest. Each tree was the responsibility of its owner who alone could harvest it. He would climb the tree with the aid of vines. Toe holes were forbidden in case of injury to the tree and unauthorised cutting was punished by law. Today, many bunya trees have toeholds, apparently made after traditional authority had been destroyed.

Bunya nuts were either eaten raw or roasted and were also stored to be eaten perhaps months later. People came from far and wide to the festival — from the Burnett, Wide Bay, Bundaberg, Mount Perry, Gympie, Bribie, Fraser Island, Gayndah, Kilcoy, Mount Brisbane and even Brisbane itself. Hundreds of family groups, speaking more than a dozen languages, came to enjoy the nuts and the great variety of food which accompanied them.

Tom Petrie, as a boy of 14 in 1845, attended a bunya festival and specially mentioned the delicacy of the tops of the cabbage tree palms, served with honey. The festivals were times of singing, dancing and ritual fights between clans, but there was also time for the sacred ceremonies and the education of young men seeking special skills.

Sadly the people have now vanished like the mist at dawn but the bunya trees remain and perhaps in the future there will be a revival of one of the oldest festivals ever celebrated by humankind.

The war of resistance against the white invaders continued throughout the nineteenth century. Following the death of Dundalli in Brisbane, the black nations intensified their attacks on settlements and, in the 1860s, the Governor of Queensland asked London for reinforcements.

In the Dawson River area, the war continued until 1879 and fighting in the Cardwell district (on the Palmer River and the Atherton Tablelands) continued into the 1880s. The final defeat of the mighty Kalkadoons (at Battle Mountain, in 1884) marked the close of a desperate hundred year war.

The result of this protracted conflict was the complete dispossesion of the people from their homelands, and the break-up of traditional society and

Bunya nuts, macadamias and quandong seeds. The almond-shaped bunya nuts were either eaten raw or roasted and their annual harvest was a time for ceremonial exchange between clans. Although the trees fruit each year, every three years there is a particularly plentiful harvest. Photo by Leo Meier/Weldon Trannies.

the laws which governed it. The survivors were forced into specially created settlements. Different people with different languages, and often of degrees of kinship which prevented them from mixing, were herded together as the land was 'cleared' for development.

The aim of the policy was to remove the people from their land and to exclude them from the towns established by white settlers. With no land, no access to their food and water supplies, however, they were driven into the towns to beg for food. On Fraser Island in 1897 the Bogimbah Creek Mission, built on a major Badjala campsite, became home — or prison — for Aboriginal people from many parts of Queensland.

The Kabi Kabi people at Gympie retained their independence until 1870. Zachariah Skyring, who arrived in 1868 (at the age of nine) with his father to develop land near Zachariah Creek, at Green Swamp, befriended the Kabi people and gave an accurate account of their lifestyles. The district was then known as Mumbeanna after Mumbea, a leader of the local people, who adopted young Zachariah as his 'son', teaching him the local language and how to hunt and forage for food. In his memoirs Zachariah described how up to sixty hunters at a time would combine for a major hunt. The hunters would march in open order and when a kangaroo was sighted a signal would be given for silence along the line, which would gradually bend until the quarry was encircled, when it was trapped and killed.

In traditional times, Mooloo (meaning black snake) was a major gathering place not only for ceremonies but also for formal dispute settlements. Young Zachariah watched a fight in the 1870s between the people of the Widgee, Tin Can and Gympie districts on one side, and the Maroochy people on the other. The battle lasted three hours and although there were some injuries, no one was fatally injured.

Today, only the wind visits the ceremonial grounds and the Kabi Kabi people, along with so many others, were moved into Cherbourg, where the administration had absolute control. The government-appointed manager (or camp commandant) made all the rules, and anyone who failed to toe the line was simply banished from home and family.

In two generations, these settlements, which were created by the colonial Queensland government in anticipation that the people would either die out or be assimilated into white society, became the new home of these people. Four generations have now lived in these settlements, which today seek a new independence.

Carnarvon Gorge, west of Rock-hampton, the only section of the 217 000 hectare Carnarvon National Park which is accessible to visitors. A variety of walking trails offer the chance to see the bush close at hand. Photos by (top left) Robbi Newman, (bottom left) Philip Green, (far right) Tony Gordon.

Waterlilies at Maryborough. Photo by Philip Green.

From the Kabi Kabi people at Gympie we travel north to Maryborough, through the lands of the Badjala people. Mount Bauple (which means frilled lizard), marks the border between the Dowarbara and Badjala peoples. Mount Bauple is a site of great relgious and economic significance. Stone from its slopes was quarried for tools and weapons, and to protect its taboos and fearful stories of evil spirits and beings with great powers were attached to the mountain. There was a spirit in lizard form (from which the mountain got its name), a cave-dwelling *melong* (a spirit in human form), a spirit with power over rain, thunder and lightning, and a man touched with madness who bit people.

One story about the melong relates how a senior man named Mooging, who had many stone tomahawks and spearheads to trade at the bunya festival, was robbed by a visitor and his four wives from Fraser Island. Thinking the spirit of the mountain had taken them, Mooging went to visit the melong with a gift and apologised for taking his stones without permission. The melong laughed, and inviting him into his cave used his power to reveal the thieves. An ancestral spirit, Yindingie, intervened and made the women empty their string bags. The stolen artefacts tumbled into the Mary River and Yindingie made them into Baddow Island. Then he turned the thief and his wives into birds.

The path followed by the thieves in the Mooging story is identical with the track generally followed by travellers from Mount Bauple to Urangan and Fraser Island. Along the way they would come to Saltwater Creek near the road from Maryborough to Pialba. Here there was a much used crossing and a path that led to a popular campsite where remains of regular occupation can still be found. The track continued past a bora ring and on towards Booral. Reports indicate that there was plenty of food in the creek and that people probably stayed there for long intervals.

Two methods for making rain are described for the Maryborough region. One involved a senior man of high degree cutting up pieces of a water-bearing vine on top of a high mountain and scattering the pieces in the direction of those areas needing rain. This form of rain-making took place at Mount Urah where the water-bearing vine grew. At Maryborough, senior men burned a particular moss-draped tree on which the drooping moss had the appearance of falling rain.

Rockhampton, situated on the Fitzroy River a few kilometres north of the Tropic of Capricorn, is the main town of central Queensland. During traditional times, 'Rocky' was clearly a centre for the Darambal people, who were spread over the undulating country of the Fitzroy region.

Babinda Boulders. Photo by Reg Morrison.

The tale of Oolana

The beliefs of the original Australians were born from respect for the landscape and the power of its creators, and many places were considered taboo. A classic example is the legend of the Babinda Boulders.

Oolana, a princess of the Babinda people, was promised to the elder, Waroonoo. Trouble came with the arrival of a handsome young warrior, Dyga, who found Oolana one day, collecting yams. Realising that they were soulmates, the two decided to elope. They ran up the creek and into the mountains, hoping no one would find them, and stayed together in the rugged rainforests. Waroonoo sent the hunters and trackers out and they found Oolana and forced her to return to the camp. Realising she would never see Dyga again, Oolana threw herself off the cliff into the racing white water of the river below, crying out to her soulmate: 'Dyga, Dyga, Dyga . . . ' And it's said that her tormented soul is in the river to this day, drawing young men to their death. In the past ten years, ten people have drowned in the swirling waters of the river: all white and under 30 years of age.

Fig trees provided many useful resources. Blankets were made from the bark and shields carved from the softwood of the buttress roots. Photo by Tony Gordon.

The Darambal people enjoyed a rich diet of game, fish, fruits and vegetables and, like the people of Asia , they prized the dugong as a delicacy.

As in the rest of the continent, every piece of land had its traditional history and belonged by law to one family group. According to Lorna McDonald in her *Rockhampton: a History of City and District,* each clan of the Darambal people had a name which ended in *bura* meaning 'men of' or 'belonging to'. The Torilla Plains clan, near Shoalwater Bay was called *Kuinmer-bura* or 'men of the plains', while the people at the top end of Torilla Peninsula were *Kuta-bura* meaning 'men of the end'. The land on the river near Rockhampton itself was part of the *Bikal-bura,* derived from *bikal,* the name of an edible grub found in trees on the river flats.

Many of these original names have long been replaced by English names, though one of the most beautiful lagoons is still called Padygole, which was a translation of *ba-dul,* and a dwelling place for many generations. It was also a ceremonial centre.

One custom described by McDonald and apparently unique to Darambal ceremonies involved a peg in an open space, about 2 metres by 6 metres.

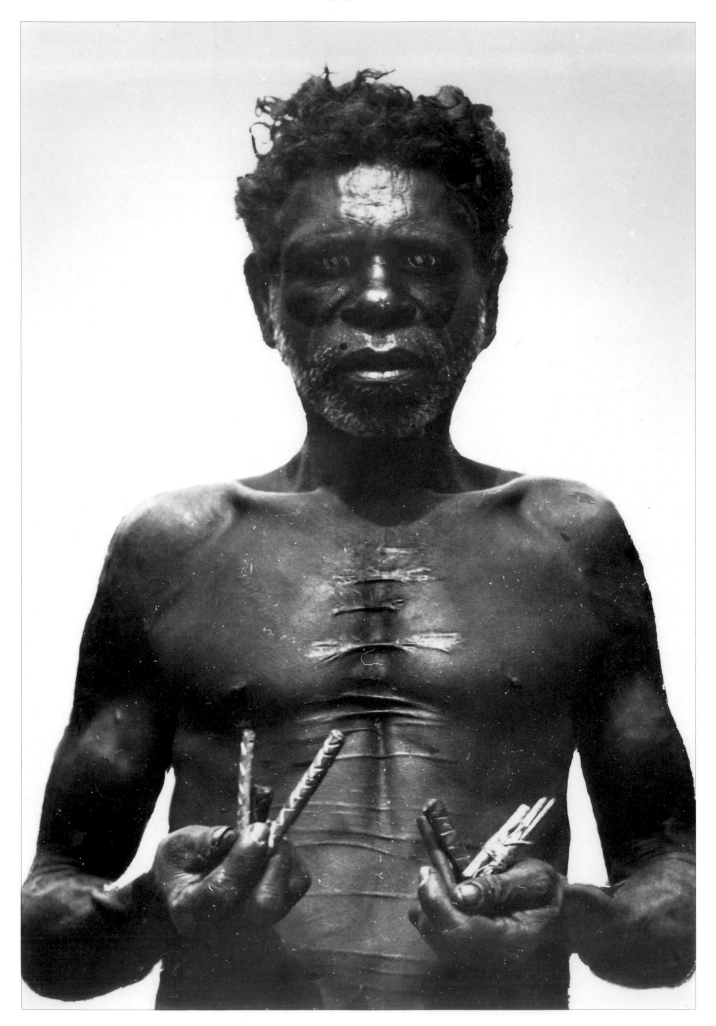

Each of the visiting warriors would take turns to stand at the opposite end and throw a nulla nulla at the peg, saying 'My country is . . .' and explain where he lived while putting his hands behind his back. He would then receive a welcoming present, never turning to see who gave it.

About every two years a bora ceremony was held, at a time and place determined by the elders. Messages were sent out to the scattered clans by message stick, which was 15 centimetres long and smooth on both sides and bore symbols to remind the messenger of the date and place. The runners who carried these messages were warmly greeted, provided with food and shelter and allocated women to look after them.

During full moon ceremonies at the main bora ground at Gavial Creek, the rituals began with bullroarers, which marked the arrival of warriors from far and near. As the young men to be initiated came forward, the women and children retired. Three weeks of instruction were required before the young men passed into adulthood.

As in all parts of Australia, Darambal marriage rules were very strict and betrothal ceremonies were as elaborate as those of the courts of Europe. Once a young man had found a woman of the right kinship category into which he was permitted to marry, he would make overtures to her brothers, presenting them with gifts. If and when the 'uncles' (mother's brothers) of the girl agreed with the match, the suitor would be so advised.

The man would go away to dress up in his finest, complete with paint and feathers, then make his way to the home of the bride's father. The mother and the girl's brothers would arrive with her and she would be seated immediately behind the would-be bridegroom. Her 'uncles' would rise one by one, taking a feather from the man's hair and placing it in the girl's. Then he would leave, without looking at her once. In the next stage of this complex courtship ritual the girl's mother would visit him, and would be received with honour and gifts.

The day would finally come when he received permission to claim his bride. She would be sent out gathering food. He would appear and ceremonially take her by the wrist to lead her home. Tradition demanded that she struggle, but not too much.

Darambal lands included the Keppel Islands, known in the old days as Woppa, and the Woppa-bura clan had a distinctive dialect.

Opposite Message sticks were used to convey invitations of ceremonial gatherings to neighbouring clans. Photo by Donald Thomson, courtesy of Mrs Thomson.

Dingoes have only inhabited the Australian continent for the past 5000 years and are believed to have been brought here by Aboriginal people as pets. Photo by Gary Steer.

The Keppels

It's a proud boast of Ansett Airlines that Great Keppel Island is the most successful resort anywhere in the world. As we have seen elsewhere around the coast, this popularity goes back way before its 'discovery' by modern holidaymakers.

We know that Aborigines have been visiting North Keppel for more than 4000 years and Great Keppel for at least 700 years. The Woppa-bura were not only skilful in the use of boats; they built sophisticated shelters near the coast from saplings bent into an arch and covered with tea-tree bark. Stones and earth were piled around the sides. Archaeologists have uncovered one such structure on the island, which is close to tools, fireplace and a shell midden, and probably accommodated a family of five to ten people. Each day the women and children would forage among the rocks and mangroves, collecting shellfish in strong, bark-twine dilly bags. Plant foods were also collected from further inland, using pointed wooden digging sticks. The most popular vegetables included the fruit of the grey mangrove — which was baked and rinsed before being pounded into a damper — baked pandanus nuts, sword grass nuts and orchid roots. Some sixty different plants were eaten, including wild oranges, grapes, figs, cherries and the flowers and roots of the native hibiscus tree.

While shellfish, marine life and vegetables were plentiful, game was less predictable. The limited game foods on the island included birds, lizards, snakes and bats. Kangaroos and wallabies may have been there in the early days, but they didn't survive long, though it appears that the koala survived on the island until quite recently.

Rainfall in winter is light, so the early Keppel Islanders chose to live near reliable creeks, concentrating their efforts on fishing, at which they were highly skilled.

In 1867, it was reported that sixty people were living on Great Keppel and about twenty-five on North Keppel. These people made trips to the mainland in bark canoes, where they traded foods for stone, vital for cutting tools and spearheads.

The islanders had limited contact with mainlanders, which led to the development of languages different from those in Rockhampton and Yeppoon, as well as different physical characteristics. They were described in early times as being short of stature, with reddish-brown hair. They also worked with a limited range of tools and had no boomerangs or shields. Measurements of skeletal remains support the view that they were of different stature to the mainland Aborigines, though with no remaining members of the clan, results and clear determinations are difficult.

Below *An aerial view of Great Keppel Island. Photo by Leo Meier/Weldon Trannies.*
Right *The Great Barrier Reef. Photo by Robbi Newman.*

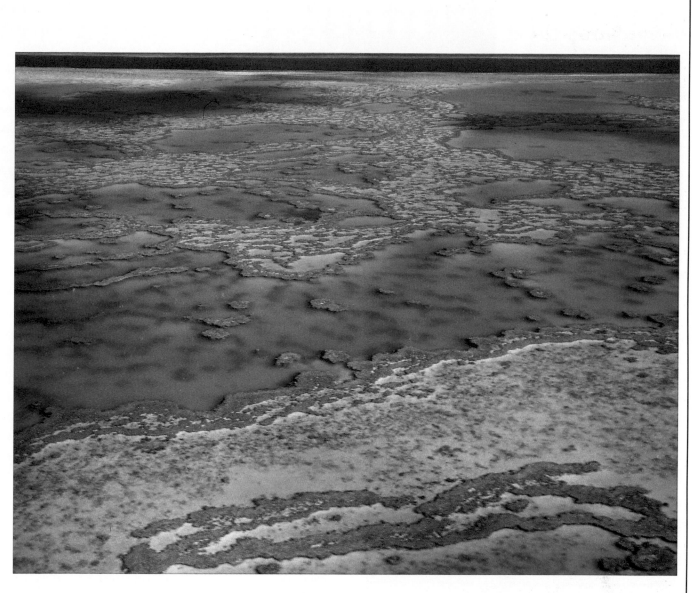

Cook visited the Keppels in 1770 and Flinders in 1803, but serious settlement attempts on the islands did not come until the 1880s. The original inhabitants of the islands were doomed once the push for settlement gained momentum. Many were killed, others fled to the mainland and those left in 1903 were rounded up and dispatched to Fraser Island.

In 1854 the colonial authorities proclaimed the traditional lands of the Darambal to be 'Waste Lands of the Crown', and the clans — with thousands of people — were living on borrowed time. Within 40 years of the white invasion, the original people had been reduced to a handful; in the same period, in Rockhampton itself, the once proud Darambal clan had been cut down to seven adults and three children. This story was repeated throughout the clans.

The survivors tended to be women, as the men had all been killed in the long struggle against the invading settlers. Often the majority of a clan would be wiped out in a single engagement.

The island of North Keppel was 'given' to a man named Ross after he had driven off the entire population, who retreated to Ross Creek at Yeppoon, where they died at the rate of one every two days.

After their defeat in battle, the Darambal people were forced to work for their new masters, some of whom paid them in opium. In the end they were herded into cattle trucks and sent to distant reserves.

The decimation of the Darambal recalls the Dreamtime story of the whistler ducks and the porcupines, who used to share all the land and the harvests of the sea between them. But one day a duck required a quill for his nose pin and took one from the porcupine's back without asking his permission. The porcupine took offence and began a fight. But the duck called all the other kinds of ducks to join him in the fight and eventually they took over all the land and water, driving the porcupine into holes in the ground for the rest of eternity.

North Queensland offers an almost tropical environment. Warm all year round, with heavy seasonal rains, the region was resource rich and its isolation from major population centres enabled the culture to survive longer than those further south. Mossman Gorge National Park. Photo by AusChromes.

The cassowary is the lesser known of Australia's two flightless birds, the survivors of a much larger species, the Genyornis which lived on the continent some 40 000 years ago. Cassowaries are found in north Queensland rainforest — as far south as Cardwell — and although generally timid, these birds can be dangerous when cornered. Their kicks have proven fatal. Photo by Philip Green.

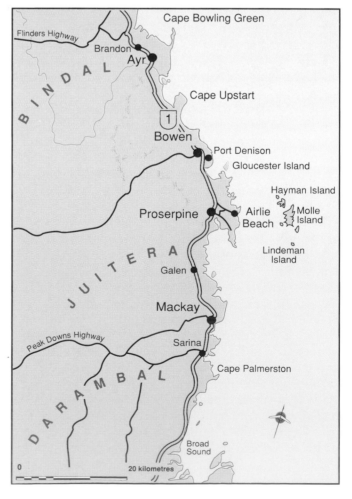

# North Queensland

orth of Rockhampton the next major population centre is the sugar capital of Mackay, a district once occupied by the Juitera people. Their traditional lands — and much of the flora and fauna — have disappeared under the intensive cultivation of sugar-cane.

These people made great use of the local orchids as a medicine and food: they were employed as a cure for dysentery and also for ringworm. In the Mackay area, the canes of the orchid, *Dendrobium discolor*, were used to prepare poultices and linaments. The cane was bruised with a hammer and the juice extracted for the liniment, which was used as a general cure-all. The starch from the pseudobulbs of orchids was also used to complement the meat and fish diet of the Juitera people.

The lands of the Bindal centred on Ayr, another area now overwhelmed by the sugar industry, while to the north was the country of the Juru and the Gia, which encompassed today's port of Bowen. The first outside contact with these people was made by an Englishman named James Morrill, who was wrecked on the Great Barrier Reef in 1846.

With six other survivors he drifted for 42 days on a raft, and was eventually washed ashore on the mainland near Cape Cleveland. Three men died shortly after, but the remaining four were cared for by the local people. They thought these strange white people must be long-dead relatives returning for a second life. A Mount Elliot clan looked after Morrill and a young English boy, while the others — the ship's captain and his wife — were taken in by the Cape Cleveland people.

Eventually the four survivors came together in the Port Denison district, waiting to be rescued. After a couple more years Morrill went back to the

Mount Elliott people. Some 13 years later he heard that some more strange white beings had travelled up from the south. Morrill approached them and their surprise must have been considerable at finding an Englishman in the guise of an Aboriginal warrior. Morrill related his experiences to a journalist, R. E. Johns, and this material provides invaluable insights into traditional life and society.

Every aspect of the heavens and earth was explained in Aboriginal tradition. For example, day and night were created when the Dreamtime heroes threw the sun and moon one to another; an eclipse was caused by an ancestral warrior putting a sheet of bark in front of the sun; and thunder and lightning were the manifestations of evil spirit beings. The benevolent spirits were clouds responsible for all the fish in the water and the vegetation on the land.

They believed in life after death — comets and meteors were the spirits of the dead returning to earth — but cremated their dead, keeping the ashes for twelve months before burial. Different burial customs were found among the Cape River people, who prepared a body in much the same way as today's embalmers. After three weeks the remains were placed on a tree platform where they rested a further three months. After that the bones were cared for by members of the family.

The people of this region wore necklaces, armlets, girdles and headbands, and made neck ornaments of shell. They also used cockatoo feathers as decoration, and wore small possum-skin cloaks, presumably in winter.

Around Townsville, the arid semi-desert area of western Queensland extends right to the coastline. The area enjoys the most predictably beautiful dry season in Australia with temperatures around 30 C and no rainfall for months on end. To the north of Innisfail is the highest rainfall in Australia averaging 25 millimetres per day over the year.

Townsville's weather is conducive to winter sport and year-round holiday travel; it is the largest city in Australia north of the Tropic of Capricorn, larger even than Darwin. It is a major terminal for rail and sea transport, and the commercial and educational centre of the north, having the James Cook University.

From Townsville to north of Cairns thirteen distinctly different nations lived, each with numerous clans.

The lands of the Wulgurukada people included the port of Townsville and Palm Island, established as a Devil's Island of the antipodes and used to incarcerate those people considered troublemakers. The black Australian author, Bill Rosser, has written an angry book on Palm Island, which has now been home for three generations of people. Today they are making a valiant attempt to build a new and proud community from fragments of Queensland's defeated nations.

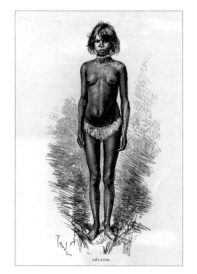

Kélamni, a Queensland girl, from Among Cannibals, *by Carl Lumholtz, London (1890). Courtesy National Library of Australia.*

A community school

I had a chance to be a part of the creation of a black Community School in Townsville in 1971 after I attended a seminar of teachers appointed to state schools with large Aboriginal and Islander populations.

The idea was to introduce black subjects into the curriculum and consequently courses covering language, dance, boat building (outriggers, canoes, etc) storytelling, traditional cooking and bush food were taught by the parents and grandparents.

Many people condemned the concept but it was something the people created themselves, particularly Eddie and Netta Mabo, who played a major role after the concept got off the ground. Unfortunately, the school lasted only ten years but it was an important step in the self-determination process.

Unlike the nations of Europe, Aboriginal nations did not seek to expand their borders through warfare. The special spiritual relationship Aboriginal people have with their own lands, and the spiritual perils they might encounter on other people's lands explains why.

This special relationship is expressed in a loving regard for the land and in the care and respect that is shown it. The thirteen nations who shared the lands between Townsville and Cairns enjoyed a unique environment: densely forested coastal lowlands and adjacent mountains with a heavy rainfall.

A group of Warrgamaygan people, photographed in 1900, from several clans in the area around Hinchinbrook Island, Ingham and Cardwell. Courtesy The Australian Museum.

Palm and Fantome Islands

Located 70 kilometres north-east of Townsville off the Queensland coast and set in the tranquillity of the Great Barrier Reef, Palm Island is absolutely exquisite.

The island features an abrupt mountain range, running east-west, with flat coastal plains densely populated with tropical plants, including towering coconut plantations laden with fruit, on the edge of a narrow coral beach leading into crystal clear water.

Set in the middle of the coconut palms, the Aboriginal reserve contains 1000 inhabitants, all of whom are victims of the infamous Queensland 'Removal Clause'. Palm Island was established as a penal colony for Aborigines from all over Queensland who were deported for trivial reasons. If a white superintendent simply didn't like the look of an Aborigine, he could have that person removed under police guard to Palm Island and kept there until he died.

It has been said that the apartheid system of South Africa was moulded on the Queensland

model. South Africa, however, allows blacks to own property whereas blacks in Queensland were precluded from any ownership of property, including their traditional homelands.

Located 3 kilometres north-west of Palm Island, Fantome Island was established as a leper colony for Aboriginal people during the nineteenth century and continued in that function until medical science discovered a cure for this dreaded disease. Victims were left in the care of an order of nursing nuns, awaiting a slow and painful death.

As the cure began to take effect, the victims filtered back to Palm Island with limbs missing and scars all over their body and face. On one visit to Palm Island I had the harrowing experience of greeting and shaking hands with a number of old friends whose hands were half missing. In a real sense these people were never to be seen again on mainland Australia because of the stigma attached to the disease, and the shame and attention their physical appearance attracted.

Shelters were dome-shaped frames 2 or 3 metres in diameter, covered with tea-tree bark and thatched with grass or lawyer-cane leaves. The largest dwellings were 3 metres high and 9 metres in diameter, and fires could be lit inside them. Blankets were created from tea tree or wild fig bark, beaten until it was as pliable as cloth.

Weirs were built as fish traps and examples can still be seen on Hinchinbrook Island, a wall of stones behind which fish were caught as the tide ebbed. Poisons were also used to catch fish, which rose to the surface when stunned.

One distinctive feature of life in the north was the custom of storing water in bark bags coated inside with wax. Baskets of different types were used to collect vegetables and fish, and to carry other items.

The people of north-east Queensland also boasted heavy hardwood swords, some 120 centimetres long, weighing 2 or 3 kilograms. These swords were unique in Australia, as were the long oval shields which protected the body from shoulders to ankles.

The massive swords and shields, used with great skill, made the northern warrior a formidable opponent. They were also in demand for trade, and recognised manufacturers allocated time in the community schedule for their production.

Trading routes in old Australia spanned the entire continent and the ceremonial gatherings were used for trading between the nations. The antiquity of these trading relationships can be gauged by the fact that they form the subject of many Dreamtime stories.

Men and women travelled on foot and by water, in canoes, or sometimes on simple log rafts. Their canoes were propelled by paddles with shaped handles and blades.

The people of the north loved decoration. Their personal ornaments included shells for the hair or beard, a bone through the septum of the nose, a feather in the hair, headdresses of net, wax and feathers, and bracelets and necklaces of hair, shell or berries.

Natural art galleries feature engravings and paintings of geometric designs as well as representations of animals, and carved trees are still scattered across north Queensland. One surviving art gallery is Jiyer Cave on the Russell River.

Central to the orderly life of the people were the gatherings which brought the clans together to trade and barter, settle disputes, fulfil religious duties and graduate young men into adulthood and the special responsibilities which they would follow for the rest of their lives. Called *pruns* in north Queensland, these meetings were held in various locations and it was vital that the dates be fixed and known well in advance so that allowance could be made for the distances to be travelled and to ensure there was no clash of engagements. Above all, the organisation of pruns depended on the availability of food resources both for the journeys and during the gatherings. In the year the Commonwealth of Australia was born, 1901, a prun was held on the lower Tully River either every seventh or thirteenth day from the termination of the previous proceedings. On the upper Tully, the prun was on the eighth or thirteenth day, while in the Cairns area it was held regularly on the twelfth day.

This calendar lasted the whole of the dry season and it could be shortened or lengthened according to the determination of the people. At the end of each prun the senior men decided where and when the next would be held. Once the date was determined a messenger was dispatched to advise the clans. Each of the nations (and sometimes the clans) had their own calendars which meant that names of days did not always correspond. Various methods were used to record accurately the details of time and place. The message stick, with its informative nicks and symbols, was a basic tool, but the fingers and different parts of the hand were used to record the number of days to the next gathering.

The arrival of the messengers was attended by the kind of pomp and ceremony seen today when an ambassador presents his credentials to the

Two north Queenslanders, with the hardwood broadsword found only in this region. Their shields were carved from the softwood buttresses of fig trees and were important in warding off blows during combat. Although this wood is very light, its complex grain structure ensures it will not split or break under attack. Courtesy National Library of Australia.

Hinchinbrook Island remains one of Australia's great paradises and Australia's largest national park island. The only dwellings are found at the tip of the island's north-eastern arm. Here, many of the streams and ridges have not even been named. Photo by Philip Green.

Head of State of a foreign power. The messenger would halt on the edge of the settlement until someone was sent to invite him in. There would be excitement as he produced his message stick, which invited the people to gather in ten days time. On occasions a messenger from another nation would arrive with a similar invitation. The decision as to which gatherings the clan would attend was reached after discussion among clan members. Some would want to go to one because their relatives might be attending, others might prefer one gathering over another because of better hunting, or perhaps the need to end a dispute with a man of another nation.

Yarrabah

The traditional ways of the north have been changed forever. No place illustrates the change more vividly than Yarrabah peninsula, about 55 kilometres by road south of Cairns and once the home of up to 2000 people. It was first visited by outsiders when Joseph Banks went ashore there during the voyage of Captain James Cook. He saw the fires of the Jirrbal people but made no contact with them.

The next European to visit this area was John Gribble, a missionary, who had previously tried to prevent atrocities against Aboriginal people in Western Australia. He had been threatened by hungry white landseekers who wanted no interference in their policies of genocide. Gribble received much the same reception in Cairns but pushed out to found Yarrabah mission, where the Gungandji people chose to settle and were joined by black refugees from throughout the state. John Gribble worked frantically to create a zone of peace and safety and when he collapsed from the strain, his son, Ernest, took over. Yarrabah became nearly self-sufficient with its industry, agriculture and fishing.

Sadly, the Gribbles left and Yarrabah became a barely disguised prison. Men and women had to live in separate quarters, children were seized at birth and brought up as pseudo-whites. Family, traditions and heritage were destroyed when the state took control in the 1960s.

Today the people of Yarrabah are taking control of their own destiny for the first time in a hundred years. Imprisoned and dispossessed for four generations, they are now rebuilding shattered families and traditions.

The area is host to an important legend, which lives in the landscape to this day. Embedded in the mountain backdrop to this reserve, on a mountain face denuded of cover, rests the giant crab. In the Dreamtime, this mythical

Opposite *Turtles were a favourite delicacy of the peoples of the north. Photo by Donald Thomson, courtesy of Mrs Thomson.*

being literally clawed its way ashore, leaving a gaping hole in the reef which allows the sea swell to penetrate the reef and break gently on the shorefront at Back Beach, the path taken by the crab as it crawled ashore to find its final resting place. This is the only beach on the 3000 kilometre coastline adjacent to the reef where any swell penetrates the outer reef.

When the world was young in the Dreamtime, the Tully River area, of which Cairns is the main centre, was the home of the Jirrbalngan people. Their neighbours comprised the Warrgamaygan, Girramaygan, Dulgubarra, Ngajanji and Yindini.

A group of people from the Cooktown area. Photo courtesy Macleay Museum.

Co-operative fishing with woven nets was a successful method of ensuring supplies of fresh fish. Photo by Donald Thomson, courtesy of Mrs Thomson.

The art treasures of Cape York

Discoveries over the last thirty years have shown that Cape York has a rich tradition of art and an important place in any assessment of Aboriginal achievement.

Until 1873 the people of the Palmer River region had hardly seen a white man, but in that year gold was discovered on the river. What followed was one of the most violent passages in Australia's history of race relations, with indiscriminate massacres of the traditional custodians of this art. As in Victoria, Chinese gold-hunters arrived from sea in their thousands and contributed greatly to the genocide.

A few people survived the turn of the century in the hills, only to be wiped out by a devastating wave of pneumonia in 1922. They lived long enough to record their new enemies in the art that adorned the walls of their shelters.

Since 1960 hundreds of these painted shelters have been discovered around the small town of Laura, featuring animals, birds, spirit beings and people. The dazzling form and colour of the Laura paintings has attracted worldwide attention to the area.

Right *The Giant Wallaroo Gallery.*
Below *The Magnificent Gallery. Photos by Jutta Malnic.*

Language

The Jirrbal language is described by Bob Dixon in *Australians to 1788*. It has a system of genders similar to French: every noun must have a gender mark in front of it. For example, *bayi barrngan* means young teenage boy, while *balan burrmbil* refers to a teenage girl. *Bayi* is masculine and is used with any noun referring to a male; *balan* is feminine, *balam* refers to food; *bala* is inanimate and is used with words such as *diban* (stone) or *mangan* (mountain).

Unlike English, Jirrbal had the same courtesy styles of Spanish and Italian in the use of different forms of 'you' to show respect. It was mandatory for a man to use a respectful style of speech, called *jalnguy,* in communicating with his future in-laws.

The majestic ritual of language was carried into the songs of the people. *Burran*-style songs were about love, jealousy or anger and were sung high and loud to the rhythmic beat of sticks. The *gama* style or ceremonial songs, describing events such as hunting or battle, are acompanied by the tapping of two boomerangs. They have a strict meter and each line must be of eleven syllables.

Rainforest on Cape Tribulation, north Queensland. Photo by Colin Totterdell.

137

Oppposite *A mourning ritual practised on Cape York. Photo by Donald Thomson, courtesy of Mrs Thomson.*

A Henry King photo of a man called Arillda, of the Wallinu-man clan, on the Gilbert River in north Queensland. Courtesy The Australian Museum.

All of the traditional knowledge, the calendars, the system of family, government and religion, was ignored by the white invaders who believed they had a divine right to shoot the game, take the fish and plough up the fruits and vegetables, while banning the traditional landowners from their own food and water supplies. Anyone who sought to share the animals brought in to replace the native fauna was shot.

Before general warfare broke out, gatherings of the clans had debated how to deal with the intruders. Should they be invited to a corroboree to show their superiority in single combat? No, it was decided: they would not accept. The newcomers relied on their *marrgin*, or guns, and their success came out of the barrels of those guns. The shooting has long since stopped but memories remain.

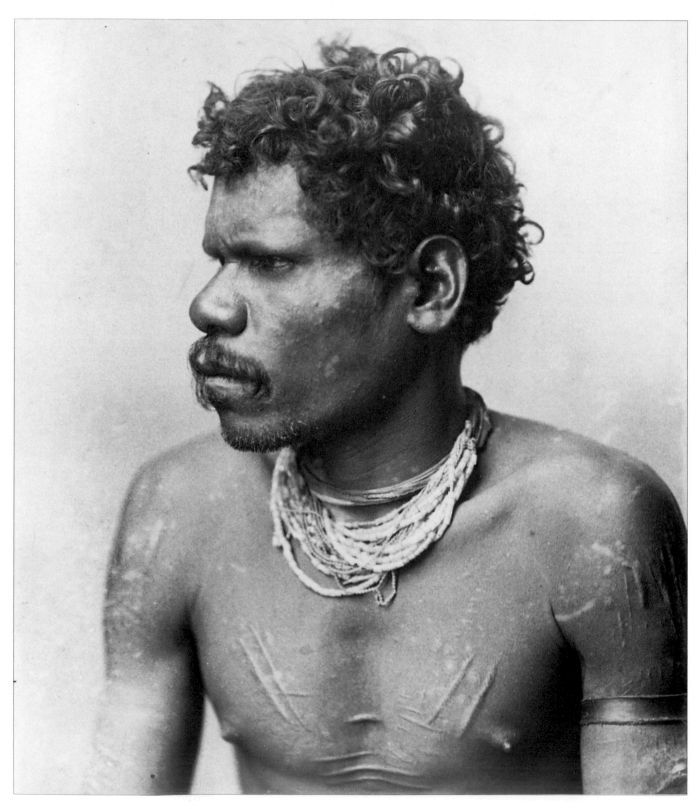

138

Kakadu National Park, one of
Australia's natural treasures.
Photo by Carmen Ky.

Townsville to Darwin

 AUSTRALIA has often been called a land of contrasts and the next stage of our journey — west from Townsville through the great expanse of central Australia, then north to Darwin — shows that contrast clearly. From the dry, flat and sunbaked world of north-western Queensland, we build in anticipation as we approach the jewel at the end of our journey, Kakadu National Park.

141

The Queensland Native Police were developed as a means of 'pacifying' outlying and troublesome clans or individuals. Queensland blacks were clothed and trained to ride against their own people, although interclan rivalries were also exploited by the authorities. From Among Cannibals, *by Carl Lumholtz, London (1890), courtesy National Library of Australia.*

Leaving the east coast at Townsville, we head south-west into the dry heart of Queensland and the lands of the famous Kalkadoons. The Great Dividing Range forms a natural barrier between the coastal regions and the vast interior, an area which supported many clans. The mighty Burdekin River, which we cross around 30 kilometres east of Charters Towers, represented a barrier, conduit and life support system for the Warungu people, and their neighbours, the Kutjala and Iiba.

At Townsville we note that, unlike at Cairns (to the north) and Mackay (to the south), the dry interior extends all the way to the coast, through a break in the Great Divide. After Charters Towers we see a subtle but steady change in the flora and the landscape.

This section of our journey takes us west on the Flinders Highway and covers some very flat country, with its own characteristics and hazards. During the daytime large flocks of emus can be seen from the road, but at night drivers should be on constant alert for very large kangaroos, big reds, which cross the highway and can easily be mesmerised by headlights. Yet the rewards of driving slowly at night (over very good road surfaces) are worth the effort. The coolness of the nights presents such a contrast to the harsh heat of the daytime. And the open skies accentuate the galaxy of stars.

It is on this stretch that one is constantly reminded of the size of Australia. The vegetation and general landscape changes every hundred kilometres or so, and the monotony of driving vast distances seems to add a meditational factor to the experience; ultimately you begin to understand what it meant to worship the landscape.

The town of Hughenden represents the heart of Jirandali country, and at Richmond we enter the the lands of the Wanamara, and then those of the once-mighty nation of the Kalkadoons.

The Kalkadoons

It was the Kalkadoons who stood last and longest against the European invaders, a ten-year struggle which culminated in a major battle in 1884.

As a result of the guerilla war carried on by many of the Queensland peoples, a strong paramilitary force — the Queensland Native Police — was assembled and despatched to ride against them. The attacking forces, under Frederick Charles Urquhart, numbered about 200 and they blazed through Kalkadoon country, until the two forces finally confronted each other near today's Mount Isa.

The Kalkadoon forces, which are believed to have been at least 600 strong, had been assembled after messages were sent the length and breadth of the nation, and had taken up a strong and well-armed position on the top of what was to become known as Battle Mountain. Their leader (who has never been identified by name) was identified by a thick possum-string hanging around his neck, which was hitched to another string passing around the waist, and wore a headdress of white down.

Three northern Australian women. Photos by Henry King, courtesy The Australian Museum.

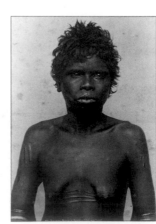
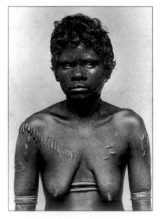

Australia's only cavalry charge

In full view of the Kalkadoon warriors, Urquhart mustered his men for the attack but wisely kept them out of the range of the deadly long spears. Before leading the charge, he called upon the Kalkadoons to 'Stand in the Queen's name'.

The Kalkadoons answered with a shower of missiles and a ferocious roar of defiance. Urquhart then signalled the only old-style European cavalry charge in Australia's history. But the Kalkadoons were ready for their assault. Under a hail of missiles the cavalry charge broke and the men took cover behind rocks at the bottom of the mountain. Urquhart rallied his men for a second charge up the slope on foot. Again they were repelled and Urquhart was seriously injured.

With their commander critically wounded, the confidence of the Europeans was badly shaken. They abandoned their attack on the summit, and the Kalkadoons believed they had won. Urquhart, however, recovered sufficiently to take command once more and divided his forces for an attack from two directions. As the Kalkadoon warriors moved from one side of the mountain to the other, to counter the two-pronged thrust on their stronghold, they were picked off by marksmen stationed at strategic points around the mountain.

Their numbers dwindling, the Kalkadoons formed up in lines and, carrying their spears like lances, charged down the mountain. It was a magnificent gesture but they were slaughtered.

The passing of years has partly healed the scars and the centenary of the battle was recognised in October 1984, by the Kalkadoon Cultural Festival held in Mount Isa. On 21 October of that year over a hundred people gathered at Kajabbi, just 20 kilometres from Battle Mountain, where a monument to the gallant Kalkadoons who fell in battle that day was unveiled as a permanent tribute.

This date has been proclaimed as Memorial Day by the Kalkadoon Council, which operates today from headquarters in the heart of Mount Isa. The town also boasts the Baiame Health Centre (administered by Kalkadoons), the Kalkadoon Cultural Centre, Kalkadoon Park, Kalkadoon High School, the Kalkadoon Indoor Soccer Club and the Kalkadoon Sobriety House.

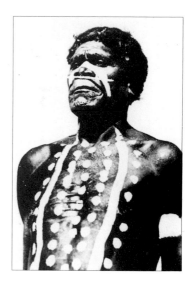

A Queensland Aborigine in full war paint. Courage, tradition and honour however were no match for European firepower. Courtesy National Library of Australia.

A gathering of tribal elders in northern Australia. Courtesy National Library of Australia.

Kalkadoon Cultural Centre

The Kalkadoon Cultural Centre is located in the grounds of the Frank Aston Underground Museum and occupies the lower floor of a large renovated reservoir at the top of Rotary Hill. The centre features a display of Kalkadoon tools and weapons and a simulated cave with rock paintings. Another reconstruction shows a traditional camp with a full-sized *wulliberri* (house), complete with fireplace and implements.

Children from the district, both white and black, visit the centre to experience 40 000 years of culture and history, together with the Kalkadoon secrets of food and water supplies. Every year people get lost in the Australian bush, often dying of hunger and thirst with food and water all around them. The Kalkadoon Cultural Centre teaches children where to look and how to survive in the bush under all conditions. They are also taught about the healing methods used by the original people, as well as about their tools and weapons.

The centre has also created a bush educational centre 20 kilometres from town so that all people, old and young, can have the practical experience of living the traditional lifestyle, even if only for a day or two.

The best local example of rock art, known as Sun Rock, was painted in red ochre many thousands of years ago. Although the rock face is near water and has probably been occasionally washed by floods, it may be extremely old. Geologists have found out that when fine-grained red ochre has been used on quartzite, a 'bonding' tends to develop between the two materials. In this case, the fine grains of ochre have penetrated into the minute cracks in the quartzite and perhaps the painting will survive for many more hundreds of years.

A trip to Battle Mountain is possible, but involves crossing many creeks and gullies and requires a four-wheel-drive vehicle. Along the way the soil changes from bright red to grey black then back to red again. Armies of red ant hills point the way to Battle Mountain itself, still eerie in its lonely majesty.

Trade between clans was an essential part of survival in traditional times, particularly in arid areas, where natural resources were scarce. Courtesy Macleay Museum.

Trade routes

Trade routes have criss-crossed north Queensland since the Dreamtime. Each nation and each district had its localised resources which were traded far and wide for the materials unavailable in their district. For example, the Mitakoodi people in the Cloncurry district used a small type of net which they obtained in trading from the Woonamurra people who lived to the north. The Kalkadoons acquired *kunti* (porcupine or spinifex grass gum) from the Buckingham Downs region to the south.

In the whole region from Bedourie down to Birdsville, no spears were manufactured. All the weaponry in that area was obtained by trading with surrounding peoples.

The Boulia district was the main centre for manufacturing acicular-tip spears, although they were also made around Leichhardt-Selwyn, Cloncurry and the Upper Diamantina. These spears were traded in the surrounding areas of the Upper Georgina and Lower Diamantina. The secret of these spears — and the reason for their popularity — is a particular kind of water reed from which the butt is made, which is obtained from the Woolgar district.

Spears with barbed prongs of sharpened wood were used for catching fish and were made by the Karunti who came from the other side of Normanton and traded with people along the Upper Leichhardt River. Other traders came in search of *pituri,* a plant which grows in the semi-arid regions north of Lake Eyre.

Shelter and lifestyle

The design of houses in north-west Queensland varied according to environmental need. Some were built on high ground, to withstand the rain, with frameworks of bush material consolidated with mud.

When houses were built especially for warmth, the mud floor was up to 60 centimetres thick and was below ground level. Grass was wedged into the space between the scaffolding of saplings and plastered with mud. Sometimes bark sheets were used as a final outside covering.

A ring of mud at the entrance formed a decorative door frame. Fires were kindled in the corner opposite the door and sapling wind breaks were often built on each side of the front entrance. Household possessions might be left inside or outside the dwelling, but spears were always stuck into the walls.

The peoples of north, west and central Queensland shared many Dreamtime traditions and legends, and there were complex laws and customs governing trade and social intercourse. This reflects the challenge of living in mostly dry areas where particular resources were limited to certain areas and co-operation between nations was critical to survival.

Both men and women liked dressing up and putting on their best paint, especially for ceremonial occasions. Hair was grown long so it could be greased up and combed into braids. Head nets were popular, along with forehead nets, head bands, kerchiefs, feathers and even artificial whiskers. Feather ornaments, made of various types of feathers, were tied on to a small sprig and stuck through the hair in irregular patterns.

Earrings of knuckle bone about 5 centimetres in length were tied with twine to the tuft of hair over the temple, so that they dangled in front of the ears.

One of two flightless birds in Australia, the emu is among Australia's best known birds. Once they were hunted widely and emus still represent an important food source for people living traditional lifestyles. The inquisitive nature of these birds was often their downfall. Hunters would mimic their call, attracting them close enough to club or spear. Photo by Densey Clyne/Mantis Wildlife.

Artificial whiskers were made with locks of hair, glued together with beef-wood gum and hung from the hair in front of each ear below the jaw. Head nets prevented long hair from getting into the eyes and bands of fine netting were worn across the forehead to keep the hair well back. This adornment was known as *mi-ri-mi-ri* and used all over north Queensland as a badge by those who had completed their education and initiation. These *mi-ri-mi-ri* were made by the men but they were worn by both sexes.

One splendid ornament, popular throughout the north, was made from two kangaroo teeth set in an oval-shaped base and hung from a lock of hair in the centre of the forehead. Red possum-string ornaments were worn in the hair, or as necklaces and armlets. In the Boulia district, a version of the Davy Crockett coonskin cap with a dingo tail was often worn. Ears and the septum of the nose were often pierced to hold decoration. The two front teeth were often removed as a part of initiation.

Beards were made to look stylish by tying them close to the base of the chin. Women favoured red reed necklaces, armlets, anklets and body cords.

Jean Chayet collection, courtesy National Library of Australia

Pituri

Throughout Australia there was a complex pattern of trading between nations, often involving travel over many hundreds of kilometres. Some lands were rich in the best materials for shields and swords, others had food resources, or perhaps quarries providing stone for implements. Areas such as the Flinders Ranges were rich in deposits of ochre and were regularly visited by expeditions from far afield, who came with items to trade for the precious pigments. But one of the most extensive trading patterns in north-east Australia was based around the supply and distribution of *pituri,* a powerful stimulant prepared from the leaves of the pituri bush.

Pituri, which was an important part of ceremonial occasions in many regions, contains more nicotine than modern tobacco products and was chewed, rather than smoked. The bush grows over much of the arid centre of Australia, although the Mulligan-Georgina district (on the eastern border of the Simpson Desert) was considered the richest source and traders came from far away for prized leaves. These were then distributed over an area of half a million square kilometres, from north Queensland to the Lake Eyre Basin and north-west New South Wales.

The *pituri* bushes were carefully nurtured and their location kept secret from all outsiders. Specialised preparation of the leaves to gain the maximum narcotic effect was crucial and was passed on from the elders to the younger men, but only when they were a little *pinnaru,* when their beards first began to turn grey.

It was the specialised methods of preparation which made the pituri from the Mulligan-Georgina district the most popular source. The leaves were mixed with the alkali ash of the wirra bush (*Acacia salicina*), significantly enhancing the power of the *pituri.* Expeditions came from far afield, with grinding stones, ochres or other items of significant value to trade for the *pituri* from this district.

Around Camooweal, the people used stone and barbed spears which came from the north and west. Woomeras used by the northern Kalkadoons were made with *melo* shell discs obtained in the Normanton area. Shields and *coolamons* (elongated wooden troughs) were also manufactured in the Boulia district (where particularly suitable timber was available), and were a great item of trade at Roxburgh and along the Upper Georgina.

The material used for making grinding stones came from around Walaya and the Toko Ranges. It was cut and ground into the required shapes before being taken to trade with a score of nations in the north. These great slabs were carried substantial distances, an indication of the acceptance of these routes by all nations.

Eagle-hawk claws and shells of all shapes and sizes were used as chest orna-ments. The decoration styles for both men and women showed great imagination (and vanity) and frequently it was the men who dressed up more often and more colourfully.

For ceremonial dances and celebrations the men not only painted their faces with yellow, red and white ochres, but decorated their entire bodies with paint and feathers in striking patterns. Preparations for the night's cele-brations could take all day. For some ceremonies the men assembled privately to put on their body paint, then suddenly appeared before the women and children.

Waist belts and aprons were worn and very fancy 'sporrans' or tassels —hung from waist belts and coloured red or white — were worn by the men on public occasions. The thick waist belts made of double plaited hair twine could measure up to 25 metres when unravelled. Feather ornaments were often attached to the belt at each hip and women also wore red tassels to cover their genitals on public occasions. After the arrival of Europeans both men and women learned to wear the tassels in their presence or even in an area which they were known to frequent.

Body scars were widely used, often extending from the nipples to the navel with patterns of dashes and dots.

Just as today's Australians are great sports fans, so it was in traditional times, though the accent was on participation. Using a ball made from possum skin, they played a version of basketball, either in teams or as indi-viduals, throwing the ball from one to the other while their opponents tried to intercept it.

Another ball game, similar to hockey, was played with a stone ball. The teams of men stood 20 metres apart and the object of the game was to inter-cept the ball with the playing stick. Another popular ball game (in which gambling was involved) used a lump of lime, ashes and clay baked into a

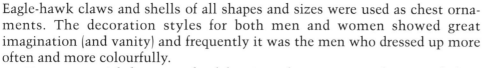

Husbands often cut their wife's hair for making string, whilst maintaining an elaborate beard and hairstyle. From the Michael Terry Collection, courtesy National Library of Australia.

A group of people from Crown Point and Horseshoe Bend, Northern Territory. Courtesy National Library of Australia.

Almost invariably it was the men who dressed and painted themselves elaborately for corroborees and other ceremonies. Courtesy National Library of Australia.

Two examples of ceremonial paint and preparation. Courtesy National Library of Australia (left), and The Australian Museum (right).

small, hard ball and painted red or yellow. The ball was spun on a hard surface and teams of two or three would compete to spin it the longest.

Skipping ropes were used and a form of hide and seek, in which everyone was involved, was popular on no-work days. Smoke spirals were another diversion. Leaves, bark and even mussel shells were thrown into a smoking fire to rise with the smoke. The highest lift won the prize.

Friendly competition took place in mimicking birds and animals and drawing the tracks of people, birds and animals (including Europeans, whose long boots always provoked great amusement).

In some areas, a form of bloodless coursing was traditional: a wallaby or dingo rat, caught in a net, was freed and the challenge was to recapture it with bare hands. No weapon or missile could be used.

A variation on throwing horseshoes was also popular. A large bone was thrown at a net with a narrow aperture. The objective was to put the bone into the hole without touching the net.

Toy boomerangs, often ornamentally carved and painted, were used in games. Teams of five or six would stand in line, each man with his hands on the shoulders of the man in front. A boomerang was thrown over their heads and as it circled (sometimes several times), they tried to avoid being hit. Team members each took turns at throwing and the team suffering the fewest hits won the game. In some places, the toy boomerang was used to throw at a peg fixed in the ground. Toy throwing sticks, up to 50 centimetres long, were also used in contests similiar to javelin throwing.

The whirler or bullroarer was used for fun and as the background for serious ceremonies. It could also be employed to charm a cold lover.

The playgrounds of the north-west have long since vanished but some of the games, the skills and the traditions live on in the people intent on rediscovering their colourful past.

T Over the border

he road from Mount Isa to Camooweal is hilly, bumpy and narrow, to the point of being dangerous. On this stretch a more enthusiastic traveller (with lots of time to spare) could branch north to the Gulf of Carpenteria, to Burketown, Normanton and other Aboriginal settlements such as Doomadgee and Borroloola.

Camooweal is the last major town before we cross the border and it's always a welcome sight to me. The Aboriginal people of this town are very friendly and the local service station has a hot shower and a modern caravan park. Just west of town there's a peaceful place by the river where I always take the opportunity to rest for a couple of hours.

The luxury highway from Camooweal to the Three Ways, fenceless as it is, is cattle-free most of the day, though care should taken to avoid any surprise encounters. Visibility is good though, because the country is dead flat, which gives one a good feeling for Australia's size. I always find this part of the journey a good time to meditate to the strains of Mozart.

As Highway One, now the Barkly Highway, crosses the border from Queensland to the Northern Territory, we pass from Wakaja country into the territory of the Warumungu, today centred on Tennant Creek. The first European incursion into these lands was led by Stuart's expedition of 1860, and within ten years the Overland Telegraph Line was snaking through their territories. With it came permanent occupation by foreigners.

As we head west we pass vast areas without human occupation. To the north, the Barkly Tablelands hide a vast treasury of ancient Australian history — recent discoveries have revealed huge prehistoric animal remains.

The story of the area is the familiar one of attack, defeat and dispossession, and the black population of Tennant Creek today is drawn from several remnant nations. The traditional owners of the area, the Warumungu, were forced to evacuate their lands in the rush of development late in the nineteenth century, but drifted back whenever they could.

Other peoples — particularly those on lands sought for pastoral leases — found themselves forced into Tennant Creek, including the Warlpiri, Warlmanpa, Alyawarra and Kaytej.

In an area of powerful snake dreaming legends, it's not surprising that these granite boulders — generally known as the Devils Marbles — are seen by Aboriginal people as eggs of the Rainbow Serpent. Photo by Trevern Dawes.

149

The Devils Marbles are one of Australia's most prominent landmarks. As part of an 1800 hectare conservation park, right on the main highway, they attract many thousands of tourists each year. Photo by Trevern Dawes.

The stark beauty of ghost gums at Camooweal. These trees are common in the drier areas of the Northern Territory, although they are also found in other tropical areas. Photo by Philip Green.

The Warumungu people have maintained a steady drift into Tennant Creek, while the Warlpiri have begun moving to outstations and camps outside the town, with people of six other nations. The old law and traditions are difficult to maintain with so many different peoples in one place. The bush camps that surround Tennant Creek are virtual refugee centres.

Poor living conditions have diminished health standards and a recent survey showed that not one man or woman in the camps surrounding the town had a full-time job. Yet the sharing spirit of kinship has been maintained and no one is ever abandoned. The reserve which was set aside for the Warumungu people was overwhelmed in the gold rushes of the 1930s and argument continues today as to what land should be given back to the original owners.

In the days of their independence, the Warumungu were great traders, mainly in shields and softwood spears. The central trade route stretched from Darwin in the north, south to Alice Springs and the lands of the Arunta, Laritja and Urabunna.

The frilled lizard is the largest and most bizarre of Australia's dragon lizards. Found across most of northern Australia, it puffs out its frills when alarmed. Photo by Jim Frazier/Mantis Wildlife.

Right *The Woomah clan, of the Northern Territory, gathered in ceremonial paint. Courtesy National Library of Australia.*
Opposite *Ceremonial decoration. Courtesy The Australian Museum.*

Djingali lands

North of Tennant Creek and Warumungu country, we cross an unseen border at Elliott, into the lands of the Djingali.

The formation of the great plains of Djingali is recorded in the Dreamtime stories. This plain is still inhabited by snakes, made enemies of the people when a hunter named Meindejala broke the sacred law forbidding those of the totem of any creature from hunting that creature. His story is told in a powerful epic poem.

PHOTO BY COLIN TOTTERDELL

The Snake Dreaming

From Malindji, the legend goes,
The mighty Dreamtime snake arose,
It crawled across the black soil plain
To Yumbe where it sank again.

A dyke of stone still marks the trail,
And those who see it dare not fail
To call their children near and tell
The talk how Mein-djala fell.

One day while hunting in the heat
His dogs had lost an emu fleet
Right near Malindji - fatal spot.
Striding up thirsty, hungry and hot,
He tapped a bloodwood tree and drank
The sweet Karimbi from its 'tank'.
Then sitting down 'neath shady tree,
Looked at that Dream-stone longingly.
His body tired, his eyes near blind,
He craved for food he could not find.
He knew the lore which elders tell,
That shades who guard these places well,
Must not be asked for food, or they
Will smite and kill in magic way.

But Mein-djala was fainting-weak;
He struck the stone: 'Food! food I seek.'
'Old man send me a snake,' he cried;
The Umbe stone in kind replied.
For as he spoke a snake he saw;
Then snakes, and on came more, and more.

He moved to get a stick, alas!
They blocked his path; he could not pass.
He tried to dodge; they hemmed him round;
They forced the hunter to the ground.
A writhing mass of snakes was there;
He cried aloud in his despair.
He fought and struggled hard for breath
As he was slowly crushed to death.

And Mein-djala was no more —
Just a warning gone before
Thus all who imitate the great,
Will likewise meet a dreadful fate.

(From W. E. Harney, and A. P. Elkin, Songs of the Songmen: Aboriginal Myths Retold, *Cheshire*, *Melbourne, 1949.*)

Barrumundi was appreciated as a fine eating fish long before the arrival of European chefs. Courtesy The Australian Museum.

A whistling kite watches over the sunset. Photo by Philip Green.

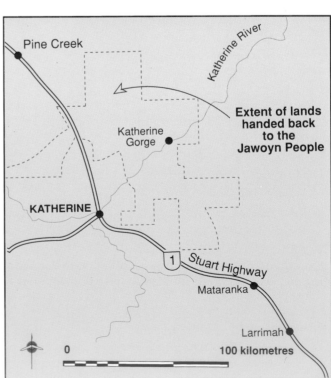

Pine Creek

Katherine River

Katherine Gorge

Extent of lands handed back to the Jawoyn People

KATHERINE

Stuart Highway

1

Mataranka

Larrimah

0   100 kilometres

Jawoyn country

urther north, the Djingali lands — and the Plain of the Serpents — give way to the territories of the Mangarai and Katamen (of which Mataranka is the centre). Katherine, heart of Jawoyn country, offers some of the most spectacular landscapes found anywhere in Australia.

The explorer Leichhardt by-passed the lands of the Jawoyn on his historic expedition of 1844-45 and it was left to the Gregory expedition, eleven years later, to claim the honour of being the first outsiders to invade their territory.

In 1862 John McDouall Stuart and his party found their way to the Katherine River itself and within another ten years the European settlers and pastoralists began in earnest to take over the traditional Jawoyn lands. Among the pastoral empires established in the lands of the Jawoyn was Elsey Station, made famous by Mrs Aeneas Gunn in her book *We of the Never Never*.

The discovery of gold at Pine Creek in 1872 brought an invasion of miners and then, in quick succession, copper, tin and tungsten were found in the region. In the 1950s, uranium was also discovered, which lifted the interest of mineral companies to new levels.

The completion of the Overland Telegraph in 1872 (and the railway in 1928) saw the dispossession process reach its final stages.

Katherine Gorge. Photo by Robbi Newman.

PHOTO BY AUSCHROMES

Koopoo, the red plains kangaroo

In the Dreamtime, a red plains kangaroo named Koopoo came from the River Mulunbar, which today is Katherine. Koopoo brought with him many of his family, including women and children, and led them far and wide over the dry country until he found a spring.

Koopoo brought his people to the spring at Chumbulmee, where the Flying Fox River begins. He told them he had created a waterhole so deep that no one could survive in it but it could be used for fishing and drinking.

Koopoo and his people moved on to Bulookchallum, lower on the Flying Fox River, and then to Boguoongguoong, still lower down on the same creek. It was at this camp that Kandagun, the dingo, came to kill Koopoo and his people, who were split up by the repeated attacks of Kandagun. Some went to Balyoorah, on today's Elsey Station and crossed the river; others went to Narrmingun, or red lily lagoon, and yet others went to Oogalah on the Waterhouse River. It was here that the refugee kangaroo descended into a deep waterhole and turned into a rainbow snake.

In the mountains where a stream flows from Toomdoouk down to meet the Flying Fox River, the black-nosed rock snake, Julungwee, came out of the wide and bottomless spring which he created and named the place and decided to settle there.

But Kandagun the dingo, who had been responsible for all the trouble, chased Kodding, the rock wallaby, to the edge of the deep water spring at Toomdooruk and jumped into the water, never to be seen again.

(Adapted from Roland Robinson, Legend & Dreaming, *Edwards & Shaw, Sydney, 1967.)*

Within a short time, the Jawoyn were working on the railway and tele-graph lines and running mail delivery wagons south and east of Katherine. Other Jawoyn worked as trackers. As the Europeans established farms through the area the Jawoyn continued to cling to the river banks. Whenever an effort was made to set aside some land for them, it was 'reserved' either for mining or agriculture.

Labour camps, called 'native control camps', were set up near mining areas and Jawoyn men were turned to underground work. World War II saw the establishment of Aboriginal compounds and residential institutions. From August 1942, Aborigines were officially prohibited from living north of the Edith River and people of many different nations were thrown together in virtual concentration camps, where soldiers doled out rations. Aboriginal men were put to work cutting wood, maintaining roads and railways, carting ammunition and assembling motors.

Katherine was bombed by Japanese planes in 1942 and many Aborigines died or were badly injured. One woman, whose arm was severely injured in the attack, was given the name *Ngal-marnak-bom*, or 'arm bomb'.

Europeans, Chinese and some Jawoyn were evacuated from Katherine under the threat of further bombing attacks. After the war the army gave up the camps and a new compound was established on the upper King River, where more than 400 people were 'housed'. Ruins of this camp still stand. Another settlement was established at Tandangal but was later moved to Bamyili, on Beswick Creek, where the white administration again herded people of many nations together.

Others worked on stations for 5 shillings per week (until 1957), plus a hand-out of tobacco and clothing. Many have drifted into Katherine where the Aboriginal population today numbers more than three hundred. Many more have settled in camps outside the town. The Kalano Association, estab-lished in 1974, provides community, health and recreational services for the Aboriginal population. It also runs an old people's home at Prior Court.

Before World War II a 'half-caste home' existed in Pine Creek, where young children were sent after being taken from their parents. Today, a number of Aboriginal camps exist around Pine Creek, which are mainly occupied by the Wagiman people, though Jawoyn and Mayali are found in a camp near the old train station.

A major part of the traditional responsibility of the Jawoyn people to their land included flora management by firestick farming, which involved burning off the dry summer grass in August or September. This encouraged the growth of tender green shoots, and the process was considered essential to fatten game.

It was the responsibility of the elders to ensure that young men and women knew the locations of the sacred sites, the measures to be taken when visiting these sites and the precautions necessary to protect them from desecration. Education also covered the geography of the land, the location of food and supplies and, above all, the religious training which provided the explanation for the creation of land, sea, sky and all the creatures of their world.

The dominant figure of the Dreamtime is *Bolung,* the rainbow serpent who is a central figure in the religious beliefs of most of the people of the Top End and Kimberley region. Bolung could take the form of a lightning bolt who brought the monsoonal rains. Sometimes he was destructive but more often he was a creative and life-giving spirit. The Jawoyn do not pray or implore him, preferring to leave him undisturbed, and ensuring others did the same.

Fishing was forbidden in the deep green pools where Bolung was believed to live. When fishing close to the pools, it was considered proper to take only a portion of the catch and throw the rest back. When the Jawoyn found Europeans using explosives in these pools, there was considerable anger and conflict.

Another powerful Dreaming figure is *Bula* (also called *Bulardemo*) and the Jawoyn believed that if his sacred sites were disturbed widespread destruc-

Australia's northern rivers have always offered a bountiful supply of fish. Courtesy The Australian Museum.

tion to black and white alike would follow. Miners disturbed one such site in the 1950s and an epidemic followed which threatened the lives of everyone in the area. The Jawoyn said Bula had shown his displeasure. The spiritual life of Bula and his role today are considered to be so sacred that they are not discussed in public and the full story cannot be told here.

Another Dreamtime figure is *Ngalcurlum* ('whirlwind') who moved around the Dook Creek area and is also associated with Gawucwucmar, a place near the Low Level Crossing in Katherine. *Bemang,* the blue-tongued lizard, left his place near Katherine Gorge and went to Seventeen Mile Creek and the pool at Edith Falls. *Wirk,* the possum, left several sites in the Dook Creek and Gundi areas. Several *gupu,* or plains kangaroos, feature in the array of Dreamtime creators and are represented at sites to the north of Katherine.

All Jawoyn adults were expected to know the location of the sacred sites and to visit them. Standing before the site they would offer the following spiritual address:

> *yo! Ngarrk ngagangan, najorr nga-ganay (from somewhere) garrk marrk berndak nga-dul? miwungu. Niyarngula dara nga-jabakmanggu ngan-gulk-wo, nyanu-worlk-wo.*

In translation: *(Name) I am here! I came on foot (from where) but the grass is high. I'll burn it. I want to fish here, too. Give me flesh. Give us fat.*

All of the Top End suffers from the severity of the wet and dry seasons. Major rivers can be reduced to dry creek beds in a matter of months. In the Gunumeleng season (October to December), the pre-monsoon humidity builds anticipation of the coming rains. The billabongs dry and crack, awaiting the renewal that comes with the wet. Photo by Bill Bachman.

Typical of these sites is a stone at Jurrangluk, said to represent a taipan's head, which visitors must rub with 'sweat from their armpits'. Another sacred stone, at Yombolyarriyn near the the junction of the Edith and Ferguson Rivers, was left there by an ancestral being called *Nagorrko*. When the river floods during the wet season, the Jawoyn people must move the stone to higher ground until the water recedes.

At Wungurri, on a spur of the Katherine River, there are two lizard dreaming places. The ritual responsibility of the people is to remove rubbish from the site and 'purify it by burning "ironwood" '.

The funeral rites of the people in the Katherine region vary from tree platform burials to bone bundles placed in burial logs. A distinctive custom of the area recognised the need for boys to grow into hunters. Often when a small boy first sighted an animal, such as a kangaroo, a carving was made and sent to the boy's relatives as an invitation to meet with the senders and discuss his future, perhaps with thoughts of marriage at some future time.

Before their graduation, Jawoyn boys went into a period of seclusion with the elders, who provided instruction in social and personal responsibilties, hunting, general knowledge, religious belief and rituals.

The bones of large animals killed in hunting by the boys were collected in one place. When the boys began to grow facial hair, the bones were painted and placed in a special pattern as a preparation for the graduation. These customs are maintained today and despite the loss of their traditional lands, the Jawoyn still hunt and fish in the traditonal way for turtles, goanna, wallaby and fish. This is one of the few remaining areas of Australia where traditional life goes on as it has for endless generations.

Senior men usually have detailed knowledge of more than two hundred different plant species, and it is a part of 'homework' for young men to study all the plants and their use in food and medicine.

To the Jawoyn, the land is the repository of the soul and they have names which relate to their birth place. Other nations have personal names which are guarded in privacy, but the Jawoyn wear their names publicly, though the names of the dead are not mentioned for a considerable time after their passing.

So close is the relationship between the people and the land that they believe the land will reject unknown persons, who will find it difficult to get fish, game or access to natural resources. In a strange locality, it is customary for the Jawoyn to anoint their head with water or to 'introduce'

Fire was a constant means of regenerating growth in the Australian bush. Not only did the fire keep plains open for hunting, but it drew kangaroos, wallabies and smaller game back into the area to feed on the fresh grass, seeds and berries which followed. Recent research has encouraged authorities to return to the regular burning of lands, as a vital part of earth and plant renewal. Photo by Bill Bachman.

159

themselves to the locality (usually with a song) and ask for fish or other food. It is the land which has the cultural identity.

Land use is governed strictly by laws which require certain localities to be treated with respect and caution. Deep green waterholes (because of the rainbow serpent) and ceremonial grounds must be respected. Women are not permitted to approach sacred sites where men perform their distinctive ceremonies and men must likewise respect women's ceremonial grounds.

Despite the long agony of dispossession from their lands, the ceremonial life of the people goes on. A complex ritual called *Gunabibi* (which can go for several weeks) was brought to the territory by *Nagorrko,* the Dreamtime hero, and continues to this day.

The *Marayin* ceremony is dedicated to the totem figures and the elaborate funeral proceedings continue, along with ceremonies to mark the end of the mourning period. In one, known as *Murlarra,* the personal effects of the deceased are burned; the house is fumigated and the widow and relations ritually bathed.

Initiation ceremonies are still held throughout the north of Australia and more than a score of distinctive nations in the north share common beliefs.

One example of the way the traditional people have come to grips with the occupation is found near Katherine Gorge, where *didjeridus* are made for sale. Throughout the area there has been a resurgence in the manufacture of artefacts, due in no small measure to the supportive role of Mimi Aboriginal Arts and Crafts acting as buying agents.

Katherine Gorge

Every year, more than 70 000 people visit Katherine Gorge by boat, which gives visitors a rare chance to experience one of the great natural wonders of the world. The gorge winds between towering sandstone walls (up to 100 metres high), snaking some 12 kilometres upstream before opening out into a broad valley at the southernmost edge of the Arnhem Land Plateau. The gorge supports a great variety of animal and plant life, from fish and amphibians to ferns and figs (which emerge from small cracks in the face of the cliffs). Katherine Gorge has only recently been handed back to the traditional owners, creating a significant tourist trade for the local people, although the decision has caused some anger among the local whites.

The gorge remains a permanent water source for the Jawoyn. Other permanent water is found south at the sacred hot springs at Mataranka and north at the Douglas hot springs.

PHOTO BY ROBBI NEWMAN

A The Darwin area

s we leave the Katherine area and head north to Darwin, the heritage we have explored can serve as an introduction to the lands and traditions of the Larrakia people, on which Darwin stands today.

Surrounding the Larrakia are the Tiwi (to the north) on Bathurst and Melville Islands, Wulna and Limilngan (to the east), the Wadjiginy, Wagaydy and Giyug (to the south and west) and the Gunga Ragany, Malag Malag and Waway, all south of Darwin.

Ever since Europeans established Port Darwin, Palmerston or Darwin as they have variously called it, the Larrakia people have been recognised as the owners of the land although, today, people come to Darwin from north-east Arnhem Land and Alice Springs, and as far west as Western Australia. Tiwis and Torres Strait Islanders complete the mixture.

In the seventeenth century the Dutch sailed through Darwin waters and the Macassans maintained semi-permanent settlements on the northern coastline for their seasonal visits for nearly 200 years. The English arrived in 1818 when Phillip Parker King anchored in Port Patterson, some 50 kilometres west of Darwin.

The English soon set up forts on Melville Island (1824) and at Raffles Bay (1827). Almost immediately there was bloodshed but the English persisted with their plans for domination of the area and, in 1865, the first pastoral settlement was set up at Escape Cliffs (by B. T. Finniss) in the Darwin area of today. A general influx of Europeans followed, with the Chinese arriving some time later.

The painter Thomas Baines with Aborigines near the mouth of the Victoria River, Northern Territory. Oil on canvas, Rex Nan Kivell Collection. Courtesy National Library of Australia.

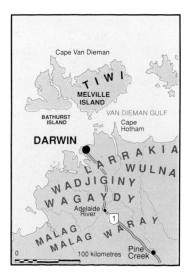

161

The Larrakia attempted to limit the expropriation of their lands but they were overwhelmed by the sheer numbers (and firepower) of intruders. By 1872, there were over 300 Englishmen and other Europeans in Darwin, as well as 140 Chinese, and the numbers grew with every passing week.

The Larrakia people shared the belief of their southern neighbours in the great Rainbow Serpent, which is sometimes accompanied by a whale, at other times by an orphan. However, they had quite distinctive customs. The girls underwent puberty rites at special sites and the boys were the focal point of the *marerlma* or *mordag* (yam) ceremony, a sacred ritual performed at sites which are only now being identified and preserved.

The women of the Darwin area shared a strong heritage. Not only were young girls given training courses in traditional life but they were involved in organising the men's ceremonies. After the men's initiation, men and women would come together for a grand ceremony.

The ceremony associated with mortuary rites, *gapuk* (or ceremonial washing), was the responsibility of women. The widow cleaned the house, while her older brother ritually burned all clothes and possessions. Then the widow gathered the children and washed their heads, arms and legs. The dancing continued, then the burnt possessions were buried.

Today, Darwin women not only hold the ancient faith but work to keep the house and feed the family as well as playing a leading role in teaching ancient skills to the younger generations. They are also negotiating the protection of sacred sites and recognition of traditional rights.

Darwin is rich in the old culture. Within the town both Gundal-Madla-maning (Emery Point) and Kalalak are sacred sites. Nearby Dariba Nunggalinya is important in the ceremonial cycle. Above all, Darwin is the gateway to the wonders of Kakadu National Park, to the Tiwi Islands, to Arnhem Land and to the beginning of the next stage of our journey through the north and north-west of the continent.

Like Mackay and Cairns in Queensland, Darwin is an impressive 'catchment area' for humans of all shapes, sizes and colour. Darwin is also a modern tourism centre with international hotels to cater for the well heeled. The multicultural feeling in the street and the constant heat and humidity are reminiscent of Honolulu.

I enjoy many Aboriginal friends in Darwin, particularly Bernard Valadian and his family. Aboriginal Hostels is well represented and the Daisy Wagbara Hostel — named after my friend from Elcho Island — is an important place for transient Aboriginals.

South of Darwin, many stories and paintings record Yagjadbulu and Jabaringi, the Lightning Brothers. They were always associated with the coming of rain, a much awaited event after a long dry period. Photos by Robert Douglas, courtesy Institute of Aboriginal Studies.

Island life

From Darwin it is possible to visit the Twi people on Bathurst and Melville Islands, some 80 kilometres north of Darwin, separated from the mainland by Clarence and Dundas Straits. The two islands, which are separated by the very narrow Apsley Strait, comprise about 8000 square kilometres, Mclville being Australia's largest offshore island other than Tasmania.

The Tiwi people, who have inhabited these islands for thousands of years, have enjoyed a sense of separation from mainland Australia and survived happily without any contact until the late nineteenth century.

Bathurst and Melville Islands now offer tourism packages where the Tiwi people share their culture with visitors on their terms.

Above *Sewing bark bags in the traditional style, Bathurst Island. Photo by Reg Morrison.*
Background *Much of the Tiwi lifestyle remains unchanged. Photo by Jennifer Isaacs.*

The use of burial poles by the Tiwi is quite different to elsewhere in Australia, though reminiscent of the use of carved trees for grave sites in New South Wales. Photo by Barry Skipsey, courtesy Northern Territory Tourist Commission.

According to Bunitj tradition, all of the landscape was created by Indjuwanydjuwa, an ancestral being who turned a blank plain into the splendour of Arnhem Land as part of his travels, rituals and hunting. After his creation work was finished he turned himself into a rock, surrounded by pink lotus flowers. That rock is just one of many sacred places in the park and can be seen in the left middleground of this photograph. Photo by Carmen Ky.

It is worth remembering that Kakadu National Park was only created by an extraordinary act of generosity on the part of the Bunitj people, who felt that all Australians should share access to a permanent natural area such as this. Photo by Carmen Ky.

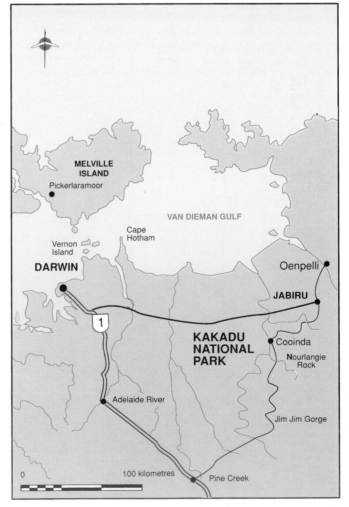

S Kakadu National Park

ome three to four hours drive south-east from Darwin is Kakadu National Park, a strange blend of unique wilderness, mining development and tourism. The park was declared in 1979, by the then Governor-General of Australia, Sir Zelman Cowan. The area of Stage 1 was 6144 square kilometres, which was more than doubled by the addition of Stage 2 in 1983.

The intriguing problems and conflicts associated with mining an area of unique wilderness led to the setting up of the Ranger Uranium Environmental Inquiry. In their report of 1977, the commissioners made the recommendation that: '. . . uranium mining proceed at Ranger subject to strict enviromental controls; Aboriginal land rights be granted to part of the Alligator Rivers Region; and a major national park be established'.

Once these recommendations were accepted, the traditional owners of the land — the Bunitj clan of the Gagadju language group — leased much of their 'estate' (on a 100-year lease) to the Director of the National Parks and Wildlife Service, to be managed as a park for the benefit of all Australians.

Every formation in the park has a meaning to the Bunitj people, and their story is written in the sacred places of the landscape. Photos by Carmen Ky.

165

'Powerful biological and geological evolutionary processes' have shaped
the landscape of Kakadu National Park. When humans settled the area,
probably around 40 000 years ago, the wilderness underwent further change;
some species of wildlife became extinct after extensive 'firestick' farming
changed the habitat. The Gagadju calendar identifies six periods of the year,
though to the casual observer the area would appear to have only two
distinct seasons: the Wet (from May to September) and the Dry (from
November to March).

The arrival of the monsoonal rains, usually in late November, quickly
turns dusty clay plains into lakes and waterways, allowing lilies, rushes and
other wild plants to flower and spread across the shallow water. Waterfowl
arrive in vast numbers and the whole region comes alive with birds, insects
and luxuriant plant growth. Within the park over 1000 plant species, nearly
300 different birds, 75 reptile species, 50 native mammals, 30 amphibians, a
quarter of all the Australian freshwater fish species and thousands of different insects have been identified.

With the end of the Wet, the waters dry up. The grasses die and are swept
away with the winter fires which spread through the desiccated woodlands,
usually sparked by lightning, although the Aborigines regularly fire the land
themselves as part of the ritual of growth and regrowth.

Introduced species, such as water buffalo, have caused substantial
damage to areas in the park although management programs (which include
an abattoir inside the park) have allowed a measure of control.

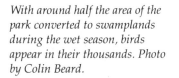

*With around half the area of the
park converted to swamplands
during the wet season, birds
appear in their thousands. Photo
by Colin Beard.*

Crocodiles had been hunted to the edge of extinction before Acts protecting them were enforced in the 1960s. Now they are a powerful tourism magnet, helping to make Kakadu one of the most fascinating parks found anywhere in the world.

Kakadu National Park stretches almost 200 kilometres, north to south, and over 100 kilometres west to east. It is crossed by four major rivers: the West, South and East Alligator Rivers and the Wildman River, all fed by a vast network of creeks and streams. In the wet season the waters expand significantly, often extending from the Arnhem Land Plateau to Van Diemen Gulf. This monsoonal wet season follows a long and dry winter and sustains a variety of landscapes, including coastal swamps, tidal flats, floodplains, lowland hills, escarpment and the plateau.

Big Bill Neidjie, of the Bunitj clan, with an old friend, Felix Holmes. Bill lived at Ubir (Obiri Rock) for a time when he was young, learning to hunt and manage the environment according to the law of his people. He has watched the modern world change his people and is committed to maintaining traditional law and keeping his homelands open to appreciation from the outside. Photo by Carmen Ky.

Classic Kakadu landscape. Photo by Bill Bachman.

Right *The tawny frogmouth, just one of thousands of bird species in the park. Photo by Philip Green.*

Far right *Waterlilies, abundant in the park during the wet season, are an important part of the Bunitj diet. The stems and seeds of three different lilies — the white, pink and blue — are all eaten. Photo by Carmen Ky.*

Opposite *The Jabiru, Australia's own stork, is found through the top of the continent, as well as New Guinea, Indonesia and southern Asia. They are sometimes found much further south, in fact the first settlers at Botany Bay reported the bird present there. Jabirus use their strong bills to feed on crabs and fish along foreshores, particularly at low tide. Photo by Philip Green.*

Pandanus trees against the late afternoon light. It is not hard to see why the people saw so much to nourish in their environment. Photo by Carmen Ky.

According to Dreamtime traditions, the creation of Kakadu centres on a female ancestral being, *Warramurrungundji,* who came out of the sea to the north-east and formed the landscape with her deeds. During her travel and exploits, she left many spirit children in various places and taught them the different languages they were to speak. Warramurrungundji distributed various plant foods, and then, at the end of her travels, she turned into a rock which remains to this day as her dreaming place. A blue-tongued lizard (another of the ancestral beings) created the totemic sites for all animal and plant species in Kakadu, which is full of such totemic sites — reminders of the travels, adventures and achievements of the ancestral beings.

Throughout Kakadu are many wonderful natural art galleries, some 5000 in all. The escarpment areas contain sandstone rock with excellent surfaces for painting the important images of the Dreamtime events and totemic beings.

At Obiri Rock (*Ubir*) there are outstanding examples of Aboriginal art in large outcrops of rock, open for tourists to visit. Some thirty-six sites have been identified near the impressive main gallery, on the western side of a comparatively small, isolated monolith.

Fire renewed the land and traditions. At right, raptors can be seen preying on insects forced from cover by fire. Photos by Jim Frazier/Mantis Wildlife.

The back wall of the gallery is smooth and curved, a vertical face of rock about 15 metres long and 2 metres high, covered with excellent examples of 'x-ray' paintings depicting a variety of species of fish. Painted in many colours, they clearly represent external shape, as well as internal structures: backbone, lungs, heart, kidneys and other organs.

A great overhang of rock forms a protective roof over the painted walls and gives the cave a cathedral-like atmosphere. Other paintings are found on a flat, smooth wall of an open shelter opposite the main Obiri gallery. The images here show a series of men running across the wall in a style known as Mimi, found throughout the region and believed by locals to be very old. Mimi figures are characterised by slender, stick-like bodies — usually painted in one of the red ochre shades — portraying action scenes: running, hunting, throwing weapons and dancing. Aborigines believe these figures to be the work of the benevolent (but timid) Mimi spirits who inhabit the caves and clefts of rocks in the escarpment.

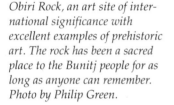

Obiri Rock, an art site of international significance with excellent examples of prehistoric art. The rock has been a sacred place to the Bunitj people for as long as anyone can remember. Photo by Philip Green.

The images at Obiri Rock show complete cross-sections of animals, with subject matter featuring a wide variety of fish, animals and people (even Europeans with guns). These are some of the best examples of Aboriginal art to be found anywhere in Arnhem Land and among the best in Australia. In international terms they rate favourably with the great Palaeolithic art sites of France and Spain and the Bushman paintings of Africa.

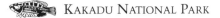

Far left *These paintings from the main gallery at Obiri Rock are excellent examples of the x-ray style, which depicts internal organ and bone structure. Photo by Colin Beard.*
Left and below *Nourlangie Rock, another of the park's famous art sites. Photos by Colin Beard (left), and AusChromes.*

171

In 1845 Ludwig Leichhardt became one the first white men to set eyes on land that is now a part of the park. In his diaries Leichhardt wrote about the friendly locals, who led his party through a maze of swamps, waterholes and wetlands which 'extended beyond the reach of sight, seeming to form the whole country, where flocks of ducks and geese rose in noisy clouds when disturbed'. Photo by Carmen Ky.

The white egret is the largest of the 4 species that occur in Australia. Found all over the continent, this egret seems very happy here. Photo by Colin Beard.

This natural rock shelter was, according to Big Bill Neidjie, in use until around 40 years ago. A grinding stone can still be seen, left of centre, together with evidence of fires and recent human occupation. Photo by Carmen Ky.

Overlooking the flood plains, these shelters were important living places during the wet season, when there was plenty of time to work on the paintings. Photo by Carmen Ky.

Arnhem Land

rnhem Land remains relatively untouched by European settlement, an area where traditional Aboriginal lifestyles continue to flourish, and still dominate over the introduced ways of the Europeans. Formal education is presented through mobile units which allows traditional learning to provide a healthy balance. Traditional healers, balanced and supported by the availability of Western health care, continue to practise their ancient and effective discipline. Because of its immense beauty and natural setting, Arnhem Land is beginning to attract significant numbers of tourists and visitors have the chance to understand and participate in traditional lifestyles. Arnhem Land is also the home of the didjeridoo and the circular breathing required to play this instrument is now attracting wide interest for its value as a yogic and healing discipline. The Northern Lands Council is a most effective mechanism to protect the interests of the Arnhem Land community.

Opposite *In Arnhem Land, bush foods are still collected and prepared in the traditional way. Photos by Jennifer Isaacs.*
Above *Arnhem Land children. Photo by Jennifer Isaacs.*
Left *A variety of yams and (far left) the highly sought after mud oyster. Photos by Jennifer Isaacs.*

Crocodiles

rocodylus porosus, commonly known as the saltwater or estuarine crocodile, is the largest living reptile on earth, and one of the few animals which refuses to be tamed. Many have tried, including a northern Australian resident who reared one from the egg-hatching stage, who daily took his 'pet' down to the ocean for a morning dip only to drive home one morning missing one arm.

Around the world there are some twenty-six different types of crocodile and alligator, but in Australia only two: the saltwater crocodile and the freshwater or Johnston's crocodile (*Crocodylus johnstoni*).

Once hunted extensively in the Northern Territory, Australian crocodiles have been totally protected since 1972. They are now growing in number, size and area of distribution and Australia is a stronghold for the species worldwide.

News headlines periodically. puncture Australian life with horror stories of a crocodile attack, somewhere in the top half of the continent. Tropical beaches maintain a comfortable heat at night (ideal for sleeping on) but many an unwary traveller has awoken to discover a crocodile planning breakfast just a touch too close.

Australia has many bizarre outback hazards, from aggressive (and very deadly) snakes to 'dive-bombing' magpies (during the September egg hatching-season in southern Australia), but few can compare with a crocodile attack. The Aboriginal people have shared the oceans and rivers of north Australia with crocodiles, sea wasps, stone fish and

sharks for many thousands of years. And when someone gets attacked there is often an explanation, quite reasonable to people in touch with traditional beliefs.

The story of *Numuwwari*, the giant mythological crocodile from Arnhem Land (claimed to be 10 metres in length and 2 tonnes in weight) reflects a spiritual relationship with the clan. Numuwwari was once a man who came from the stone country and, during a very bad dry spell, took to the billabong and turned into a crocodile. When he came to sunbake on the beach the people would present him with food, mainly kangaroo meat or fish. When Numuwwari helped himself to a small boy, who was ill from birth, there was a certain acceptance of events as part of the grand plan.

The legend of Numuwwari was the subject of a feature movie, *Dark Age,* the first 35mm movie based on an Aboriginal story. I had the honour to play the role of Oondabund, the keeper of the Numuwwari story.

The crocodile provides us with a direct link to animal life on earth some 190 million years ago, as it has changed very little during this time, living on in northern Australia as a living fossil of our prehistoric past. Crocodiles were once widely distributed from India through South-east Asia, the Philipines, New Guinea and as far south as Mackay.

Crocodiles are known to be among the largest of the reptile family, frequently exceeding 6 metres in length (with reports of animals up to 10 metres). The skin is heavily armoured on the upper or dorsal surface where individual scutes (or scales) are strengthened with deposits of bone. On the underside or ventral surface, the scutes are smooth and usually squarish; it is this part of the skin which is prized as high quality leather.

The tail is about half the total body length. The hind limbs are more powerfully developed than the fore limbs and both the hind and fore feet are webbed.

The head shows a number of adaptations to the aquatic lifestyle. The eyes have elevated above the general line of the snout and have upper and lower eyelids and a third lid, the nictitating membrane, which is clear and through which the crocodile can see without the eye being exposed. The pupil contracts to a vertical slit in bright light and the cells of the retina are adapted for vision in reduced light levels. The reflective tapetum at the back of the eye reflects light, so that the eyes glow red in the beam of a spotlight.

The ears are immediately behind the eyes and are protected by two flaps, which can be closed tightly against the skull. The conical teeth are deep-socketed and are replaced throughout life. The front teeth of the lower jaw may penetrate through the upper jaw, and the fourth tooth back from the front on the lower jaw is enlarged and fits into a notch in the upper jaw. In alligators, this tooth fits into a socket in the much broader upper jaw and it is this feature which is commonly used to distinguish alligators from crododiles. The brain is encased within a very solid bone cage.

The saltwater crocodile lays an average of fifty eggs in nests 1.8 metres long, 1.6 metres wide and 0.5 metre high. The eggs are white, hard-shelled and weigh between 90 and 130 grams. Survival from the egg stage to full growth is generally 50 per cent, although this varies with seasonal conditions.

Hatching occurs at various times between late February and June depending on the time of nest construction and probably on the incubation temperatures. The hatchlings are equipped with a small tooth-like structure in the tip of the snout called a caruncle which they use to slice through the egg membrane and shell. When the young are ready to hatch they call or squeak — while still within the egg — in response to loud noises or disturbances from outside the nest. In response to their call, the mother uncovers the nest. Both parents carry the hatchlings (in their mouth) down to the water. Once there, the egg gets gently rolled and squeezed by a parent until hatching takes place.

Young saltwater crocodiles eat mainly small crabs and prawns until they reach about 2 metres in length. As they grow they move on to larger crabs as well as fish, reptiles, birds and small mammals. Any saltwater crocodile over 3 metres in length is a real threat to the unwary human.

When travelling north towards Darwin visitors may first get a glimpse of a crocodile when they least expect it. These are large and dangerous animals and when you enter the muddy waters of the Top End's streams and creeks be aware: the danger is no tourist hype. If you want to see crocs up close without danger, the crocodile farm just south of Darwin is a great tourist drawcard, especially during feeding time.

In the East Alligator River, tourists are able to feed crocodiles from the side of a boat. But you need to exercise caution at all times as crocodiles have been known to leap 3 metres high after food.

Opposite and **below** *Saltwater crocodiles. Photos by Robbi Newman.*

The Bungle Bungles, south of Kununurra were avoided, it seems, by the original Australians as well as the newcomers, at least until recently, when this unique landform has become one of Australia's most characteristic landmarks. Photo by Grenville Turner/Wildlight.

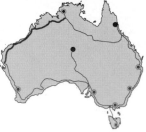

Katherine to Carnarvon

SOUTH from Katherine, Highway One takes us into Western Australia and some of Australia's most stunning and mineral-rich landscapes. Our journey passes the Kimberley and on to Broome — and the extraordinary Wandjina paintings — before we follow the barren, rugged west coast south to Carnarvon.

At the Ord River, we enter the country of the Miriwung people at Kununurra and we are set to explore the Kimberleys, one of the most fascinating regions anywhere in Australia.

South of Kununurra towards Turkey Creek, we cross into the lands of the Kitja. Many stories of the old days in this region have been related by Jack Sullivan to Bruce Shaw in *Banggaiyerri: the Story of Jack Sullivan*, published in Canberra by the Australian Institute of Aboriginal Studies.

Jack Sullivan was born in the year of Australia's Federation, 1901, near Soda Creek on Argyle Downs Station. His mother was a woman of the Djamindjong people, his father a European. He became a stockman and worked on the stations of Argyle, Rosewood, Ivanhoe, Dunham River, Mabel Downs and Lissadell. He lives today at Turkey Creek, 150 kilometres south from Kununurra.

Wherever he lived and worked — during a life spaning most of the century — he saw a new world, with English names for towns, mountains and rivers. The Dreamtime names have long given way to names commemorating the invaders, their homelands and sometimes their wives or girlfriends.

The East Kimberley region remained independent longer than most of Australia. But the advance of the Europeans was relentless and, by the late 1800s, giant cattle stations dominated the entire region.

These new pastoral empires completely replaced the traditional power centres of the northern nations and were to be followed by a series of atrocities. Christian missions followed the spread of the new cattle empires and the Church of England established Forrest River Mission in 1897-98. A year later it was abandoned, but reopened when the frontier war cooled in 1912. This mission was the site of the Onmalmeri massacres in 1926, a significant event in the history of Western Australian race relations.

It took half a century for the invaders to conquer the East Kimberley region, the black nations fighting a guerilla war of resistance from the late 1800s to the 1930s. Their desperate stand, which allowed the original people to keep their lands and independence for a generation, was made easier by the hostile climate and the terrain. In the wet season, for example, tracks turned to mud and created havoc for soldiers and policemen on horseback.

A fish image — probably a barramundi — painted over older stick-like figures at Kununurra. Photo by Jutta Malnic.

Turkey Creek

In the days of independence Turkey Creek was a traditional camping place. Following the 1967 pastoral award in Western Australia, many Aborigines were expelled from cattle properties and Turkey Creek became a refugee centre. Basic facilities were made available to attract people driven to the fringes of their traditional lands. In European times it has also been the site of a ration depot, a police station and a telegraph station. There are now more than 250 people here, nearly half of them under 21.

Below *Mixing ochres, keeping traditional skills alive, Kununurra. Photo by Colin Totterdell.* **Below right** *The man-made Lake Argyle, part of the Ord River scheme in the Kimberley. Photo by Philip Green.*

Above *The Keep River National Park, near Kununurra. Photo by Bill Bachman.*
Left *An aerial view of the Durack River, south of Wyndham, showing the salt-encrusted tidal flats, cut by drainage channels lined with mangroves. Photo by AusChromes.*

An art site on the Keep River. Photo by Barry Skipsey, courtesy Northern Territory Tourist Commission.

The Bungle Bungles cover an area of 700 square kilometres with sheer cliffs, striated walls and deep gullies. The formation is around 350 million years old, formed in the Devonian period. The Bungle Bungles were of little interest to the Kimberley cattlemen who arrived in the area at the end of the nineteenth century. There is no evidence of Aboriginal occupation. Photo by Grenville Turner/Wildlight.

Right, far right and below *A selection of photos of people from the north of Western Australia. From the Crooks Collection, courtesy Macleay Museum.*

Left *A group of men from the Kolaia clan, Cambridge Gulf. Their hair has been tied around a pod of emu feathers. Courtesy National Museum of Australia.*
Below *The King Leopold Range. Photo by AusChromes.*

Today the bulk of people are without work, but the Warmun people run a community store and receive recognition both from the Federal Government and from Argyle Diamond Mines, a multi-million dollar venture which pays $133 000 annually for use of the land and its rich harvest of diamonds.

The movement from a refugee settlement to a government reserve and then to an independent community represents an enormous achievement for a community which, after all, is an historic accident which groups together people from an area larger than some European countries. The community is linked with various Aboriginal organisations — the Balangarra Aboriginal Association, the Kimberley Land Council and the North Eastern Aboriginal Affairs Consultative Committee — and is also part of the European-style Shire of Halls Creek.

The representative for the area (the electorate of Kimberley) in the Parliament of Western Australia is a distinguished Aboriginal, Mr Ernie Bridge, who is also a Cabinet Minister.

Warmun Community is also the centre for a number of outstations which provide social, political and economic alternatives. These include Mandangala (Glen Hill), Rugan (Crocodile Hole), Jalarlu (Frog Hollow), Baulu-Wah (Violet Valley), Rarragun (Chinaman's Garden) and Kawarra (Bungle Bungle). These small communities, while representing independence and an alternative way of life, have few facilities. They lack a secure economic base and are almost entirely dependent on social security payments.

There are no post offices, no mail deliveries, no banking facilities, no television, poor radio reception (only shortwave), no airstrips, no sewerage, no resident doctor or nurse, and the water supply contains salmonella.

The Kimberley people had a commitment to scarification unmatched elsewhere. Photos courtesy The National Museum, (left), and the Battye Library of Western Australia.

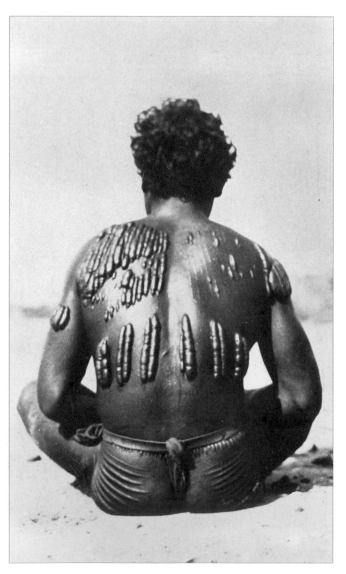

Above and **left** *People from the Kimberley region of Western Australia. Photos courtesy Battye Library of Western Australia (top left), and The Australian Museum (above and left).*

Cattle were introduced into the Kimberley at the end of the nineteenth century, and led to clashes with the traditional owners of the land, who had escaped the march of civilisation to that point. Once the conflict had been resolved, the cattle industry provided jobs. Photo courtesy National Library of Australia.

The Kimberley is an area quite
different from the rest of the
continent, an ancient rock
plateau, carved by erosion over
millions of years. Photo by Colin
Totterdell.

Only on Australia's west coast
can sunsets over water be fully
appreciated. North Kimberley
coast. Photo by Colin Totterdell.

D The Kitja and Djaru

own the highway (now the Great Northern Highway) from Turkey Creek to Violet Valley and Halls Creek, we enter the lands of two important nations, the Kitja and Djaru. In fact Halls Creek itself is still the centre for the Kitja people whose traditional lands lie to the north and west of the town. The Djaru people's land extends to the south and east of the town. The town today is not only close to the frontier between the two peoples but marks the boundary between two languages.

The Kitja and Djaru peoples have traditionally been friendly, although intermarriage and the adoption of each other's language is not common. The Djaru sometimes intermarry with the Walmadjari and Gugadja peoples, whose language structure is similar. The multilingual Djaru often speak Walmadjari as a second language.

On the other hand the Kitja mix more with the people of Turkey Creek and tend to intermarry with the Miriwung and other northern nations. Despite this, both the Kitja and Djaru peoples share common culture and religious disciplines.

In this area land ownership descended through father or mother. In most cases men look upon their father's land as their primary affiliation but some women claim their father's or their mother's. In these days of exile from their ancestral lands, birth place is also taken into account.

A distinctive Kimberley hairstyle of 1910. Photo courtesy National Library of Australia.

In the Dreamtime, *Narangarni* (in Kitja) or *Waldjiri* (in Djaru) was the Ancestral Being who laid down the eternal and immutable laws. Following in his footsteps were other great creators such as *Djamandi*, the hill kangaroo, who moved from the Oombulgurri area to Balgo and, in the process, established clear marriage laws based on kinship. Throughout this area are sacred sites. Some are visited only by men, others only by women and some by both. In their world desecration of a sacred site is an affront to the spirits, a disaster which invites divine retribution.

The people of Halls Creek have the religious responsibility to care for their sacred sites, to learn the song cycles and ceremonies associated with their country, and to ensure that these are properly learned and transmitted. The more songs a person knows, the higher their status, and pride is taken in passing songs on to others. Songs may be shared by men and women or may be the property of either sex. Ceremonies are commonly passed from one group to another with whom there is a ritual relationship along recognisable Dreamtime tracks.

The law of the people still governs the land, flora and fauna, behaviour towards kin and others and particularly the marriage customs. There is a fearful respect of the powers of sacred sites and of the *maban*, or traditional doctors and sorcerers.

Marriage partners are determined by the category into which each person is born. There are eight such categories for this region (sometimes known as 'skin' groups), which determine who each person can marry, appropriate behaviour to other members of the group and social obligations.

This complex system means an exchange of relations. For example, it is possible for women of two separate categories to marry each other's sons and become each other's mother-in-law.

These days promised marriages are on the decline, but all children enjoy a secure social position, cared for by all kin but being 'owned' by no single family. They are independent from a very early age, often helping themselves to food from parental and other family households. They find playmates wherever they wish and stay with them without hindrance.

Wolf Creek Crater

Wolf Creek crater, located 510 kilometres south of Kununurra and named after a meandering water course to the east, is the second largest crater to be found anywhere on earth. Caused by the impact of a huge iron meteorite striking the ground, this almost perfecly round crater is 50 metres deep, with a diameter of 850 metres. Although generally thought to be between 1 and 2 million years old, the crater remains in a remarkable state of preservation. The formation of the crater remains sharp and complete. Scientists have suggested this state of preservation is due to the arid, desert climate of the region. Photo by Robbi Newman.

The peoples of north-western Australia had elaborate headwear which was worn on ceremonial occasions. Lieron Bay, Sunday Island. Courtesy National Museum of Australia.

Great affection exists between adults and children and between younger and older children. Unlike the generation gaps found in European society, the young people of this area often take small children with them, carried on their hips. Warnings about strangers and fear of abuse within the family (now common in all urban communities) are still unknown in this culture.

In traditional times men hunted for larger game while women gathered vegetable foods and small animals. Both went fishing, using poison or nets. Cooking was usually done directly on the coals. Concave stones were used for containing liquids. Fish and meat were often wrapped in leaves and paperbark for cooking in earth ovens.

The prized possessions are still connected with hunting, vegetable collecting, cooking or making music. Today, the favoured weapons for hunting are rifles, but they are in short supply. Property circulates freely among kinfolk, including expensive items such as cassette players. What is owned by one is shared by many.

Despite all the pressures of contemporary Anglo-Australian society, most have retained their names and language. Many Djaru and Kitja people used the name of their country or their birth site as their main personal name. Many have completed the educational courses leading to initiation, and most are still enthusiastic participants in traditional gatherings.

Traditional camps probably consisted of 15 to 40 people, the size varying with seasons. Unlike the permanent stone houses of Victoria, or the semi-permanent beehive clusters of north Queensland, the desert peoples such as those in the Halls Creek area found it necessary to use more temporary dwellings.

European conquest has meant that thousands of people of many different nations, clans and localities were herded together irrespective of language and tradition. This has diluted the law and the authority of the elders.

Camps in this part of Western Australia reflected the social organisation of the people, as they did throughout traditional Australia. The cluster of dwellings within a camp was sometimes orientated towards the homeland, sometimes arranged according to social and site consideration.

According A. H. Ross, who made a detailed study of traditional housing and living environments, a traditional camp is made up of 'hearth groups' and households in which you find a man, his wives and their young children. There are women's camps for widows and their young children together with those women who are not married. You will also find camps for men (catering for the single and widowed). Ross says that these arrangements are a way of keeping young people in check.

Newcomers to the camp built their dwellings near those of the members of the clan with whom they had the closest affiliations. The layout of the camp was designed so that it was necessary to walk in a specified direction

A woman from the Kimberley area. Courtesy National Museum of Australia.

189

Opposite *The baobab tree is one of the few trees to have adapted itself to life in semi-arid regions. The name comes from similar trees found in East Africa. The tree has adapted well to this environment and retains water in small pockets inside its trunk. This was known to Aborigines, and utilised; some trees have yielded up to 860 litres of fresh water. When cut, the trunk releases a white gum, which can be mixed with water and drunk, or fermented into an intoxicating liquid. Aborigines also ate the flowers and nuts, which are often the size of emu eggs. Photo by Bill Bachman.*

around the circle to visit members of another sector. All camps had an activity area used by everyone — a kind of village green, a refuse zone, and the main shelter.

The camp plan allowed a certain amount of flexibility so that households wanting to draw closer together could do so, but those in dispute could put distance between them before open confrontation. Childless couples might move frequently between their respective parents' households, one week helping the woman's mother and another week going to the man's family to assist with hunting.

One man, discovering his wife was having an affair, used the layout of the camp to resolve his problem. He moved his dwellling 300 metres across the camp to an area where he had no close relations but where his wife had many and where there was a large women's household. This provided his wife with company and monitored her activities. It was not long before the affair was over.

Older people often move to the outskirts of the camp to avoid noise at night and the system had to be flexible to cater for this. After a death it was customary to burn the dwelling and all possessions. Today this tradition has been modified.

The entire camp might be relocated if the site became unhealthy or unsafe. This might be to avoid accumulations of rubbish and excreta, or flooding or other natural phenomena. In the event of a serious dispute involving an extended family, it was possible for a group to leave camp altogether and move to an entirely new area to set up an independent community.

Leaving the country of the Kitja and Djaru people and Halls Creek behind us, we follow the highway south and west in a great curve that touches Margaret River before arriving at the small town of Fitzroy Crossing. This is the border of Bunuba, Konejandi and Njikena territory and it is in this region that Windjana Gorge is located, the site of the battle in 1895 between the Europeans and a resistance party led by the black leader Jundumurra.

Bell Creek, west Kimberley. Photo by Bill Bachman.

Jundumurra: resistance hero

Jundumurra — or Pigeon, as he became known — was born to the Bunuba people in West Kimberley and was a local hero of the region's long-running war with the invaders.

White settlement initially respected the lands of the Bunuba, but, during the l880s two stations were established in the shadow of the Napier Ranges on land the young Bunuba men used for hunting.

As a young man, Jundumurra was enticed into working on William Lukin's Lennard River Station and it was Lukin who gave him the nickname of 'Pigeon', because he was such a sunny personality, small and fast-footed. He became a gun shearer, the best horseman on the property and was fluent in English by the time it came for him to complete his traditional education and to learn the history, lore and faith of his people.

Very much influenced by a daring warrior friend, Ellemarra, who challenged all Europeans (whether armed or not), Jundumurra built his own reputation first as a hunter and then as a committed war leader, determined to recapture the Bunuba lands taken by Europeans. The colonial authorities despatched a strong force of troopers, who set up a military post near Windjana Gorge. It was there that both Jundumurra and Ellemarra were captured and sent to Derby in chains.

Jundumurra escaped and returned to his own people but was recaptured, after which attempts were made to use him in military operations against his own people. Returning home, he found Bunuba land had been invaded, sixteen of his fellow countrymen were being held prisoner, and a trooper at Fitzroy Crossing was shooting his people at will. Jundumurra managed to release his compatriots and assumed the role of war leader. His old hero Ellemarra agreed to serve under him in a major resistance campaign.

Jundumurra recognised that if he was to win the war he must match the firepower of the whites, so he ambushed a wagon train (in the same Windjana Gorge where he had been first captured). With a large store of captured arms and ammunition he set about training his men in preparation to ambush the reinforcements being sent to the area by the colonial authorities.

Like so many other resistance heroes, Jundumurra finally fell victim to deceit, betrayed by six black stockmen from Queensland who were sent by the white commander to infiltrate his forces. They spied on his camp, noted his strength, and reported back to his enemies.

Jundumurra had planned to ambush the colonial forces in Windjana Gorge. Forewarned by his black spies, the white commander divided his force into three columns and made surprise attacks from three directions. Ellemarra was wounded and Jundumurra was shot three times before he was forced to retreat. For two years he hid in Tunnel Creek Cave, about 50 kilometres from Windjana before re-emerging to take up the fight once more. Trying to free Bunuba prisoners he was wounded once more, but again escaped death and fought on, although Ellemarra and all his old companions had been shot or hanged.

The end for Jundumurra came after his final attack on the Oscar Range Station. Wounded yet again, he made his way back to his Tunnel Creek hideout, but a black tracker named Micki led the colonial forces there and Jundumurra, slowed by many wounds, was finally killed.

During his life Jundumurra did not see his country occupied, but soon after his death Leopold Downs Station took over the land he had fought so hard to defend.

Sporadic fighting continued until early this century, when a series of massacres finally crushed the resistance. Today the shooting has stopped, but the wounds have yet to heal.

Below *Windjana Gorge, the site of so much of the conflict which followed Jundumurra's resistance to the invaders. Photo by Philip Green.*
Opposite *Tunnel Creek, where Jundumurra met his end. Photo by Philip Green.*

Noonkanbah

As we head west towards the coastal town of Derby, Noonkanbah country extends west and south. Noonkanbah was a sheep station until 1972, when more than 12 000 head of cattle were introduced. Black labour kept the enterprise alive but the harsh conditions drove the people off the property, despite the fact that it embraced a number of sacred sites.

The station went downhill until it was brought by the Aboriginal Land Commission and became the responsibility of the Yungngora community, who found on their return that overstocking and mismanagement had caused significant damage to their beloved lands.

So successful were they with their restoration work that, within two years, they had sold more than $100 000 worth of cattle. This pastoral operation (without any government funds) provided the people with food, cash and self-determination. Noonkanbah became an important cultural and educational centre with a bilingual school and a large regional festival.

However, while the Yungngora people were re-establishing themselves and their shattered lives, their lands had attracted the attention of mining companies interested in diamonds and oil.

The great Noonkanbah dispute, which attracted international attention, began in 1977, when the Western Australian Government issued oil exploration permits on the land to private corporations. In November 1978 the Yungngora people, using white man's law, lodged 95 objections to incursions on their land, asserting desecration of sacred sites and damage to fences, equipment and stock.

Despite advice from its own authorities that sacred sites would be desecrated, the Perth administration granted approval for drilling on Yungngora land and a foreign company, Amax, protected by 35 white police, invaded their land once more. As the world watched, Amax's convoy, with paramilitary protection, pushed on to Noonkanbah. The confrontation strengthened the community and rallied thousands of Australians — black and white — to their support. But it failed to stop the mining.

Drilling and mining are still being carried out in the Kimberleys but awareness has been aroused and three major projects are in the national (and international) spotlight. These are in the Balgo–Malan–Billiluna country at Lake Gregory (extending south to the Stansmore Range), the Lake Argyle–Turkey Creek area near the Ord River and the Mitchell Plateau on Admiralty Gulf. Continuing surveys of all these areas are being carried out to ensure Aboriginal people are not further disadvantaged as mineral deposits in the area continue to be discovered.

Mowanjum

Our highway journey takes us west to Derby and the Mowanjum Aboriginal Settlement, the sea gateway to the Kimberleys and its people. One of the many storytellers from the region is Jean Wungunyet, who has recounted how, in the Dreamtime, all the world was one and it was only after the flood that islands and divisions appeared.

At that time a woman lived in coastal country where there was plenty of food all the year around. Each day her people went turtle hunting and speared fish, as well gathering turtle eggs and shellfish. The woman's husband never shared his catch with her, although he gave it to other kinfolk.

After suffering this for a long time she determined on revenge. Setting out in her canoe to live alone on the coast she reached a reef off the shore and used her spear to stir up the sea. Immediately the waters began to bubble and rise. As the waters rose higher and higher, flooding the land, she walked across the reef and climbed the highest hill. Her husband and his kinfolk saw her on the hill and realised she was causing all the trouble. They caught and killed her with their spears but it was already too late. The waters rose and drowned them all.

Even today, on the islands off the coast there are blowholes where the water boils madly if you throw in a stone. So the local people do not go anywhere near this place, where the water can boil over to flood the world.

Another story of the Halls Point area explains the particular pit, shaped like a well, which, according to legend, has been there since time began. Another traditional story told by Jean is about a husband and wife who went out to collect some baobab nuts. They climbed a big tree and when they had gathered enough nuts the wife took the ladder down, leaving her husband stranded at the top of the tree. She told him she was going home to cook the nuts. 'Why do you do that?' he asked. She said she was sorry but then started to sing, cursing the tree so it would grow taller and her husband would never get down.

Using his axe, he cut bark from the tree for a new ladder, which he used to get down, but his wife had foreseen such a possibility and, along the path back to their dwelling, had dug a deep trap and covered it with grass.

On her arrival home the woman was asked 'Where is your husband?'

'I don't know', she replied. Someone said, 'I think you've killed him'. They waited for a long time for his return but when the fires burned low the old men said, 'We'll sleep now but at first light we'll look for him.'

They picked up his tracks in the early morning light and as they neared the trap they heard him calling. 'I'm here in the ground. My wife left me in the tree and then laid a trap for me. Where is she now?'

They put down forked sticks to help him escape and then took him to water where he soon recovered. On his return home he beat his wife with a heavy stick until she was sorry for what she had done. Then the couple decided to leave home, and lived happily in another country until they found themselves in the middle of a war between two clans. The raiders burned down the dwellings and killed all but the re-united couple, who escaped and returned to their own country to live happily every after. The pit remains today as a reminder of their adventure.

In traditional times, a man was not allowed to go near any girls except his betrothed or promised one. As he grew older and the time came for him to marry, the families would have to agree to the match, including all her brothers and uncles.

After the marriage agreement was made, the great hunt began for the feast. The men chased kangaroos and emus, the women dug for yams and searched for wild honey in the trees. Then everybody got ready for the celebration, painting themselves with ochre and putting on all kinds of ornaments — all except the young couple who came forward naked before the lawman. He pronounced them man and wife before sending them off to a place where there was plenty of meat, honey, yams and water to drink so they could live together happily.

(*Adapted from* Visions of Mowanjum: Aboriginal writings from the Kimberley, *Adelaide, Rigby, 1980.*)

Burning the scrub, Derby. Photo by Philip Green.

The Wandjinas

erby, the southern port of the Kimberley region, is world famous for its Wandjina rock paintings. These extraordinary paintings of huge man-like beings sometimes measure more than 6 metres in length and have spectacular colours — black, red or yellow, over a white background.

I. M. Crawford, a leading authority on Wandjina paintings, says they represent the 'spirit in the cloud', and they are believed to have both human and cloud-like forms. Characteristic of Wandjina figures are their large, mouthless heads surrounded by hair which may also be seen as a cloud, and feather-like strokes which are both the feathers worn by these beings and the lightning they control. The cumulo-nimbus clouds that herald the arrival of the monsoon season are believed to be the Wandjina beings themselves.

The human-like images of the beings show the head and shoulders with the body tapering away. In some a halo surrounds the face, in others the halo becomes concentric lines 'with only the eyes peering through'.

The ancient tradition is that the Wandjina paintings were not created but inherited from the spirits themselves. The great god of the Wandjinas — *Wallanganda* — came down to earth before returning to the Milky Way. The central event in all Wandjina stories is the conflict between the Wandjinas (led by *Wodjin*) and the people of the land. The Wandjinas, unhappy with the people, met in council and decided to drown everybody. The spirits live on in the paintings symbolic of the bodies of dead Wandjinas.

Wandjinas have names and each cave dedicated to a particular Wandjina being has a special name. Wandjinas have special powers and their paintings must be approached with great care. If they are offended they may bring devastating storms and floods. Frivolous behaviour is not permitted and in many places there is a law against even touching a painting. It is believed that an angry Wandjina could call up lightning to strike dead the offender.

Wandjina and Galan snake images at the Mandangarri Place, Gibb River, Kimberley. Photo by Jutta Malnic.

Opposite *The Wandjina Rowalumbin, Barker River, Napier Range, Kimberley. Photo by Jutta Malnic.*

197

The protocol usually followed provides that the individual or party halt several metres away and indicate, in an introductory speech, that no harm is intended from their visit. They might indicate their own totemic spirit, or perhaps those relatives who have an affinity with the site, and even add that, since their last visit, they have faithfully observed all the laws.

Wandjina beings have beneficial powers as well as destructive ones. They are associated with fertility and reproduction, and are responsible for the spirit children who live in some freshwater pools. A man eating food from such a pool might actually eat a spirit child, or be followed home by one. He will then dream of the spirit child and so it will enter the mother. Should the ritual obligations associated with the paintings cease, so too will reproduction.

At Windjana Gorge, in the Napier Range (where Jundumurra fought his battle) there is a rock in a small pool in the middle of the gorge. Here, it's said, the baby spirits wait for fathers and mothers.

The north-west Kimberley area is rich in the art galleries, while paintings have also been recorded in the Oscar and Napier Ranges in the south. Central Kimberley is also extraordinarily rich in art, mostly located in shallow caves with an overhang to keep off the rain. These places are positioned not far from waterholes for the convenience of the artists, but not too close in case of flooding.

Right *Perilana or 'Dingo Spring', Napier Range, Kimberley. Two dogs — Yeddigee, the male and Lumbiella, the female — wait in a shallow cave, preparing an ambush on the kangaroo.*
Far right *Wunggadinda's snake image at Manning Creek.*
Below *Snake Cove, Gibb River. Photos by Jutta Malnic.*

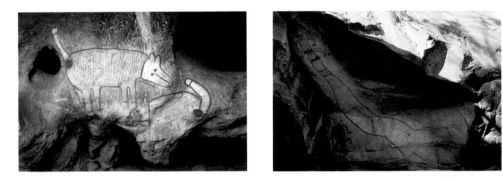

S Broome

outh to the land of the Nigina and the port of pearls, Broome, spread along the curve of the bay at the edge of mangroves, with a long stretch of unbroken beach.

The area is a riot of trees: poincianas, mango trees, whitewoods, gum trees, bauhinias, coconut palms, travellers palms and bougainvillea, as well as dozens of shrubs and grasses of many colours.

Roebuck Bay and Broome represented the most southerly point reached by the friendly Macassan invasion of Australia. Each year a fleet of praus from the south-west Celebes sailed with the north-west monsoon for the coast of Australia which they called *Kayu Djawa* or 'Land rising out of the sea like Java'.

They came to harvest trepang or bêche-de-mer (sea cucumber), which was sought as a delicacy throughout Asia. Men of the Bugis, Timor and Papua often came with them. Arriving in December or January they divided up into groups and systematically harvested the reefs, before coming together in April for their return to Macassar on the south-east monsoon.

The Macassans and Australians met, traded for metals, rice and dugout canoes, and often worked together. Today, the language of the north Australia contains many Macassan words. It was a happy association which lasted nearly 200 years until British colonial administrations called a halt.

Not far from the centre of today's Broome is Buccaneer Rock where the Englishman, William Dampier, repaired his ship, the *Roebuck,* in 1699. Out of fresh water and suffering from scurvy, he and his crew attempted to make contact with the people of the area. They landed with guns, fired on anyone they saw and got neither water nor help. They discovered some water at what is now called Dampier's Creek, but in the face of hostility, he sailed off, never to return.

In the 1850s shallow-water pearling began at Shark Bay, some thousand sea miles to the south of Roebuck Bay. The town of Onslow had a brief burst of glory and was succeeded by Cossack, where, in 1873, eighty boats were searching for pearl shell and pearls. By 1880 it was the turn of Broome to play host to the pearlers, who had moved up from Onslow and Cossack, down from Darwin and even from far away Thursday Island.

It was in 1883 that Broome was formally proclaimed a town, named after the then governor of Western Australian. By 1900, some four hundred luggers worked out of Roebuck Bay. The crews were from Timor, the Philippines,

A Kimberley corroboree, performed in 1926 for visitors on HMAS Geranium. Courtesy National Library of Australia.

Aborigines had dived for the pearl shell long before Broome became the pearl-hunting capital of Australia. Courtesy Macleay Museum.

This baobob tree, just outside Derby, was used as an emergency prison at one time. It is said that up to 20 blacks could be kept in it overnight. Photo by Philip Green.

Malaysia and Indonesia, while the divers were mainly Japanese or Malay. Most of the owners were European and the shops and trade were in the hands of the Chinese, Japanese and Europeans. In those days Broome boasted of being the most cosmopolitan town in Australia.

The original Australians worked among them, diving naked in shallow waters from stationary boats. But, with a growing demand for the local treasure, they quickly gave way to the helmeted diver with diving suit and lead-weighted boots. As the divers were forced to increasing depths the dangers increased, especially the phenomenon known as 'the bends' (diver's paralysis) which can kill or maim. In one year alone thirty-three men lost their lives in the risky pursuit of the prized pearl.

By 1910 Broome had reached the peak of its prosperity. But while the master pearlers built opulent tropical bungalows in styles which reflected their status, the founding people of the continent were often to be found in a humpy at the back of the house, from which the man did the gardening, his wife the house cleaning.

In the bad old days apartheid reigned supreme, with each ethnic group distinct and separate. The biggest division was between the Anglo-Australians and all others. Intermarriage was rare and there was no social mixing. The original people were even banned from the local hospital. They went to one for 'blacks only'.

After a hundred years, the old barriers have gone and, in many ways, Broome has been in the vanguard of Australia's development as a multicultural society. As development spread north and west from Broome and Derby, the Nigina people and the Ngarinyin, Wanambul and Worora nations to the north were all overwhelmed by the influx, their land overrun and the traditional way of life broken like a reed in a storm.

Today, there is a new pride among the original people and a determination to overcome the problems which have followed dispossession and years of despair. The memories (and photographs) remain of old-time chain gangs of black prisoners, cleaning the streets and gardens of the wealthy. They were barefoot, clad in trousers that ended between the knee and ankle and chained in pairs, with just enough slack on the chain to let them work. The ever watchful khaki-clad guards, with rifles slung over their shoulders, completed a picture of tyranny.

In 1920, the bad feelings between ethnic groups spilled over in a race riot that lasted three days and nights. During World War II the airfield and bay were bombed by Japanese planes and more than a hundred people were killed.

Today the Port of Pearls is at peace, with a new jetty and a new scientific face for the industry, following the introduction of cultured pearls by a Japanese businessman named Kuribayashi, one of the founders of the original

Japanese–Australian joint venture to produce cultured pearl. The port has acknowledged his contribution. Kuri Bay was named after him and at the entrance to Chinatown there is a life-size bronze likeness of Kuribayashi, which stands alongside that of a Japanese-Australian, both recognised for their contribution to Broome.

From Broome, the Great Northern Highway runs south past Eighty Mile Beach to Port Hedland and the Strelley community, which border on the lands of the Kariara and Njamal peoples.

The creation of Strelley Station is a one-off in Australian history, because it is not the result of forced migration, or the creation of refugee camps by white administrations, but was founded by traditional people from the Western Desert and Pilbara regions who came together themselves.

More than 500 people with common cultural links and a shared history of struggle against outside invasions live on Strelley Station. At a series of historic meetings held at Skull Springs in 1942, a grand alliance was forged on the western margin of the Gibson Desert. The ultimate aim was to preserve traditional culture and free the people from economic oppression.

In the early 1920s they won access to a pastoral lease known as Strelley Station, about 60 kilometres east of Port Hedland. In the final hours of the Whitlam Goverment (in 1975) Strelley was told that federal funds would be available to start a community school.

The school began in February 1976 and was a triumph for the community, which saw it as a means for self-determination — both social and economic — and a chance to ensure the cultural and religious development of future genterations. In 1978 an additional school was established at Warralong Station, some 90 kilometres east of Strelley, which operates as an offshoot to the main community school. A third school was set up in 1980 at Lalla Rookh and yet another in 1981 north-east of Jigalong.

This network of educational institutions augurs well for the continuation of the people's culture and offers some security that ancient languages and traditions will not be allowed to die.

On the road once more we pass the old pearling towns of Roebourne, Cossack and Onslow. Further south we reach Carnarvon, on the southern bank of the Gascoyne River, which has become a centre for more than 200 Mandi people who have moved in from the surrounding countryside.

Leaving Carnarvon behind, we head south to the Murchison River and the land of the mighty Nyungar people whose many clans were the traditional owners of a vast estate of land along the ocean and hinterlands, from the Murchison River to Albany.

South of Carnarvon, the mighty Murchison River makes its way to the coast. Photo by Philip Green.

Traditional medicine

With 6000 non-Aboriginal inhabitants in Carnarvon, the local people have had to contend with massive unemployment, locked out of traditional lands except for seasonal jobs as stockmen, and no real educational system. Despite this, elements of traditional life have survived and in recent years there has been a revival, due in part to the reappearance of the traditional doctors or healers.

Their medicine is based on the use of copious plant materials and this knowledge is shared generally among adults. It also involves diagnosis and therapies that treat the spiritual causes of illness, believed to be supernaturally imposed punishments. These people also accept the benefits of modern medicine and when a person falls ill the decision has to be made whether a western doctor or a traditional doctor should be employed.

A second tier of healers are called *maban* men or *jamadji* doctors. The word *maban* is used in Carnarvon to refer both to the spiritual power of the doctors and to the substances they are believed to carry in their bodies and which they use to bring about cures. Most doctors are also lawmakers.

Today the Mandi people have been joined by Wadjari speakers from the Upper Gascoyne and Murchison region, although they are distinct nations. The Wadjari, for example, practice circumcision: their Mandi neighbours do not. These cultural barriers run far deeper than white administrators could or would accept.

Great diversity has developed within the community and today three traditional doctors speak Wadjari, one Warianga and one Dargari. Becoming a doctor in this region simply involves acquiring the knowledge, which is passed from father to son.

Often the graduation of a doctor is associated with a religious ritual in which the apprentice receives the power. In one case, a *maban* man told of being taken to rest at a site sacred to the duck spirit. During the night the *ngarua* spirit took him on a journey to show him different places and give him the power of healing.

The apprentice works for up to two years with his father, learning to use his spiritual power and the small multi-coloured stones which are kept in the stomach and used to treat different illnesses. The healing power can be lost by illness, accident or old age and must be passed on while the doctor is spiritually strong and vigorous.

Opposite *Two Aborigines in from the desert at Marble Bar. Their heights were recorded at 6'7 (2.0 metres) and 6'5" (1.95 metres). Courtesy Battye Library of Western Australia.*

Below *The Zuytdorp Cliffs, north of Kalbarri, stretch for almost 200 kilometres, their limestone cliffs — 250 metres high in places — being constantly pounded by the Indian Ocean. The cliffs were named after the Dutch ship* Zuytdorp, *wrecked in 1712 some 64 kilometres north of Kalbarri. Photo by Bill Bachman.*

The Nyungar burnt their land on a regular basis. Such fires were carefully planned and controlled, often timed so that a wind change later in the day would extinguish the fire. Banksias, so abundant in this region, actually need fire to germinate their seeds. Photo by Philip Green.

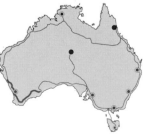

Geraldton to Esperance

THE great fertile region stretching from Geraldton to Esperance comprises the territory of the Nyungar people who, through a complex relationship between clans and bands, ruled an empire large enough to embrace six European kingdoms. Their territories represented an area of some three million hectares, with 1600 kilometres of coastline.

Opposite *Top left, the black swan, emblem of Western Australia, which can still be seen around Perth and the Swan River. Top right, Bluff Knoll, the highest point in the Stirling Ranges National Park. This park attracts many visitors each year for the spectacular wildflowers in spring and early summer. Photos by Robbi Newman (left), and Colin Totterdell.*

Right Xanthorrhoea *sunset, western style. Photo by Philip Green.*

Situated near Hyden, 160 kilometres east of Perth, Wave Rock is a wonderful geological oddity. Formed in pre-Cambrian granite which crystallised some 2700 million years ago, the rock has been eroded and undercut in the process of weathering, forming the overhang from which it earned its name. The process of erosion has exposed pronounced vertical bands of colour in the rock, which vary from deep grey to rusty red. Photo by Philip Green.

The ancestors of the Nyungar lived and flourished in what is now metropolitan Perth at least 38 000 years ago, 35 000 years before the seige of Troy and 34 000 years before the great Pyramids of Egypt were begun.

According to the local Dreamtime saga, the offshore islands including Garden, Carnac and Rottnest, were created when the ocean swept in and separated them from continental Australia.

The Nyungar nation, numbering about 7000 at the time of the European invasion, was quite distinctive in language and custom. The clans came together regularly in gatherings for religious observances, trading, educational necessities and to arrange marriages. Bailup (near Perth), because of its plentiful food supplies, was a major centre.

The orange banksia, a member of the Proteaceae family, is found throughout this region. There are 71 species, 57 of which occur in Western Australia. Photo by Philip Green.

The state capital, Perth, was originally called Boorloo. At the time the English arrived in 1829, a sprawling, slow-moving river reached across Perth Water from *Matta Gerup* ('knee deep' crossing) at the present causeway to Goodrool. The once lovely Eliza Bay is now buried beneath the freeway. Freshwater springs fed by lakes to the north surfaced below the high ridge of sloping land where Perth City today is built.

Nyungar people had a body of laws similar to other Australian nations. Although the senior men controlled this domain of life, women were also influential and could be accorded the high status of 'wise women'.

The cold winters dictated the need to construct bark houses and for the people to wear *buka* (or cloaks), usually made from kangaroo skins sewn together with the fur inside. The women carried *gundir* (kangaroo-skin bags) for transporting babies.

The evil spirit of the Nyungar was *Cienga* who lived in the centre the earth. It was *Cienga* who released the whirlwinds and cloudbursts and killed children. In the traditions of the Nyungar, the moon is an evil man who wanders the sky (accompanied by many dogs) stealing from earthlings. His wife, the sun, is the friend of all. The stars are joined in marriage and have many children. The planet Venus was an attractive young woman who practised sorcery.

Burial traditions varied from the people of the mountain to the lowlands. Usually a corpse was buried in its cloak and, as among other black Australian nations, a doctor was present at the funeral to make sure the spirit had departed the body. A small tomb of reeds or boughs was constructed over the grave and a fire lit at the entrance to make the place more comfortable and home-like for the spirit. The soul of the newly dead would go to *Kurannup*, the home of the dead beyond the western sea. Here the old skins were discarded and the dead appeared white. The arrival of the first Europeans was at first believed to be the return of the dead.

Perth today

Perth has a large Aboriginal population, many of whom have enjoyed considerable success in their chosen field of endeavour. Sport has always offered Aboriginal people the most obvious opportunity to excel and Perth has nurtured some great football talent over the years, including Polly Farmer, Barry Cable, Phil and Jimmy Krakour and Maurice Rioli, all of whom have enjoyed Australia-wide respect for their commitment and prowess. Other successful Perth people include Ken Colbung, chairperson of the Australian Institute of Aboriginal Studies and Revel Cooper and Yibujung, who have enjoyed recognition for their art.

The traditional lands of the Nyungar.

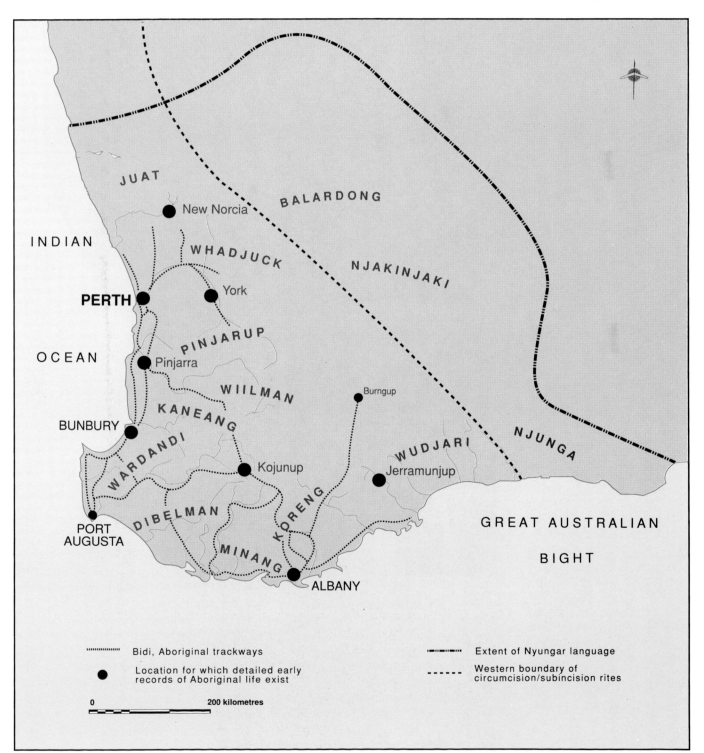

Bidi, Aboriginal trackways

● Location for which detailed early records of Aboriginal life exist

Extent of Nyungar language

Western boundary of circumcision/subincision rites

0   200 kilometres

Nyungar natural resources

The Nyungar lived well, in a world of harsh and often unpredictable seasons. The south-western region was serviced by some twenty rivers flowing to the coast from their watershed in the Darling Ranges. In this lush country, kangaroos roamed in mobs of more than 500. Ducks were plentiful and fish abundant. The Nyungar family also enjoyed an inexhaustible summer diet of turtle, fish, marron (a freshwater crayfish) and frogs.

In the drier regions — between Geraldton and Northampton — the predominantly flat country carried turkeys, as well as pigeons, emus, cockatoos and parakeets. The Swan coastal plain is a stronghold for waterbirds, including the famous black swan, the emblem of Western Australia. Around 20 000 black swans have been counted on Wandering Lake, near Woodanilling, with similar numbers of ducks.

The Darling Plateau is a series of contrasts: dense forest and high broken country, with poor soil and difficult terrain. Firestick farming by the Nyungar kept the valley floors open.

Throughout the south-west, snakes and lizards are numerous and they formed a major part of the Nyungar diet. Fish were caught with spears, by trapping, or by hand. Fish traps were a reliable source of food and when catches were substantial they were preserved by being cooked, wrapped in bark and then buried.

The principal vegetable was a native potato, although many plants were eaten. The Nyungar had special techniques for dealing with noxious substances in plant foods. *Haemodorum* roots were thought to cause dysentery when eaten alone, so they were roasted and ground with mould, which women carried in their bags especially for that purpose. The poisonous nuts of the zamia palm were popular, but they had to be harvested at the right time, soaked in water and then buried, after which they could be eaten raw or roasted.

The Nyungar employed simple farming techniques. Those soils carrying concentrations of edible plants were regularly turned over, and often over areas of many hectares. Firestick farming was practised to improve the grass and *typha* roots. The native potato areas on the alluvial flats were kept open by firing and good harvests assured by reducing plant competition.

Basic conservation was also practised and the law required that no seed-bearing plant could be dug up until after it had flowered. This was one of the first Nyungar laws broken by the white invaders.

Trees provided most of the material necessary for the manufacture of implements, from spears to spinning spindles. Drinking vessels were also made of timber, and bark provided roofing material as well as cooking wrap for fish. Gum (extracted from grass trees) was used in making implements, and stone was quarried from a wide area for many purposes: grindstones, tools and for trade across national boundaries. There was also a brisk trade in ochres and clays for cosmetic, ceremonial and ritual uses.

Black cockatoos in the Stirling Range. These birds were often seen as signalling the coming of rain and the black feathers were often used in rain-making ceremonies. They were hunted with boomerangs. Photo by AusChromes.

Salvado

The great observer of the Nyungar people was a Spanish Benedictine, Rosendo Salvado. He is remembered in both Australia and Spain, by a statue in his home town of Tuy, in Galicia, and by his greatest monument, the Benedictine Monastery at New Norcia.

Salvado described the Nyungar people as a fine race, tall and well-built, whose bodies would have delighted the eye of any artist.

He savagely criticised the English for taking black Australians (such as Bennelong) to London and showing them off as 'noble savages'. His condemnation of the massacres was equally blunt and he highlighted the predominant view of European settlers at the time, expressed by a barrister defending a European accused of killing a black, that the killing of Aborigines was no crime at all, as they were 'cannibal savages'. The good Salvado was happy to find they believed the soul immortal.

Salvado, among the first to study the language of the Nyungar, acknowledged their religious belief in the all-powerful creator of life, *Motogon*, who stood strong, tall and wise and said: 'Land, come forth!' and the land was created. Then: 'Water, come forth!' and the waters were created.

Rottnest Island was established as an Aboriginal penal settlement in 1839. Troublesome blacks from all over the state were incarcerated here. Photo by Greenham and Evans, courtesy National Library of Australia.

New Norcia

A unique settlement in Australia, the Benedictine monastery New Norcia was founded in 1846 by the Spanish fathers, Salvado and Serra, who had been sent as missionaries to Black Australia by Pope Gregory XVI. The church, mission building and extensive grazing land along the Moore River north of Perth were designed to offer the Nyungar a new way of life. The mission was established eighteen years after the English settlement on the Swan River.

A Nyungar girl called Kookina was first to be baptised. It was typical of Salvado's pragmatism that, although Kookina was christened Mary Christian, he ensured she kept her original name as her surname.

Salvado saw no evil in nudity and observed that when he travelled and slept with his black brothers and sisters he never saw an 'unchaste or improper' action. This was quite different to the usual missionary approach of the time, which was to condemn all beliefs and customs of the 'pagan savages'.

Today New Norcia stands serene and beautiful, a treasure house of history drawn from Australia, Spain and Rome containing invaluable paintings and artefacts from kings and popes testifying to their admiration for Salvado, whose own tribute to Aboriginal Australians was his desire to die as a member of the Nyungar people.

Two early guests of the New Norcia mission. Courtesy The Library Board of Western Australia.

An ancient trading centre

South of Perth and Pinjarra is the city of Bunbury, heart of the Pindjarup people and an important trading centre of traditional Australia.

The major trading items made by the people of the Bunbury district were superb spears of local 'spear wood' which grew plentifully in the coastal swamps. These were traded for a special kind of red ochre called *wil-gi*, which was mixed with fat and used as a body paint on ceremonial occasions.

Quartz (called *bwor-ral*) came from the Darling Ranges and was used for spearheads. Later this was replaced by glass introduced by Europeans. Stone tomahawks were another major trading commodity brought from the distant ranges. Woomeras, known to the Nyungar as *mi-ra*, came from even further away and were made from the 'raspberry jam' wattle *Acacia acuminata*. Cork-wood shields (*hi-la-man*) and throwing sticks (*dau-ak*), also made of wattle wood, were additional items of trade from the Avon area.

A major trading route (*bidi*) extended from the south-west through the Murchison and Gascoyne districts, as far north as the Kimberleys, where stone for axes was exported to the south.

Below left *The Stirling Range.* **Below** *The koala, protected but still at risk. Photos by Robbi Newman.*

Yellagonga

This man's offence is not known, nor his fate. Courtesy The Library Board of Western Australia.

King Billy, of the Karridale district. Courtesy The Library Board of Western Australia.

The most prominent Nyungar leader at the time of the arrival of the English in 1829 was Yellagonga, whose clan boundaries stretched from the Indian Ocean in the west to Ellen Brook in the east and from Melville Water and the Swan River north to the Moore River.

Yellagonga's camp (*kaleep*) was in the heart of today's Perth, on a sloping hill called *Byerbup*, where the Anglican Bishop's House in Spring Street now stands. From this spot he commanded a view of the river flats and the approach of any visitors.

Symbolically, the British 63rd Regiment subsequently took possession of the hill to pitch their tents. An observer, writing four years after the occupation, said the proud companions of Yellagonga had been reduced to begging. In fact, Yellagonga and his people were driven from Perth to Galup (Mongers Lake), allowed back into town only under the watchful eye of the soldiers.

Yellagonga had been a gentle leader and had attempted to co-operate with the English in those early years, yet he was credited as being a great Nyungar warrior. The *Perth Gazette* printed his obituary on 10 June, 1843, noting that he had drowned after falling into the river.

However, it is the name of Yagan, an outstanding Nyungar warrior, who will always be remembered for his role in rallying the Swan River people to resist the invaders.

Yagan

In 1832, Yagan was accused of killing a settler and proclaimed an outlaw. Later that year, with two fellow Nyungar warriors, he was enticed into a boat and captured. They were jailed in Perth and later transferred to Carnac Island, 12 kilometres from Fremantle, but within two months Yagan and his companions had escaped to the mainland. On 4 May 1833, Yagan was wanted 'dead or alive' — after the death of two brothers — and a bounty of thirty pounds was offered.

Even though he was an outlaw, Yagan was praised in the *Perth Gazette*:

> *Yagan stands prominent in height among them, walks very*
> *erect and is accompanied by a small black dog . . . which yet by*
> *its watchfulness may render futile every attempt to take his*
> *his master by surprise.*

Yagan met his end when killed by two brothers, James and William Keates. A settler then cut off his head and skinned his body, to preserve the clan designs on his back. Yagan's head hung for three months in a hollow gum tree over a smouldering fire of green gum leaves, before being eventually sent to England and exhibited as that of a 'Swan River Chieftain'.

The Battle of Pinjarra

Weeip is another resistance leader remembered in the Upper Swan district, while Calyute and his people were the most successful resistance fighters in the south-west.

Faced with increasing resistance and responsible for the 2000 English troops and settlers, Governor Sir James Stirling, one of the most effective military governors in Australia resorted to the tried and tested strategy of divide and conquer. Having convinced Weeip not to join with the southern forces led by Calyute, Stirling concentrated on the war with the southern Nyungar. He selected Pinjarra as the site for a town and military post, knowing it was the main meeting place for all the southern Nyungar people. Here he threw down the challenge.

Calyute was not yet thirty years of age when he became leader of his people. His great height and strength meant that he stood out in battle and life. Calyute had built a remarkable unity among his people but Stirling outmanoeuvred him with a force of men from the Royal North British Fusiliers. Moving his men in three divisions, Stirling staged a surprise attack on Calyute and his people on Tuesday, 28 October 1834. The battle took place only a couple of kilometres from the main street of today's town of Pinjarra.

Trapped on all sides, the Nyungar fought frantically. Many warriors died, along with women and children, who fell to the bullets and swords of the English force. Calyute escaped but the battle had sounded the death knell for the independence of the Nyungar people. Calyute himself died an old man, unheralded by his conquerors and remembered only in the folk memory of his people who he had led so bravely.

Calyute, a leader of his clan in the south-west, who led the attack on Governor Stirling in the battle of Pinjarra in 1834. He died in 1884, when he was said to be 126 years old. Courtesy The Library Board of Western Australia.

Coastline near Cape Clairault. Photo by Andrew Witton.

Devil's Lair

In 1955, a discovery important to understanding the long history of Australia was made by palaeontologist Ernest Lundelius, who opened a cave south of Bunbury: the repository of thousands of years of history.

Called Devil's Lair, the cave is on the sheltered eastern side of the Leeuwin Ridge, 5 kilometres from the ocean and surrounded by open eucalypt forest, which gives way to stunted woodland and scrub towards the crest of the ridge.

The cave is like many in the region of limestone running between Cape Leeuwin and Cape Naturaliste. Formed over many thousands of years by the weathering processes of underground stream erosion, they were used by owls, bats, rodents and many other animals, among them Tasmanian devils (*Sarcophilus harrisii*), the voracious bone-crunching animals after which the cave is named.

The present entrance is only a few hundred years old, the original entry at the rear of the cave now being blocked by debris. The gently sloping sandy floor built up over 40 000 years, layer after layer of bonded sand, which has provided significant insights into the long use of the cave by Nyungar people.

Before the Ice Ages, inland Australia contained huge freshwater lakes abounding with wild life, including giant crocodiles. The ice ages, however, brought aridity to these regions. Glaciers and snowfields covered the highlands of southeastern Australia and Tasmania while the rest of the continent was windswept, cold and dry.

As glaciers and polar ice caps expanded, the sea level dropped. At that time — 17 000 years

ago — Devil's Lair was 40 kilometres from the coast. Around 12 000 years ago the cave was still 20 kilometres inland and it was not until 6000 years ago that the shore reached its present position.

The original coastline had great sandy plains, dominated by dunes and the ice ages brought changes not only to the sea level, but also to vegetation. Animal and human populations were also changed by this process.

Devil's Lair reflects this development and the layers disclose it as the home of Tasmanian devils, as well as rock wallabies and honey possums, which began to disappear as the once open vegetation gave way to dense thicket and forest. The cave today has its primeval darkness illuminated by electric light as work continues, probing the past. One predator which shared the cave with the Tasmanian devil was a dasyuroid, more popularly called a native cat.

Devil's Lair was used by people intermittently from some time around 30 000 years ago until 6000 years ago. It seems they used the cave for a few weeks at a time, every few years, or perhaps for a few days every year. They hunted in the bush nearby and brought back possums, wallabies and lizards, then cooked and ate them in the cave, building up rubbish heaps within the cave itself. Sometimes they went to the nearby coast or streams for shellfish. They also used the cave as a workshop for tool making, sometimes with materials traded over great distances.

Many hearths have been examined and it seems people often moved into the cave during the cold winter months. Families inhabited the

Nyungar people. Courtesy The Library Board of Western Australia.

cave, but excavations have uncovered at least one mystery yet to be solved: a pit, which was at first thought to be a grave, is now believed to have been connected with religious ritual. The cave has yet to reveal a clear answer. Devil's Lair has already yielded a wide range of stone artefacts, up to 30 000 years old, and bone beads which date back 17 000 years.

Still further mystery is added by three engraved limestone plaques, the oldest of which dates back 25 000 years. They have small four-sided figures formed by straight lines, which meet but do not cross, and curving lines, forming tiny semi-enclosed shapes. Whether they are symbols made during rituals or merely graffiti with no symbolic or ritual significance has yet to be established, although they have much in common with similar carvings discovered in two other caves near Perth. Other engravings, representing emu and kangaroo tracks, have been found near Scott River, 40 kilometres east of Devil's Lair.

Among the remains of thirty-five different animals found in the cave are koalas, ghost bats, dingoes as well as the now extinct *Protemnodon* and *Sthenurus* (giant kangaroos). Remains have also been found of an extinct wombat and a uniquely Australian marsupial lion, the *Thyla-coleo,* as well as a cow-sized marsupial, *Zygomaturus triobus,* which looked like a concertined rhinocerous. We do not yet know why they disappeared but the cave clearly records their coming and going. The bones recovered show signs of being savaged not only by Tasmanian devils or native cats, but also by domestic dogs.

A few kilometres north of Devil's Lair is the Mammoth Cave, where the 37 000 year old bones of the extinct *Zygomaturus* have been found. Between Cape Leeuwin and Cape Naturaliste are many open camp-sites of the Nyungar people. It seems that Devil's Lair and other caves were places of refuge in the glacial period. The Nyungar adapted to a new world, as different as any we could imagine. Scientists are still seeking to discover when and how these people evolved the conservation and farming techniques which ensured their survival in centuries of dramatic climatic change.

Explorations at Devil's Lair (and the south-west corner generally) have shown how the Nyungar people accepted innovation and new ideas, then regulated their food gathering as systematically as any twentieth-century farmer. Evidence of innovation is found in the artistic creativity of the diverse rock paintings and engravings, and explorers of prehistory have confirmed a continuing cultural enrichment and intellectual dynamism over thousands of years. It is this long span of history which has brought about the elaborate oral traditions of songs and Dreamtime stories, the complex and sophisticated organisation of society and the deep spiritual beliefs which so impressed even Roman, English and German clergy.

Devil's Lair ranks with the Lake Mungo discoveries of yesterday's Australia and as 95 per cent of the cave deposits are untouched the challenge for further exploration remains — and the chance for a clearer perception of the Nyungar heritage.

PHOTO BY COLIN TOTTERDELL

The Swan brothers

In the great sagas of the Nyungar Dreamtime the story is told of the coming of people to the Swan River area. The Swan brothers, who lived around the sacred ochre caves near Wandering (about 145 kilometres south-east of Perth) in the days when all the swans were glossy black, were great hunters and widely respected.

The brothers would start off for the hunt hours before anyone else, checking their range of weapons — boomerangs, spears, woomeras and nulla nullas — with great care. They would identify the feeding grounds of their prey and establish themselves in position before dawn, disguised as emus (complete with feathers) or kangaroos (complete with skins). They would strike when the time was right and lead the other hunters, who arrived later.

After it was all over, the brothers would call all the hunters together and allocate each of them a load to carry back back to camp. On arrival, preparations would begin for a night-long celebration to give thanks to the creator. Hailed as heroes, the brothers were greatly admired and when they had eaten and danced the night away, they were given permission by the elders to go to sleep.

One night they were awakened by a group of young warriors who told them that Jubuk, the wise one, wished to talk to them. They were led to a circle of fire prepared for the occasion and Jubuk raised his warnuk stick, bearing the coiled waargle or snake, the totemic symbol of the clan. He told them the creative being appeared before him in the form of a beautiful black swan which kept changing from black to white and back again. Jubuk explained that he was commanded to send the brothers to the sacred river, Warrening, and begin a new clan which would have for its totemic symbol, the swan. The brothers' names would be Moornuwooling (meaning black) and Ngnitteeyung (meaning white) and they must never make war on each other.

'Go and make many of your new people,' he said, and the two brothers became the black and white swans of the Swan River. Even today it is rare to see a black swan without a white one nearby.

(Adapted from 'The Swan Brothers' in Eddie Bennell and Anne Thomas' Aboriginal Legends from the Bibulmun Tribe, Rigby, Sydney, 1981.)

R Albany

ounding Cape Leewuin, we head for Albany, continuing our journey through the vast lands of the Nyungar nation, which terminate at Esperance. Albany was visited by the English captain Vancouver in 1791, by the French commodore Baudin soon afterwards, then by the English captains Flinders and King. In l826, the Sydncy colonial authorities sent fifty-two people, mainly soldiers of the 57th regiment, to found a settlement at King George Sound, which was originally called Frederick Town. This failed to catch on and Albany took over as the official name.

To these early English explorers, such as the medical officer Scott Nind who accompanied the first settlement to Albany, the Nyungar people looked pretty much the same as the Eora of Sydney. Nind described them as being of middle stature and slender of limb. They wore kangaroo-skin cloaks stretching to the knee, fastened on the right shoulder. In rainy weather they turned the cloaks inside out, with the fur outside for better water-proofing.

Cloaks were made by pegging out the skins on the ground to dry. Then they were cut into the desired shape with a stone knife, which was also used to scrape the inner surface, until the skin became soft and pliable. Once prepared, the skins were stitched together with animal sinews, then rubbed over with grease and red ochre. Nind noted the women wore larger cloaks than the men.

A waistband, or *noodle-bul* was also popular, 'a long yarn of worsted', spun from the fur of the possum and wound around the waist several hundred times. A similar band was sometimes worn around the left arm.

Single men wore head ornaments of feathers and dingo tails, and sometimes bound long hair around their head. In contrast, women wore their hair short. Both men and women used a special red pigment on their faces and upper body as a sunburn lotion and also to keep their skin clean. In mourning, a white streak was painted across the forehead and down the cheekbones. Body painting was also a feature at festival time or on visits to neighbouring clans. Circumcision was not practised.

Patterns of ritual scarring on the shoulders and the chest differed from clan to clan. The nose bone, also a feature in Sydney, was popular with the Nyungar. The ritual markings were considered to single out a man of distinction, but ornaments were not recognised as indicative of authority.

The coastline near Albany.
Photo by Robbi Newman.

Men and women travelling any distance from their encampment carried firesticks, not only for kindling fires, but for the sake of heat in the cold winters. Weapons consisted of two or three kinds of spear (propelled by woomeras), knives, tomahawks and boomerangs. The spears were long, slender and fire-hardened. The hunting spear was 2.5 metres long, with wooden barbs fixed with kangaroo sinew. War spears were longer and heavier, their tips barbed with pieces of sharp stone resembling the teeth of a saw and fixed with gum.

The hammer, or axe, was made from two stones embedded in gum and fixed to a handle. A unique throwing stick, narrowing at each end, served a dual purpose: the handle had a sharp-edged stone, fixed in gum, which was used to scrape the point of a blunted spear. At the other end, a small wooden peg was used to propel the spear.

A short stick (called *towk*) was used to hunt small animals, but the boomerang was seldom used as a weapon, being mostly for amusement or skinning kangaroos.

The 1.2 metre high huts were often constructed in pairs — arranged so as not to overlook each other — usually as part of a camp comprising many huts and about fifty people. Single men had a hut to themselves; children slept with the women in a large shelter near their husbands.

Scott Nind made many observations of the innovative applications of firestick farming. Torches made from dry leaves were used to fire both sides of the cover so the game in that area was trapped. Vast numbers of animals were killed for food in this way.

These fires could extend over many hectares, but control was maintained by burning in carefully selected portions. Women kindled their own fires to take bandicoots, but sometimes co-operated in larger operations with the men.

'Trained hunting dogs', presumably dingoes, were also used and their owners were awarded a larger portion of the kill. Kangaroos have acute hearing and were often hunted in the rain or when the wind was blowing hard, as it disguised the hunters' approach. Using a bush as cover the hunter would silently creep up on his prey. If the kangaroo turned round the hunter would stop still until the animal resumed eating. Spears were thrown as soon as the hunters were close enough, then they would close in for the kill with axes or hammers. Another way of hunting kangaroos was to surround an area and gradually move in until close enough to use spears. Pitfalls set in wet places were also used. Emus were usually hunted in winter, when they were laying their eggs, although kangaroos, when available, were preferred.

The *munnaar* (a large lizard) was good eating and their eggs were found in ant nests, where the *munnaar* laid them for protection and incubation. Other species of lizard hunted in this area included the *wandie*, a small, quick animal usually found among rocks, and the short-tailed *youern,* which has a large head and purple tongue.

Snakes made good bush tucker but the Nyungar, as part of their religious beliefs, always destroyed the head completely and removed any undigested food in the snake's stomach. Certain foods were never eaten, including some birds (particularly of the parrot clan), flying foxes and fish of all kinds except shark. Stingrays and oysters, although common, were never taken for food. Whales and seals were speared and eaten after stranding on beaches. The fat was often put away for lean times.

The freshwater swamps abounded in crayfish, which were roasted in ashes. The freshwater turtle, two or three species of frogs, a range of grubs and eggs, vegetables of various kinds and honey were all popular. The Nyungar diet had some intriguing customs. Quails were considered old men's food, bandicoots were not good for young girls and black eagles were believed to cause young men to have a thin beard and be poor hunters.

One of the amusing stories which has survived from the first days of the English arrival concerned their search for Nyungar kings or chiefs. Coming as they did from a society structured around a king, they thought there must be an opposite number in the Nyungar.

ALBANY

Thistle Cove, Cape le Grand National Park. Photo by Colin Totterdell.

Eventually they concluded that three tall handsome young men, who wore the most ornamental headgear, must be the chiefs. As it turned out, the three were, in fact, young single men, the only ones to wear the fancy head-pieces. The elders wore no ornament at all, but carried ritual scarring on the upper body which signified their status.

The Nyungar seem to have enjoyed the joke and one of the young men, Naikennon, felt it was great fun to be a king so he played the part, persuading his young friends to back him up. At the beginning he said little, sitting quiet and aloof and refusing to join in any activity. The English were impressed with these signs of kingly arrogance. Eventually Naikennon and his young companions began to converse with their English hosts and gave themselves away. But it was good fun while it lasted.

One feature of traditional society was the role of the doctors, who actually possessed the most influence within the community. These doctors, or *mulgarradocks*, had several grades which determined the nature and extent of their powers.

They were believed to drive away wind and rain and to bring down lightning or disease on those who earned their hatred or contempt. Standing in the open, with arms outstretched, they would command the elements to hear them. The *mulgarradock*s were believed to confer strength and healing through their hands

In traditional times, the Nyungar people had few ailments and one of the doctor's main jobs was treating spear wounds. They would first extract the spear, then apply a medicinal dust and bind the wound tightly with soft bark. Diet also played a major role in treatment: during the first stage of convalescence, only roots were eaten, followed by lizards. The cure for snake bite was to tie a ligature of rushes above the bite, enlarge the wound with the point of a spear or knife, then suck it, washing the wound (and their mouths) frequently with water.

Describing a meeting between people of neighbouring nations, Scott Nind noted that the two parties approached with all their weapons carried by one man of each nation. Each man carried a green bough and was painted, a band of grass-tree leaves around his forehead, hanging downwards over the face. After making several turns in a circle, they embraced by putting arms around the waist of their opposite number and lifting him from the ground. Then they kissed each other's hands and danced together. The green bough was their sign of peace.

There were no punitive executions, the main punishment being a spear through the leg or thigh. In duels, which were fought mostly over women, the fighting stopped once one participant was wounded.

The story of Waargle

The story of Noah and the Flood has a direct parallel in the sagas of the Nyungar relating to their belief of the second creation. After thousands of years of harmony and contact with other nations through the trade routes that criss-crossed the continent, a great many mixed marriages took place.

These worked well for a long time but then there arose a reluctance among young people to follow the laws and customs which had enabled all the nations to live in harmony. Young people failed to respect their elders and even abused them, laughing at threats that the all powerful creator would punish them. Even the strict rules of marriage were broken and young people began to marry those in prohibited categories, such as second cousins, aunts, uncles and brothers and sisters.

Such destruction and jealousy developed that warriors and hunters would not leave home in case their women were claimed by someone else because they had married their sisters, aunts, second cousins and nieces. As a result of all this incest many children were born with deformities, yet chaos continued to reign.

And the whole land, according to the story, was 'blanketed by a black cloak of evil and wickedness'. Children began to torture helpless animals and even deformed babies, and many elders joined in the debauchery. But there were seven just people — four men and three women — led by Buerrna who, although the youngest, was the most powerful because he carried the ancient law so strongly.

Buerrna was elected leader and on the seventh day after his election he called the others and told them he had dreamed he was riding on the back of Waargle, the snake, who was the All-Powerful One. All he could see on every side was water and, as he moved through the water, men, women and children everywhere called out: 'Save me! Save me!'

They attempted to climb on his back but Waargle brushed them away and suddenly Buerrna found he was on Waargle's back with his six chosen companions. They rode for many days and nights until reaching a sacred rock above water level where Waargle allowed them to disembark.

He then said, 'Children, let there be no more wickedness in your hearts and I will bless you, and you will again become a great and powerful tribe. Know that your totemic symbol shall always resemble me, the Waargle. Remember the laws you have chosen to obey and keep this rock sacred, because I will always be here.'

He then dived back into the turbulent waters and left the survivors to build the world anew. The sacred rock, Boyagin Rock, is revered today as the sleeping place of the Korrndon Marma Man in his form of Waargle, the sacred snake.

Adapted from Eddie Bennell and Anne Thomas' Aboriginal Legends from the Bibulmun Tribe, Rigby, Sydney, 1981.)

Mokare

One of the most famous of all the Australians of the Albany area was Mokare, whose father is believed to have torn down the cairn of stones erected by Captain George Vancouver in 1791, with a bottle containing a note declaring he had claimed the land of the Nyungar for the distant King of Great Britain.

Even if he had been able to read, the declaration would have meant nothing to Mokare's father, whose people had occupied these lands for thousands of years, although he was probably intrigued by the glass from the broken bottle and put it to good use. Ten years later, when Matthew Flinders arrived, life continued as it always had and when Flinders' marines began marching and drilling on the beach, the Nyungar thought they were putting on a ceremony and tried to copy the elaborate display.

In 1826 Mokare visited the French ship L'Astrolabe and sat for his portrait by a young French officer, who felt he had a young, open face and was more lively and outgoing than his companions.

These good intentions were to change once permanent settlers arrived and it was thanks to Mokare that the English and the Nyungar maintained good relations for several years.

Mokare kept the peace by insisting simply that the new arrivals abide by Nyungar laws relating to the land. The Nyungar were in the majority and at any time they could have driven the invaders into the sea before reinforcements arrived from the east. But peace persisted throughout his life, despite the disease, liquor and other degradations suffered by his people at the hands of the settlers. When the Nyungar first saw a drunk European fall down, they were convinced that the man would soon die.

Mokare was unmarried when the invaders first came, as Nyungar men remained single until at least thirty years of age. Women, on the other hand, were usually betrothed at birth and married at puberty. Mokare was betrothed when his future wife was a still small child living with her family.

Four wives were permitted in Nyungar life: Mokare's father had two. Mokare had a sister and four brothers: the eldest, Nakina, became the head of the family after the death of their father. The family always lived on their own land (on which Albany was later to be built) and wisely, the English, while taking possession (according to *their* law) of any land they fancied, did not interfere with Mokare's family.

As the family head, Nakina was treated with respect by the British. They came to him to present their compliments on arrival and departure. He never went to them.

The whole area of Mokare and his Nyungar people encompassed some 6000 square kilometres extending inland for about 70 kilometres north of Albany and along the coast for more than 120 kilometres. Their northern border ran along the base of the Stirling Mountains.

All Nyungar people were meticulously educated in the lore of land. The formal ceremony at puberty, when the nose-bone was inserted, was followed by a period when the boys left their families for what could be several years. Initiates would join one or two senior men and go to live with another family. They would then undergo strict formal instruction, and their teachers demanded discipline and physical endurance.

At this time, initiates could be betrothed to a baby girl or perhaps make a friend that would be a 'blood brother' for life. The traditional healer or doctor, in a small ceremony, would make a number of small cuts on the body. The blood from the two young men would be mixed with ashes and then massaged into the cuts resulting in patterned scarring of the body. Loyalty between the two had to transcend family feuds. After this period the initiates would be taken to other parts where further teachers continued the formal training program.

Over a period as long as four years he might stay with up to ten different familes under many instructors. He would go home with several promises of marriage and many ritual scars, indicating a network of blood brothers. All the while he would keep the bone through his nose which would remain in place until his education was complete. Only then was it time to marry.

At a 'welcome-home' ceremony the bone was finally removed by the *mulgarradock* and it was announced to all and sundry that he was an adult.

Despite all the safeguards, family feuds did break out, particularly over women. The dispute might be settled by blood brothers or by a non-fatal spearing, or a stolen girl might be returned and damages paid.

Mokare embraced the European custom of shaking hands and before long it became a recognised form of greeting among Nyungar people. The soldiers and their associates were allowed to camp on Nyungar land as long as they shook hands in peace, kept away from the women and children and were careful with fires.

Sincere attempts were made to keep to the rules and people like medical officer Nind tried hard to understand the culture of the host people. Long evenings were devoted to discussions about comparative lifestyles and religion, but when it came to claims about their respective cultures, Mokare pointed to the prevalence of strange and virulent diseases among the English which, even as early as 1830, were spreading to the Nyungar.

It was not long before Mokare himself fell victim. Returning from a bush tour he became seriously ill and the English doctor, Collis, and the Nyungar *mulgarradock,* Coolbun, tried in vain to save him. He died peacefully in his own home in the presence of his oldest brother, Nankina, and during the long day of his last hours many of his kinfolk called to pay their final respects.

Mokare was buried according to Nyungar custom, under the supervision of Nankina. No greater tribute to the peacemaker could be paid than that of Doctor Collis, who subsequently chose to have his body interred alongside his friend Mokare. It is on the two graves, one black and one white, that the present Albany Town Hall was built.

Fitzgerald River National Park.
Photo by Andrew Witton.

The emu, the possum and the brush kangaroo

A story of the emu, the possum and the brush kangaroo illustrates how Nyungar society worked in the resolution of disputes. In the Dreamtime humans wore the garb of animals, birds and reptiles and it was at that time that Quorra, the brush kangaroo, and his nephew, Waitch, the emu, lived and quarrelled. They argued for months about who was the better hunter, the uncle or the nephew. The elders and lawmakers elected Koormal the possum, himself a great hunter and lawmaker, to be the judge in a contest between them to resolve the issue.

On the night of the contest two corroborees were performed, one to bring good luck to the contestants and the other to prepare Waitch for initiation into full manhood if he won. It was then decided that Koormal would not only be the judge but also the prey.

Just before dawn, the great possum hunt began. They searched for hours, before Quorra picked up the trail and saw Koormal scurrying up a big old white gum tree. Cleverly, he trapped the possum and when Waitch turned up he found he had lost the contest. He shouted and abused everyone.

On returning home the contestants were summoned before the elders who banished Waitch for his poor sportsmanship. His uncle felt sorry and, in sympathy, asked if he could be banished too. This request was granted and today the three live quite separately: the possum, the emu and the brush kangaroo.

Adapted from Eddie Bennell and Anne Thomas' Aboriginal Legends from the Bibulmun Tribe, *Rigby, Sydney, 1981.)*

The Nullarbor Plain is bounded
to the south by steep, limestone
cliffs which extend in an almost
unbroken line for hundreds of
kilometres. Photo by Colin
Totterdell.

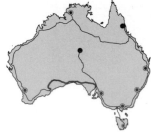

The Nullarbor to the Murray

S we head east from Esperance, leaving behind the lands of the Nyungar, we enter the Western Desert area, one of the most arid regions of the world. Our route takes us across the Nullarbor Plain, stretching 600 kilometres from Esperance east across the South Australian border.

The original telegraph station at Eucla, now abandoned to the sand. Photo by Andrew Witton.

The area of the continent now represented by the state of South Australia was once the home to nearly fifty nations, some as small as a few hundred people, others of several thousand. These people have been categorised into three broad groups: Western Desert, Central Lakes, and Murray and south-east.

In the expanse of nearly 200 000 square kilometres of the Nullarbor there is an almost complete absence of trees, hence its Latin name which means literally 'no trees'. The Nullarbor is actually a giant limestone plateau, some 300 metres deep and one of the largest areas of limestone in the world.

The region is without seasonal creeks and there is virtually no surface water of any kind, as the sparse rainfall is quickly absorbed by the porous limestone. Below the surface, underground water has produced an extensive series of caves, created over millions of years. Some are like great cathedrals, with domed ceilings and pools of crystal clear water. The underground world of the Nullarbor is a speleologists' (someone who explores underground caves) paradise and cave explorers from all over Australia are engaged in mapping it.

On the surface, low saltbush, interspersed with bluebush, extend to the far horizons, so distant in this flat world that the curve of the earth can actually be seen. These plants have adapted to a fierce environment, with leaves which enable them to survive with even a drop of dew.

Despite the formidable terrain, red and western grey kangaroos invade the area regularly and a proliferation of pock marks across the plain testify to the presence of the southern hairy-nosed wombat, which is equipped with special shovel-like nails for speedy digging. The wombats live in an underground world which they construct by lying sideways and digging with their strong forepaws, pushing the soil behind them with their rear legs. Their underground dwellings are up to 30 metres long — and wide enough to accommodate a small child — with distinctive flattened arched entrances.

Sand and spinifex, Eucla. Photo by Bill Bachman.

Wombats spend the hot days underground and come out at night to forage for the small tufted grasses which provide food as well as moisture.

The Nullarbor caves are rich in the remains of many species of small mammals which are rarely found today. One of the survivors is the kangaroo rat, bigger than a domestic rat and with large kangaroo-like hind legs, which enable it to move surprisingly fast. Kangaroo rats have large ears, a long brush-tipped tail and, despite their tiny size, they can cover a metre in one leap. Like wombats, they live below the surface, in grass-lined nesting chambers with many escape holes, and come out at night to search for seeds, fruits and leaves. They also have their own system for conserving water in their bodies — actually manufacturing additional water internally by oxidising food seeds.

The Nullarbor Plain, a harsh and unforgiving environment. Photo by Colin Totterdell.

Cocklebiddy Cave, on the western margin of the Nullarbor Plain, has extensive caverns and an underground lake some 80 metres beneath the plain. Photo by Colin Totterdell.

229

In traditional times natural wells and rock holes which accumulated water were capped with rocks to retain the water. Today, other resources are available. This rock hole at Wigunda, some 80 kilometres west of Yalata has been sealed with a tractor tyre fitted with a metal insert. A native orange tree can be seen in the background. Photo by Tom Sara.

In past years the Nullarbor was also home to the thylacine, which stalked the plains before their demise at the hands of a harsh climate and the attacks of other maurauders, like the dingo. Complete carcasses have been recovered in caves, preserved in the limestone, with even the tiger-stripes intact.

One of the most fearsome creatures found on the plain — and one of the most formidable looking animals on earth — is the thorny devil *Moloch horridus*. Despite its spines and defensive armour, which give it a ferocious appearance, the thorny devil is not dangerous. It changes colour to avoid detection and any moisture is channelled from every part of the body to the corner of the mouth, where it is absorbed internally.

Another resourceful creature of the plain is the thick-tailed or barking lizard which stands up to fight and actually barks at its opponent. It has the ability to cast away its tail if it is caught and, in time, develops a new one, sometimes growing two or three tails during a lifetime of close encounters.

The death adder, one of Australia's most dangerous snakes, is found along the coastal margin of the plain. Short and thick, the death adder uses the tip of its tail as a lure to entice and trap small ground birds and mammals. The king brown snake, which grows to 2 metres and whose venom is fatal, is another inhabitant. Emus, bustards, parrots and honeyeaters also frequent the plain, together with the quail thrush. Two species of bat have established colonies in deep caves.

Space scientists came to the Nullarbor to study the australites, small black glassy bodies which litter the plain and are now believed to come from outer space. The traditional people believed they had special powers, but also found some of them useful as tools.

The first recorded outsiders to see the Nullarbor Plain were the crew of the Dutch ship *Gulden Zeepaard* which, in 1627, explored the coast around Cape Leeuwin. They saw the towering limestone cliffs and, on their return journey, named the islands of St Francis and St Peter near Ceduna.

The French navigator d'Entrecasteaux followed the Dutch route many years later but found the coast so barren he could find nothing to say about it. The Englishman, Mathew Flinders, was next in 1802, and surveyed the southern coast, describing it as monotonous. But no Europeans explored this area seriously until 1841, when another Englishman, Edward John Eyre, crossed the Nullarbor from Fowlers Bay to Albany. The plain was given its name by another explorer, Alfred Delisser.

As time passed and invaders multiplied, a telegraph line, railway tracks and a highway traversed the plain. A colony called Eucla was set up to service the line but the heat and sand dunes of the great plain overwhelmed the settlement. Today all that is left of Eucla is a few neglected graves, and a cluster of old buildings.

In traditional times, the plain was part of the territory of a number of nations. They used it when seasons were good and retreated to less harsh areas when they were bad. The original people relied for water on small rock-holes, which they sealed with stone lids to conserve these scarce supplies.

One of the permanent settlements was located at Ooldea or *Yoodil Gabbi*, to use the original name. This Aboriginal settlement lasted until 1926, when a severe drought gripped the country and the people moved to the Koonibba and Yalata settlements.

Right *Sea lions are common on South Australia's southern shores. Photo by Bill Bachman.*

Far right *The Australian bustard, or plains turkey was a favourite food of Aborigines. Photo by Jim Frazier/Mantis Wildlife.*

Looks can be deceiving. The thorny devil has a fearsome appearance but a timid nature, using its thorny appearance as a defence against predators in the desert world to which it has adapted. Photo by Jim Frazier/Mantis Wildlife.

A selection of photographs from David Lindsey's expedition of 1891, on behalf of the pastoral company Elders. Lindsey's party explored the remote regions of north-west South Australia, crossing into Western Australia. These photos, taken on that trip, show a people who had never seen a European. Courtesy Old Parliament House Museum, Adelaide.

The Pitjantjatjara

The largest nation in the Western Desert region is that of the Pitjantjatjara, who moved eastwards at the dawn of history. The social organisation of the Pitjantjatjara is based on patrilineal descent groups, which today (as yesterday) have the responsibility for the spiritual and ritual ties to the land.

The people of the Western Desert are remarkable for their highly developed adaptability in an area so tough and barren. One of the first requirements of such an environment was that material possessions be minimal; a single weapon or tool was designed to serve a dozen different purposes.

The women's tools comprised a wooden dish, a grindstone and digging stick, all related to the collection and preparation of vegetable foods. The basic kit tools of the men — spear, spearthrower and stone knife — were all designed for hunting. Unlike many other nations, the people of the Western Desert did not specialise in a particular 'trade', so the tool and weapon makers were also the hunters.

The invasion of traditional lands by Europeans was followed by the familiar pattern of mass relocation of the clans into reserves. Only in the past ten years have negotiations with white authorities enabled the people to return to their traditional lands and revive their religious observances.

An Aborigine from the Coffin Bay area, throwing a barbed spear. Illustration by George French Angas, from South Australia Illustrated, *courtesy South Australian Museum.*

Yalata

One of the Pitjantjatjara centres today is at Yalata, near Ceduna. Yalata comprises a coastal strip 30 to 80 kilometres wide and has an an Aboriginal population of about 300 people. They use the Eyre Highway to visit the neighbouring towns of Nundroo, Penong and Ceduna.

During the early part of this century, the Yalata Pitjantjatjara migrated from the northern and western parts of the Great Victoria Desert, first to Ooldea and then to Yalata in 1952.

The word *Pitjantjatjara* means 'those having pitja' or 'those having to move'. There is a common language, spiritual beliefs, attachment to country, customs, rituals and way of life, they hold themselves as a nation distinct from all other peoples, black *and* white. The Yalata people frequently travel up to 80 kilometres north to collect wood for artefacts or hunting. It is hot, dry and sparse but kangaroos, wombats and bush turkeys help augment their diet.

The people of Yalata place themselves at the centre of the universe with other Pitjantjatjara forming their next circle, other original Australians a second circle, Europeans who are known to them and finally all strangers outside. Yalata includes a small European enclave of people who live in houses alongside their office building, stores, clinic, workshops, school, church and powerhouse. The Pitjantjatjara, true to their name of people on the move, live in their own camps, moving every ten days or so. They make a major move every six weeks.

The traditional dwellings are the *wiltja*, made from local timber, bushes and polythene sheets. Water is delivered in mobile tankers. But living conditions are poor: good drinking water is in short supply, the climate hot and dusty (in a terrain without shelter or shade) and the ground is stony and unworkable.

My blood brother Clem opted for a nomadic lifestyle and found himself living at Yalata for a number of years. His walkabout track was from Yalata to Adelaide, across to Lake Tyers, then north to Griffith via Tumut. A career in Jimmy Sharman's boxing troup and a lifetime of alcohol abuse has left him in a mental institute near Goulburn.

Koonalda Cave

Testimony to the original Australians' presence on the plain (for more than 20 000 years) is found in the great underground caverns of the Nullarbor. The greatest of all is Koonalda Cave, 85 kilometres from the state border and 20 kilometres from the southern ocean. Here, alongside a network of underground lakes, were Aboriginal workshops where weapons and tools were made.

The original miners have left an extensive array of engravings on the walls of the inner passages. Parts of the limestone are very softand the slightest touch marks the surface, while in other areas it takes considerable finger pressure to make an indentation.

These ancient finger markings are found alongside markings of more recent visitors, who have left names, initials and dates. The most visually impressive part of the underground art passage is a wall area of 20 metres long by 7 metres high, almost covered with deeply impressed grooves.

At the end of this passage is the 'squeeze', a crawl tunnel 5 metres long, 40 centimetres high and only 60 centimetres wide at the narrowest point which leads to a ledge overlooking a lake in a large cavern.

While this cave has been known to Europeans for a century, the 20 000-year-old engravings indicate there could have been a religious significance accorded the cave. It was a Dreamtime belief that the plain and its caves were guarded by *Gamba*, the giant serpent.

The mysterious markings of lines, lattices, concentric circles and grooves remain a subject of debate. Koonalda art has something in common with old galleries in Delamere and Ingaladdi in the Northern Territory, Carnarvon in Queensland, Seelands in New South Wales, Nackara Springs in South Australia, and even with some ancient European art. Indications are that this early religious art is the oldest of its kind in Australia, and perhaps in the world.

Hand stencils and engravings on the walls of Wombat Cave, 60 kilometres west of Koonalda Cave. Photo by Tom Sara.

Rain ceremony

The annual rain ceremony, held in August, superseded earlier ceremonies about the turn of the century. This ritual originated in the Kimberleys and gradually spread to other people, perhaps a testimony to its efficacy. The ceremony at Yalata was described in detail by Isobel White.

The ceremonial ground, about 2 kilometres from the Yalata Lutheran Mission, is called *Gundarbungani,* and the entire population, sometimes up to 400, moves to the site for this important event. The days leading up to the ceremony see the women busily building new shelters, the men filling water tanks, and everyone helping to prepare the ceremonial ground.

The ceremonies begin in the evening and go for three or four days, with one all-night session. The women bring brightly coloured blankets for the occasion and carry the young children on their backs, wrapped in the blankets. As darkness falls a man calls out and a party of menfolk use firesticks to mark the path to the ceremonial grounds where everyone is seated in position. In the centre are the dancers, and behind them are separate rows for the different ritual and social groups. The song leaders are in the front row, the men in the second row, then two rows of women and children. Young babies stay with their mothers but an older child is encouraged to sit with its grandmothers. There is singing and music, which is provided by boomerangs and shields specially designed for the ceremony. The women keep time, clapping their hands and thighs, sometimes beating small tin cans.

As soon as everyone is seated, the first song of the ceremony is sung, then the fires in the centre are built up so that their flames shoot high in the air as the two lines of dancers appear from behind a screen of bushes.

The kuri dance was conducted on moonlit nights. Gum leaves were attached just above the knees and ochre applied to the body, giving a 'hideous appearance' according to early accounts. Illustration by George French Angas, from South Australia Illustrated, *courtesy South Australian Museum.*

Painted and decorated, they are directed by the *bungari* and everyone carries a pole with white feathers. Kimberley shells decorate the chest and pubic area of the dancers, whose bodies are painted in white pipeclay and red and yellow ochre.

As the dance finishes and the fires begin to die down, there comes a command: 'Women under blankets'. At this point, the women and children lie face down while the sacred carved boards are revealed and ritual homage paid to the symbols of Pitjantjatjara law. After fifteen minutes they can sit up again. As the ceremony continues, the women and children are sent back to camp at certain points in the proceedings and then called back as it continues. Often, heavy rain falls during the ceremony.

Today's transcontinental railway follows an ancient Australian trade route and the sacred carved boards, which were transported over great distances by foot, are often carefully wrapped and sent as baggage. The boards range in length from a few centimetres to over 6 metres, man-made replicas of the boards that the ancestral beings carried with them. They are believed to be dangerous to the uninitiated and to women, who could turn blind or die by just by looking at them.

Yalata is the main centre of the southern Pitjantjatjara, who are steadily rebuilding a cultural heritage.

Early illustrations of dancers in the Adelaide area. Top left, a man decorated for the kuri dance, his body painted with ochre and his hair daubed with karku, *a red ochre from the Onkaparinga River. Top right, two men in the palti dance, a form of corroboree. Bottom row, two figures who led the kuri dance. The figure on the left is using a long spear with feathers attached at one end and human hair, bound together in tresses, strung along the length of the spear. The figure on the right has a* palyertatta, *made from two pieces of stick bound together with strings of possum fur. Illustration by George French Angas, from* South Australia Illustrated, *courtesy South Australian Museum.*

E The Central Lakes

ast of the Western Desert we enter the softer and richer world of the Central Lakes peoples. Their lands stretch from Spencer and St Vincent Gulfs to the Mount Lofty Ranges in the south-east and north to the Queensland border and include Lake Torrens and the Eyre Peninsula.

In this vast area, some of the twenty original nations enjoyed life by the seashore, others battled the elements in arid and semi-arid regions. These nations all practised circumcision and shared a body-scarring ceremony to mark final entry into adulthood.

One of their outstanding engineering achievements was the construction of tunnel-reservoirs in the Simpson Desert, dug as access to underground water in the same way as Europeans later dug artesian bores. In granite areas elsewhere, natural cisterns were covered with stone caps to prevent evaporation of the precious supplies.

Techniques for food conservation were equally sophisticated. Excess meat was sun-dried, while surplus vegetables were buried in skin bags. The modern Australian water bag — now seen all through the outback — was in use here for centuries, made from animal hide rather than hessian.

The Australians from this area made a kind of porridge from the *nardoo* plant (*Marsilea drummondii*), winnowing the spore cases then grinding them into a black paste, which was mixed with water.

Hunting was equally inventive and techniques included nets, snares and animal pits. The major hunting weapon was a large two-handed 'sword', similiar to a boomerang and used as a projectile.

Lake Eyre is central to the nations of the Central Lakes district. According to tradition, this lake was formed after the *wilyaru* ancestor captured and skinned a kangaroo, which had been brought down by hunting dogs. He pegged out the skin of the gigantic creature — it had to be gigantic because he himself was a giant — and the area of the skin formed the bed of the salt lake.

This region was one of the most important trading centres of the old continent, a trade which led to the import of the ground-edge axes from

The Coongie Lakes, near Innaminka. Photo by Grenville Turner.

The Diyari people of the Lake Eyre district considered dogs to be symbols of wealth and standing. Their traditional stories refer to many dogs which accompanied the ancestral heroes on their travels. These sculptures were made of resin extracted from Triodia *or spinifex, then painted with a combination of gypsum and ochre. Courtesy South Australian Museum.*

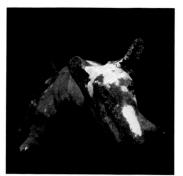

South Australian woman with child. Courtesy National Library of Australia.

Below A family out collecting food, Warburton Ranges. From the H. L. Greene Collection, courtesy South Australian Museum.
Below right 'Comet', a member of the Luritja people, in the north of South Australia. Courtesy South Australian Museum.

Queensland quarries and the much sought after *pituri* — from the narcotic plant *Duboisia hopwoodii* — which was chewed like betel nut.

In the Flinders Ranges was one of the most important red ochre quarries in Australia, prized for its high quality. It was the source of pigments which were traded all over the continent.

An early description of a trading expedition to the Flinders Ranges quarry tells of the appointment of the leader by the clan council who then selected the personnel for the journey. Everything was kept secret from the women, in case they objected to their husbands and sons undertaking such a long journey. On the day of departure the men rose early and set out singing a traditional travel song. When the women awoke, they called for the men to return and not venture into strange and hostile country.

The expedition paused, until the old men caught up, who were then left at a selected site to build a new camp for their return. Then the young men would set out on their mission to the ochre quarries, a distance of some 500 kilometres, covering around 30 kilometres a day, singing all the way. On arriving at the quarry, they would begin digging out the ochre, which was then mixed with water and made into loaves and dried.

Once the quarrying and baking were finished, each man took his burden (30 kg), which he carried on his head for the long journey home. At night they rested, occasionally spending a day trading some of their weapons or tools for other items needed at home. When within one day of their new camp they would take a break and then sneak up before dawn to surprise their families with shouts and yells.

A tumultuous welcome followed, a true hero's return, a feast was prepared and they danced till dawn. The following days were spent relating stories of the journey, the adventures, the trading and the success of the expedition.

In the Flinders Ranges there are also grindstone quarries, where flat-bedded sandstone was sought. These stones were dug out and carried hundreds of kilometres (on the head), in stacks of five or six.

These quarries were also marked by art galleries believed to be 10 000 years old. During the struggle for land which followed the arrival of the European settlers, the local population was decimated and great damage done to these sites, but today the government of South Australia has moved to conserve their heritage.

Toas

One of the nations of the Central Lakes region is the Diyari people who occupy the Lake Eyre basin, whose past glory is symbolised in their remarkable carvings, called *toas*. These finely crafted objects were both ornamental and practical: a carved length of timber, usually 15 to 45 centimetres long, sharpened at one end.

The Diyari lived in one of the world's toughest regions: a long summer with temperatures as high as 50 C, followed by short, freezing winters. The landscape is dominated by stony plains, sandhills, dry saltpans and lakes.

Every few decades Lake Eyre would fill with water, but mostly the Diyari would rely on the waterholes of Cooper Creek and the underground cisterns in the Simpson Desert. In their eyes, they lived in a vast garden, with familiar and sacred places, plentiful supplies of food and an invisible culture which only they could see.

The Lake Eyre people spoke a dozen languages, and many of them added German and English when a Lutheran mission was established at Lake Killalpaninna. The languages and boundaries of the people were established in the *Mura,* or Dreamtime. The saga tells how the heroes of the *Mura,* the *muramuras,* came out of the earth and talked to the people in their own language. But whenever they went into a new nation, they were always able to speak the local language. The tradition is continued today and Diyari people are able to speak many languages.

There was a great deal of intermarriage among the peoples of Lake Eyre and a child was expected to take on the language of his father, although this tradition was not always followed.

The resistance to European encroachment and the scourge of imported diseases all but wiped out the Diyari people. In fact the Diyari who guided the first Europeans to the area were shot, simply for 'knowing too much about them'.

Above *Some of the more than 400 toas from the Lake Eyre region collected and documented by Pastor Johann George Reuther. These sculptured wooden objects were used by the Diyari people as signposts. Each toa indicates a locality, according to topographical character and events which took place there in the Dreamtime. Courtesy South Australian Museum.*
Below *Pastor Reuther, whose painstaking work with the Diyari people and their toas has left such a rich heritage. Courtesy South Australian Museum.*

Much of the heritage of the people would have been lost without the work of Bavarian-born Johann George Reuther, who came to Diyari country as a Lutheran missionary and stayed to show the world their genius as sculptors. He collected some four hundred *toas* which were used by the Diyari as direction posts and location finders. A toa indicates a particular locality according to its topographical character: its shape is the place name reference, colours indicate the location of a camp and its geographic features.

Toas were used to tell a traveller whether the people were still in that settlement or had moved on, and to where they had gone. A *toa* would also be stuck in the ground in one of the unoccupied dwellings, to protect it from wind and weather, and provide helpful information to visiting friends.

Toas have a bewildering range of forms, including birds' feathers, lizard's feet, human hair, netting, tools and wood. Others show carved representations of boomerangs, wooden bowls, geographical features and parts of human and animal bodies. Other *toas* bear painted designs, without any carved, moulded or attached objects. The most complex *toas* have been found around Lake Gregory, and

1. This toa refers to a place near Lake Eyre where two ancestral heroes saw the souls of the dead climbing upwards. The lower white section of the toa indicates the earth, the recessed waist is the atmosphere and the upper white section the sky. The vertical lines represent the souls of the dead climbing upwards to the stars.
2. These toas represent an emu crouching (left) and an island with a hill.
3. A flat area, ringed by a sandhill (left) and a waterhole
4. A place where Kirlawilina implored his uncle to let him chase after the girls there.
5. A section of the Cooper Creek and (right) a place where an old tree was sprouting with a new branch.
6. A lake with many pelicans. Photos courtesy South Australian Museum.

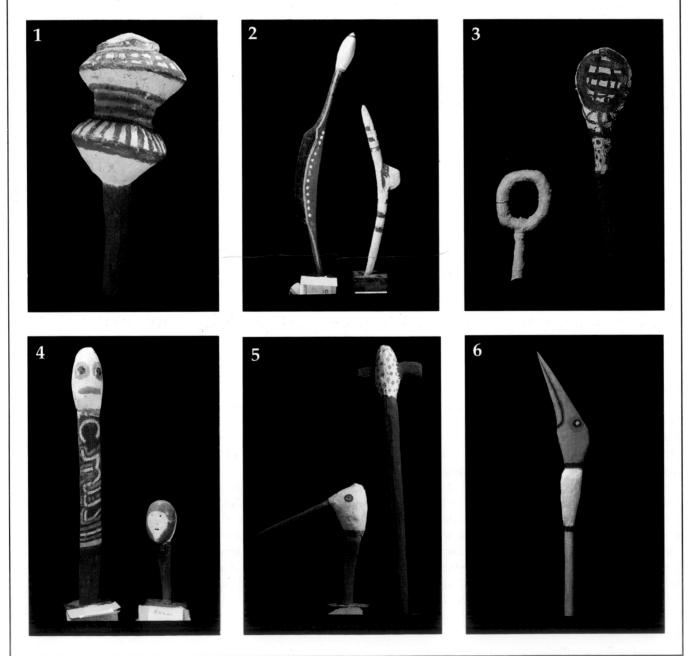

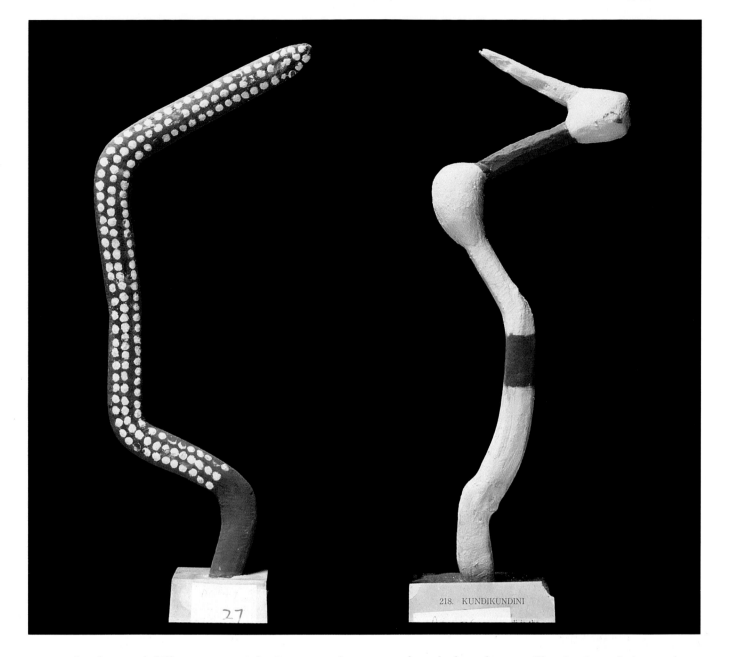

218. KUNDIKUNDINI

27

are made of several different materials. Desert mulga was preferred, though gypsum was also used. The most popular colours were red, black and yellow, the components of the modern Aboriginal national flag, which was designed by a South Australian.

Describing a Lake Gregory *toa*, Reuther said it told the story of the two female *muramuras* who found numerous eggs of the black swan. The *toa* depicts an island in Lake Gregory where the eggs were found, where the black swans lay their eggs to this day. It has two black knobs, which represent the two protruding peninsulas of the island. Black knobs at the ends of the *toa* represent the black stones found on the island; black dots are black swans and a white stripe indicates boggy ground.

One of the most widely known Dreamtime stories of South Australia explains how the people of Lake Eyre obtained fire, which had been stolen from them by predators from the Simpson Desert. One of their heroic ancestors turned into a black swan and flew south to replace the fire. Reaching Lake Gregory she discovered an old woman with a firestick. The swan struggled to get possesssion of the flame from the old woman and then flew home with it in her beak. The swan's red beak, which resulted from the extreme heat, has a special symbolism for the peoples of Lake Eyre.

In the great journey around the continent, a visit to Lake Gregory is an exciting voyage back into time and part of the saga of the *toas* which are found nowhere else in Australia.

These two toas refer to meandering sections of Cooper Creek. The white dots on the left-hand toa represent gum trees standing in the creek bed. The red banding on the right-hand toa refers to washed out waterholes in the creek bed. Courtesy South Australian Museum.

239

The Kaurna

The capital of South Australia today is Adelaide, named after the German wife of an English king in 1836, but for 40 000 years it was the home of the Kaurna people. A 'middle-sized' Australian nation, the Kaurna were a proud, dignified and gentle people, most of whom were dead within twenty years of the English invasion. Despite this, there are Kaurna people still living who can claim a link with the first inhabitants of Adelaide who called the earth 'mother'. Aspects of their life have been documented by Howard Groome.

The culture of the Kaurna people was derived from the Western Desert but, because they lived so near to the Murray River, their way of life was more like that of the peoples of south-east Australia. They enjoyed a high standard of living and a rich culture of song, dance, history, faith and law — passed from generation to generation over 40 000 years — since the beginning of the Ice Age. At that time, the weather was colder and wetter, the sea level lower and the Adelaide plains were swampy and bordered by sand dunes. Tall trees dominated the skyline and giant kangaroos, wallabies and diprotodon roamed the countryside.

But the climate deteriorated during the Ice Age, and the Kaurna had to survive significant changes to their habitat. By 18 000 years ago much of southern Australia, particularly Tasmania was covered with ice, the sea level was 100 metres below that of today, many rivers and creeks had dried up, the tall timber had disappeared and the game was gone. Great dust storms blew frequently from the interior.

The Kaurna were forced to refine their weapons and tools in order to survive in a period that must have seemed to be the end of the world. Not only did they survive, but over thousands of years these gallant people continued to develop and reinforce their culture.

With the end of the last Ice Age (some 15 000 years ago), the seas rose quickly and the Kaurna retreated inland, adjusting to a climate that was warmer and wetter than today. Once again they were forced to modify their lifestyle and technology, to adapt to a new range of foods and resources, or lack of them.

Wilpena Pound, in the Flinders Ranges, is a huge, saucer-shaped hollow in the sandstone bed of the ranges, forming a natural pound, or enclosure. Traditional stories tell of two huge Arkaroo snakes who descended on a ceremony there long ago and ate all but two of the people. These snakes then lay down and died, forming the walls of the pound. St Marys Peak, the pound's highest point, is said to be the head of the female snake. The coal deposits in the pound are said to be the remains of the ceremonial fire. Photo by Philip Green.

Custom and tradition marked every stage of Kaurna life. At birth a child was given one of nine names which indicated its place in the family. Girls were expected to marry and bear children. A girl could marry at ten years of age and at this time receive a new name, associated with her dreaming.

Boys began their long and tough initiation at about the same age. By the time a boy had reached the age of 25, he was expected to have learned all the basic lessons of lore and culture, but he still had another five stages to full adulthood. Only then was he permitted the ritual scars on back and chest, to eat the foreleg of the kangaroo and to marry.

This graduation ended a long period of instruction when boys were separated from their families to be trained by the elders and lawmakers. After circumcision, men were given two new names, one of which was used only in the company of men. The other name described the area of land they had been linked to since the Dreamtime. At this time they were also presented with an possum-skin bag containing sacred objects, and were allowed to wear a *yudna* (a fancy 'sporran') and carry a *wirri*, or carved club.

The Kaurna people occupied several different environments, from coastal mud flats and swampy areas to well-watered grassy plains, and their culture varied accordingly. They had close and friendly ties with their neighbours, the Ngarrundjeri, who lived on Yorke Peninsula, but were not so close to the Permangk people who lived in the the hills and valleys beyond the Mount Lofty Ranges, and the Ramindjeri, whose lands were in the Encounter Bay area. The nations traded peacefully, however.

The Xanthorrhoea, *or grass tree, with its long straight stems — perfect for spear shafts — is found all over the continent. Here, its distinctive profile is set against the Flinders Ranges. Photo by Bill Bachman.*

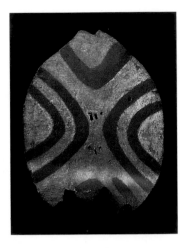

A Kaurna carved shield from the Adelaide plains. Photo by Reg Morrison, courtesy South Australian Museum.

The whole region was criss-crossed by traditional routes, the Dreaming tracks followed by the ancestral beings whose exploits were marked by trees or rocks or other features. Some of these sites are known today.

Among them is one called *Tarjndarna* in the city of Adelaide. Another is at Somerton Lake, which was once a great ceremonial and educational centre. Ngurlongga (near Winnaye) was a trading place; Willangga was a centre for skin tanning; Yankalilla, a meeting centre; Watbartok, a ceremonial place. On the border of Kaurna and Ramindjeri country is Tjilbruki's Cave, named after the heroic Ibis Man who made a famous journey from his homeland on Cape Jervis to recover the body of a dead nephew. Many freshwater springs along the south coast are said to mark his sorrowful return journey.

The most important of all the spirits and forces in their world was *Manintjeru*, who made all things on earth before retiring to heaven. Mount Lofty and Mount Bonython were *Urebilla*, or the two ears of the great giant who was killed in an Dreamtime battle. His body is represented by the hills running north to Nuriootpa.

The stars were also incorporated in their traditional stories: the Pleiades are said to young women digging for food. They are being courted by Orion, believed to be young men out hunting. Running through the the plain of the sky is the river known in English as the Milky Way, and in the black expanses between is a giant snake.

The appearance of a hawk at night was believed to be a sign that a child would die. Evil spirits brought sickness and death, while a big-bellied monster roamed at night and took people to a place of death. He was most active on dark nights, when the fires had gone out.

Right *The mission vegetable garden at Kopperamanna, near Killalpaninna, 1895. Courtesy South Australian Museum.*
Below *An Aboriginal camp near Killalpaninna, 1895. Courtesy South Australian Museum.*

Despite these fearful images, the Kaurna led a life of relative peace and plenty, with many different kinds of fish readily available in the waters and marshes. Crayfish, crabs and shellfish could be found on the beaches and large flocks of birds (especially ducks and geese) were common in the marshes. Fruit and vegetables were abundant. One feature of Kaurna hunting techniques was their use of the *munta* a large hunting net with a fine rectangular mesh made from fibre or tendons.

A *taara*, or netting belt, was worn tightly around the waist while the *gadlotti*, a girdle made from possum string, was also popular. Young and old wore the *manga*, a head band of possum fur. The *witkatja* (or carrying bag), slung casually over the shoulders by both men and women, completed the outfit. In winter, both men and women wore full-length kangaroo-skin cloaks. Kangaroo skins were used to make larger carrying bags for women as well as drums used during ceremonial occasions. The skins were also traded with northern nations for precious red ochre and flintstones, mined in the Flinders Ranges. Fighting spears were long (3–4 metres), a single shaft with a

Rock painting, Mulkat Gap, Flinders Ranges. Photo by Jutta Malnic.

Left *A collection of miniature paintings of Aboriginal artefacts by H. J. Hillier. From the Reuther Collection, courtesy South Australian Museum.*
Below *Rock carving, Chambers Gorge, Flinders Ranges. These circular motifs in association with lines are similar to designs found around Uluru. Photo by AusChromes.*

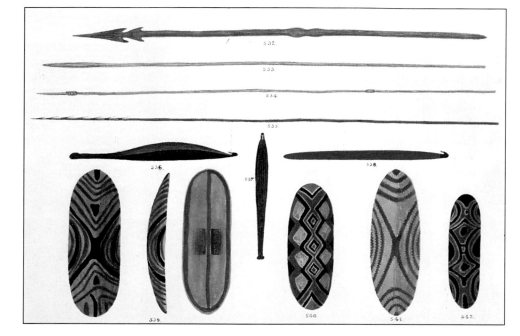

plain or quartz-tipped point. The hunting spears were shorter and made in two sections. Shields varied from a heavy model made from red gum to a lighter one made from bark. Both were painted and carved.

Night dancing was a popular pastime. Though some ceremonies were restricted to men only, most were song and dance nights in which everyone joined in.

An early form of football played with a ball of possum skin, was popular and there were plenty of opportunities for the brightly bedecked warriors to show their prowess in ceremonial jousts, where speed and dexterity were sorely tested. Injuries were common but rarely fatal.

The first invaders of Kaurna land were the sealers, who captured and enslaved the women, then introduced depravity and disease to the area.

The English settlers, who arrived in 1836, had clear instructions from London to negotiate for the purchase of land but they ignored them and simply took what they wanted. The pale skins of the Europeans were a great worry to the Kaurna, who thought they were dead relatives returning. They called them *pindi meyu,* or 'men from the grave'.

They quickly discovered the British intentions as they were driven off their lands at gunpoint and locked into reserves crowded with people of different families, clans and backgrounds and denied access to their own food. They subsisted on what they could beg or steal from their conquerors.

Within twenty years, most of the Kaurna people had been rounded up by troops and taken to Poonindie, near Port Lincoln, hundreds of kilometres from their homelands, where they were held as virtual prisoners. But the blood of the Kaurna has survived and the culture of these people is now being recognised, not only in Australia but right across the world.

As we leave Adelaide, heading east we experience the gigantic limestone landscape of the south-east, where high rainfall and rich vegetation merge with the more arid mallee country towards the border with Victoria.

Below *Arkaroo Rock, Flinders Ranges. Two snakes are crawling in parallel, a theme found throughout the Flinders Ranges, in art and legend. Photo by Jutta Malnic.*
Below right *A woven basket from the Coorong district. Photo by Reg Morrison, courtesy The Australian Museum.*

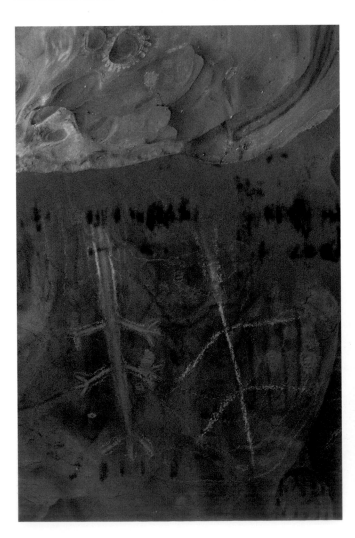

Above *Yourrambulla Cave, Flinders Ranges. These drawings feature the circular theme, with radiating dashes — probably in charcoal — forming the circle. Photo by Jutta Malnic.*

The palti dance, a popular form of corroboree. Illustration by George French Angas from South Australia Illustrated, *courtesy South Australian Museum.*

The Ngarrindjeri

The culture and later history of the Ngarrindjeri, whose country was the Lower Murray Lakes district, has been documented by the South Australian poet and academic Graham Jenkin. Their territory formed a great triangle of land from Cape Jervis north to Swanport and east to Kingston with the Southern Ocean as their south-western boundary. The Ngarrindjeri language was distinctive, with not one word in common with their Adelaide neighbours, the Kaurna.

The Ngarrindjeri nation was divided into eighteen *lakalinyeri* (groups), each of which had its own government or *tendi,* which was both parliament and high court. Men were democratically elected to sit on the *tendi,* and the 'president, or *rupulle,* was in turn elected by that body'. Matters concerning all the Ngarrindjeri were dealt with by a 'combined' *tendi.*

The Ngarrindjeri established semi-permanent villages, with dwellings large enough to house several families, built of wood, clay and grass. These dwellings were often bigger (and better) than those built by the English invaders in the 1840s. Often forty people lived in one small village, occupying three such houses.

They wore beautiful cloaks made from skins or woven seaweed, and they were well know for their baskets, nets and mats. Ngarrindjeri fish nets were large and intricate. Bark canoes and rafts were essential to their economy.

At Lake Alexandrina — south of the highway and just east of Victor Harbor — women made the rafts of layers of reeds, which were used when diving for mussels. They gathered the mussels in nets tied around their necks and cooked them on the raft, on a hearth of wet sand and water reed.

The living heart of the Ngarrindjeri country was the Murray River, one of the great trade routes of ancient Australia, which serviced a brisk and continuous trade with the nations of western Victoria, who brought polished ground-edge axes to trade. These axes were made from volcanic diorite, quarried at Mount William (and other quarries in western and central Victoria). There was vigorous trade not only with surrounding nations but between the

The fertile lower Murray River. Photo by Colin Totterdell.
Opposite *An assembly of artefacts, tools and weapons. Illustration by George French Angas, from* South Australia Illustrated, *courtesy South Australian Museum.*
Below *A man from the Milmendra clan, in the Encounter Bay area, wearing a woven seaweed cloak. Illustration by George French Angas, from* South Australia Illustrated, *courtesy South Australian Museum.*

The English missionary, George Taplin. Courtesy South Australian Museum.

The Coorong is a narrow inland waterway at the mouth of the Murray River, which once supported large Aboriginal populations. Now this area is a national park and wildlife reserve. Photo by Philip Green.

clans, as each group concentrated on producing items from its own natural resources.

Cloaks, basketware and nets formed basic items of commerce. A major import was the *wunde*, a long solid hardwood spear from the Upper Murray region. They were made from the myall tree, a species not available in their own lands. Trade was tightly controlled to prevent any unfairness. When still a child, one person from a group was chosen to be a trader when he grew up, but was forbidden to speak to his opposite number in another group, so that all business had to be conducted through a third person.

Law, justice and administration were based on religious principles, and were eminently logical and practical. The English missionary, George Taplin, felt they were 'the most law-abiding people' he had ever encountered. In fact, he believed their lives were *too* highly regulated by religion.

The power of life and death lay with the senior men, whose command of supernatural punishment ensured that the younger (and physically stronger) generation never attempted to overthrow the government by force.

Funeral ceremonies, in which the dead were cremated on raised platforms in elaborate rites, were designed to acknowledge the immortality of the soul and the ascendancy of the spirit over the physical being. The skin of the deceased was removed before burial, so the corpse was pink and called *grinkari*, or 'corpse with skin removed'. Grinkari was the name given to Europeans because of their colour.

Although the rites involved with manhood did not include circumcision, scarring or celibacy, the young Ngarrindjeri men went through a tough training period. Women were economically and culturally independent, but they had to marry outside their own group, which meant leaving family and childhood friends. This averted inbreeding and built continuing and renewable links between the clans.

Their love of music captivated early Europeans. In later years, Ngarrindjeri adult and children's choirs performed in Adelaide and other parts of South Australia. The Ngarrindjeri enjoyed sport, including a kind of football, and all the sporting aspects of hunting. Proud of their language, they made a point of speaking it accurately, despite the complexity of its structure, the

number of inflections and the precision demanded. Etiquette was observed in every aspect of life in this quite extraordinary society.

The key to the spiritual life of the people was *Ngurunderi*, the great creator of the Murray River and all the fish. The Dreamtime describes how, with his sons, he followed a massive Murray cod down the Darling and Murray River systems. The huge fish created billabongs and swamps with its tail as it swept the water aside. Long Island, near Murray Bridge, is said to be the bark canoe used on this epic voyage. Arriving at Wellington, Ngurunderi speared the giant cod which he proceeded to cut into small portions. As he threw the small pieces into the river they became the many different species of fish found in lakes and streams today.

Ngurunderi came across his two wives cooking silver bream, a fish forbidden to women. They made a raft to escape his wrath but he pursued them down the Coorong (to Kingston) and back to Cape Jervis, creating the natural features of the landscape. As he caught up with the two errant women, who were crossing to Kangaroo Island, he caused the seas to rise. The women were drowned in the flood and became rocky islands known as The Pages. Ngurunderi crossed to Kangaroo Island, cleansed himself of his old skin of life and ascended into heaven. The cleansing was perpetuated in the funeral rites with the removal of the outer skin.

The beginning of the end for this great nation came when their most westerly clans confronted the first invaders of their region, the sealers and whalers. One of the tales of their terrible slave raids recounts the escape of three women one of whom attempted to swim from Kangaroo Island to the mainland with her baby on her back. They were found by her own people on the beach, she dead from exhaustion, the baby from hunger and thirst.

The Ngarrindjeri quickly adapted to European technology. They were acknowledged as fine horsemen, sailors and shearers, and could pick up a gun and learn to use it in five minutes. But the more proficient they became, the more of a threat they presented to the invaders. Despite efforts in far-away London to provide for land rights, the dispossession process continued unabated. Driven from their food and water, death was inevitable and counter attacks provoked military intervention. Even poisoned damper was employed to wipe them out. Women were constantly captured and enslaved.

Yet among the Europeans were some who sought justice for the Ngarrindjeri, such as George Taplin, who spent his life among the Ngarrindjeri attempting to give them a new strength to cope with European values. He found white compatriots his biggest enemies: they bribed young men away from school to work for them, and took and raped women and girls whenever

Three portraits of people from the Murray River and Coorong districts. Left, Nginnimniey, a Murray River boy. Centre, Pellampellamwallah, a woman from the Milmendura clan on the Coorong, equipped for travel. She carries her net, made of woven bullrush fibres across her back with her rush basket, digging stick and fire in her hands. Right, Nyaldyalley, a girl of the lower Murray clan, near Lake Alexandria, in a small kangaroo skin cloak. Illustrations by George French Angas from South Australia Illustrated, *courtesy South Australian Museum.*

they pleased. Taplin learned the language of the people, became their teacher and champion and created a new capital at Raukkan, known to Europeans as Point McLeay, with a church, school houses and farmland.

It could be said that George Taplin almost single-handedly prevented the extinction of the Ngarrindjeri, who shrank in numbers from 3000 when the invasion began to around 600 by the time he was able to arrest the decline. It is due to his work that so many of the traditions of the people have been recorded. He died, aged 47 in 1879, at Raukkan, the village capital which he had founded with love and compassion.

The village on the southern shore of Lake Alexandrina was to flourish for many years. As the population grew, many dispersed. But a jetty was built and steamers called regularly, and Raukkan even played host to the first English prince, Alfred, ever to come to Australia.

In 1916 the South Australian government took control and, within half a century, the once idyllic lakeside village had been reduced to a rural slum. Not content with destroying what had been created, they set about destroying the very identity of the people, changing their names and dispersing them among white communities. It was not until 1974 that Raukkan was handed back to the Ngarrindjeri people, who now have the challenge of rebuilding their great nation from near extinction.

Two types of shelter employed in the Coorong district. Illustration by George French Angas, from South Australia Illustrated, *courtesy South Australian Museum.*

The inventive genius of the Ngarrindjeri people is best illustrated in the story of David Unaipon. Born in 1873 he lived until 1967, the year an Australian Government first gave Aboriginal Australians the right to vote.

During his life he witnessed the attempted destruction of his people, but chose to challenge the Europeans on their own ground. Born at Raukkan, he went to school there and learned music, becoming the church organist. Then he embarked on an intensive reading program of his own, deciding on the twin challenges of science and engineering.

He was commited to becoming an inventor and one of his first designs was an improved sheep-shearing machine. Between 1909 and 1944 he applied for nineteen separate patents for his inventions, but failed to attract financial backing for their development. Among his works were designs for perpetual motion machines, lasers and an improved helicopter. He won nationwide respect as a scientist, inventor, lecturer, writer, musician and preacher, and was described in 1931 as astonishing the professors of Sydney and Melbourne universities by the breadth of his intelligence and his capacity for absorbing knowledge. He was buried where he was born, at Raukkan.

As we leave the lands of the Ngarrindjeri people and South Australia we can salute today's generation seeking to rebuild their capital and their ancient heritage and wish them well.

David Unaipon. From an oil painting by Leslie Wilkie, courtesy South Australian Museum.

Two boys from the lower Murray. Illustration by George French Angas, from South Australia Illustrated, *courtesy South Australian Museum.*

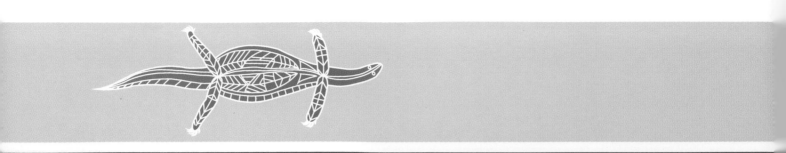

Uluru. Photo by AusChromes.

North to the centre

HE journey north from Port Augusta to Alice Springs and the red centre is one of my favourite anywhere in Australia. A real challenge, and a chance to appreciate the immensity of this, the world's largest island. At the end of our drive lies Uluru, Australia's best-known landmark.

The drive north from Port Augusta takes us through country where galahs become a regular sight. Photo by Jim Frazier/Mantis Wildlife.

Port Augusta is a major catchment area for peoples of all kinds and the Davonport reserve, just out of town, was home to my friend Pat Walsh for many years. To the east are the Flinders Ranges, home of my friend, Faith Thomas, who is the only Aboriginal woman to play cricket for Australia.

The ideal trip north from Port Augusta starts at dawn, with a southerly tailwind. The first 200 kilometres is flat and desolate, with a real chance to come to terms with the wide open spaces. Coober Pedy provides a multicultural resting point, with blacks, opal miners of many origins and travellers. The feature film, *Ground Zero*, in which I played the part of Charlie, a man blinded by the effects of the atomic testing at Maralinga, was filmed in Coober Pedy. The dazzling white landscapes in this region are unlike anything else in Australia.

North of Coober Pedy you can see signs at the side of the road indicating a 'prohibited area'. This land, which takes several hours to drive through, remains contaminated today, more than 25 years after the blasts. The local kangaroo population is depleted every night on this highway.

The Stuart Ranges at Coober Pedy yield over half the world's production of opal. Photo by Philip Green.

As you push further north, the red sand dunes begin to appear more frequently, and desert vegetation begins to dominate. In the spring this country becomes a flower garden, with a spectacular array of wildflowers, sheltered in places by native pines.

One's concentration is often disturbed by galahs in their crazy flight. Hawks, surprised by the appearance of your car, are forced off the carcasses left by the previous night's carnage, mainly caused by the massive road trains which barrel up and down this highway. Dingoes skulk warily in the scrub and the eagles soar aloft, slowly circling and watching. The boredom of driving this endlessly flat road can be broken by finding yourself parallel to a

The MacDonnell Ranges resemble a jagged spine — some 400 kilometres long — through the heart of the continent. Photo by AusChromes.

The spring near the Todd River from which Alice Springs gained its name. Photo by Philip Green.

Recent times have seen a rebirth of traditional values and skills. Here, school children at Mount Allen, an artists' community near Alice Springs, are being taught the age-old methods for grinding seeds. Photo by Claude Coirault.

Usually found in nests at the base of mulga trees in the arid areas of central Australia, honey ants are a real delicacy in an area with few sweet foods. Worker ants collect nectar from leaves of the acacia bush, which is transferred to storage ants, who remain underground. These storage ants can be as big as small grapes and are an important food source. Photo by Derek Roff.

train on the Adelaide–Alice Springs railway line, which runs adjacent to the highway for quite a stretch. The length of some of these trains is almost unbelievable.

Every now and then, dramatic ridges change into red hills, which can be seen from many kilometres away and can have a mesmerising effect.

The journey to Alice Springs through the very heart of the continent offers the chance to camp out at night under a canopy of stars stretching to the horizon for 360 degrees — truly a never-to-be-forgotten experience.

Crossing the South Australia–Northern Territory border at Kulgera always creates a sense of achievement and an air of anticipation.

Like a jagged spine, the MacDonnell Ranges — in a series of parallel ridges — cut a rugged spur some 400 kilometres long through the very heart of the Australian continent. Although it seldom rises more than 500 metres above the surrounding desert plain, the range presents a powerful visual barrier in the landscape.

Where rivers and streams once flowed through the valleys of these ranges, water is now confined to springs and pools. These lands were once the traditional territory of the Aranda people, who used the water resources of the region sparingly, sustaining themselves and their fragile environment since the *Altjira,* the Dreamtime.

The Aranda adapted quite superbly to the harsh environment of the region, preserving water supplies, nurturing game and vegetables and celebrating their survival in regular ceremonial gatherings. These were signalled throughout the lands with smoke signals and personal messengers who would be despatched to all areas to advise neighbouring clans of the time and place for the gathering. When the day approached, people would begin moving into the selected area, establishing camp for the festive and ritual ceremonies. One of the popular sports at these gatherings was throwing the *kultjera* clubs. The kultjera is around 70 centimetres long, with a carefully shaped head and handle (sanded and polished with sand) and was thrown in a contest which involved considerable rivalry and barracking. Everyone watched and cheered though only the men took part.

Firestick farming was the key to land management, and they regularly fired the scrub. Each burn was carefully controlled and restricted to specific areas, which was partly to prevent major fires, but also as a means of hunting game. It was also employed to build barriers around important trees — such as the quondong (*Santalum acuminatum*) with its plentiful fruit — or sacred sites, as a part of the Aranda's commitment to maintain these sites for the *Altjira* beings. Areas were also fired to create new shoots and feed for kangaroos and wallabies, or to encourage the growth of a particular plant.

The Aranda hunted a range of game which included wallabies and other small marsupials, rock python, carpet snakes, goannas and lizards. They had access to some 140 different species of plant food, of which 75 were used for their seeds. They used diferent timbers and stones, as well as bone, fur, hides, barks, sinews, feathers, grasses and spinifex resin to make a variety of implements, including three types of non-returning boomerang, soft and

Above *Collecting wild food within sight of Katatjuta, still officially known as the Olgas. Photo by Derek Roff.*
Below left *Skinks can be food or fun. Photo by Claude Coirault.*
Below *Photographer Claude Coirault was travelling with a group of people from Mount Allen, when a pair of bustards were spotted, killed and eaten by the side of the road.*
Bottom *Bush yams at Mount Allen, still an important food. Photo by Claude Coirault.*

257

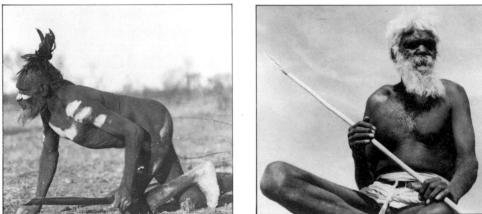

Above *A hunting party in central Australia. Photo by AIS, courtesy National Library of Australia.*
Far right *An elder from the Alice Springs district. Photo by J. Tanner, courtesy National Library of Australia.*
Right *Hunting in central Australia. Courtesy National Museum of Australia.*

hardwood dishes, digging sticks, axes, spearthrowers and knives. Spears were made with and without barbs, for different applications: heavy jabbing spears, for example, were used in ritual duels to resolve disputes.

Development of the region came with the need for a telegraph link between Darwin and Adelaide in the 1870s. A telegraph station had to be established in the centre of the continent and the site selected near a spring in a dry creek bed near the Todd River. The spring was named after Alice, the wife of the South Australian postmaster-general, Charles Todd, after whom the river had been named.

In the burst of exploration which followed the establishment of Stuart (as the town of Alice Springs was known until 1933), the MacDonnell Ranges were forced to give up their water and food resources to the pastoralists and the herds of cattle that came with them. Later these leases were revoked and the land became national park, a major part of Australia's tourist map and original history.

This area of Australia — of which Alice Springs represents the business centre and Uluru the spiritual centre — is a landscape in which each hill, river, rock and animal plays a part in the Dreamtime legends which hold everything together. The hero Yipperinya exists today in the form a red, rocky mountain, which is cut by the Stuart Highway south of Alice Springs at Heavitree Gap. This rugged range of mountains is rich in tradition and

Above, left and **right**
Painting a wooden bowl and inscribing simple patterns in rocks. Photos taken on C. P. Mountford's expedition to central Australia during the 1930s on behalf of Oxford University. Courtesy National Library of Australia.
Left *Central Australian, with spear and* woomera. *Reproduced from* Paradis Primitif, *by Jacques Villeminot, courtesy National Library of Australia.*

Some 478 kilometres south-west of Alice Springs, Uluru is a living record of many hundreds of Dreamtime events, permanently retained within its huge body. Each crack, mark, stain and indentation has an explanation in the Dreaming. The 100 metre high split in the face of Uluru (see opposite page) is ngaltawaddi, the sacred digging stick. Photos by Claude Coirault (above, below and opposite), and Barry Skipsey (right), courtesy Northern Territory Tourist Commission.

Hunting in central Australia. Courtesy National Museum of Australia.

important Aboriginal sites have been documented from Standley Chasm in the west to Coorooboree Rock in the east. Through the folds and creases of these mountains are ancient river courses. South of Alice, the Finke River is said to be one of the oldest rivers to be found anywhere in the world. Palm Valley, on the Finke River east of Alice, gives a glimpse of the combined effect of wind and floodwaters on the sandstone cliffs which enclose this unique envirnoment, where the *Livistona mariae* palms grow. Although related to other palm species found in eastern Australian, the palms which have given Palm Valley its name are found nowhere else in the world. It is likely that these are the last of what was once a common species through central Australia. The valley is now protected within the bounds of the 46 000 hectare Finke Gorge National Park.

Kings Canyon, west of the Finke River, is a breathtaking landform created by powerful rivers at a time of much greater rainfall. Although surrounding areas have numerous examples of cave art, the canyon itself has none, being held as a place of great significance since the Dreamtime. An area of some 76 000 hectares was proclaimed as the Kings Canyon National Park in 1984.

Alice Springs township provides a full spectrum of Aboriginal lifestyle, from brick veneer homes in town to camp sites along the Todd River. Church and Aboriginal hostels also cater for Aborigines who visit Alice from a radius

Wooden food bowls were also used as cradles. Courtesy National Museum of Australia.

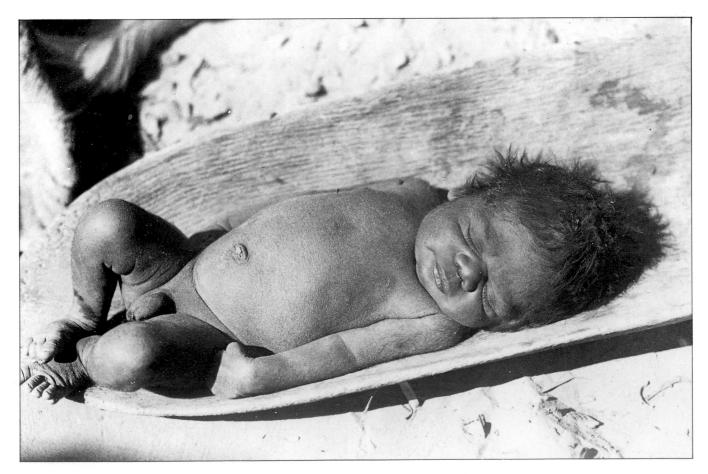

A warrior. Courtesy National Museum of Australia.

Below *Widows often daubed their hair with clay as a sign of mourning. Courtesy National Museum of Australia.*
Below left *Painting a Hunting shield in central Australia. Courtesy National Museum of Australia.*

*Uluru in the rain is a spectacu-
lar sight as the water pours off its
surface in a series of spouts and
temporary waterfalls. This runoff
during rains results in pools
and abundant plant growth
around the base. Photo by Derek
Roff.*

*Katatjuta, still officially known
as The Olgas, means 'many
heads' and is a place of great
significance. Every boulder, cave,
shrub and indentation represents
a part of the Dreaming. The big
domes on the western side of
Katatjuta are said to be the
bodies of giant cannibals who
came to eat the people long ago.
Another of the domes, on the
southern side, is explained in a
story about a kangaroo man who
died in his sister's arms after
being attacked by dingoes. Other
stories tell of Wanabi, a huge
snake who lives in a cave in
Mount Olga. According to the
story, when tribal law is broken,
Wanabi vents his anger with
great gusts of wind up the
valleys. When he is satisfied he
becomes a rainbow. Photo by
AusChromes.*

of over 700 kilometres. The area now attracts some 500 000 tourists a year
and supports a thriving art industry. Albert Namatjira was the first Aboriginal artist to enjoy success, his European-style water colour images of the
outback finding their way into houses and art galleries throughout the
country during the 1950s and 1960s. Today the local artists paint in their
traditional styles as well as carving snakes, emus, kangaroos and echidnas
out of mulga wood.

Since first sighted by Europeans in 1873 (by Willian Gosse), Uluru has
evoked an aura of mystery and attracted millions to admire its immense
form and attempt the walk to its peak, 384 metres above ground. Uluru was
once thought to be the world's largest monolith, but sčientific research has
confirmed it to be the tip of buried mountain range. Uluru now represents
the new strength of Aboriginal people. Handed back to its traditional owners,
the Pitjantjantjara, in 1985 as a freehold title, Uluru is an example of traditional people again taking responsibility for the symbols left to them since
the Dreamtime. The region has been leased back by National Parks Management for a period of 99 years.

During the 1950s concern was rising over vandalism to Ayers Rock (as
Uluru was then known) and the Northern Territory government appointed
W. E. (Bill) Harney as the rock's curator and 'keeper' in 1958. Fascinated by
the Aboriginal history of the rock (and Katatjuta, or the Olgas further to the
west), Bill Harney spent three years, until his retirement and death in 1961,

Above left *Palm Valley, home to the* Livistona mariae *palms, which grow nowhere else in the world. Photo by Robbi Newman.*
Above *Rock art at Maggie Springs, Uluru. Photo by Philip Green.*
Left *One of Kintore's resident artists, Johnny Scobie and family, in front of a recent work. Photo by Claude Coirault.*

Two central Australians.
Courtesy Macleay Museum.

documenting the stories of the area, as told to him by two local people, Kudekudeka and Imalung.

In their Dreaming the south side of the rock represents the saga of their struggle against the *Leru,* the poisonous snake people from the west, and the *Loongardi* (sleeping lizard) people. Pitting in the rock is said to show where spears struck, boulders are the bodies of attackers who were repelled by the Uluru people. On Uluru's north side, different legends explain each of the forms, twists, holes and cracks.

At the base of Uluru, among rich plant growth supported by the abundant run-off rainfall, are many sites of Aboriginal significance, some exclusively for men, some for women. To Aboriginal people, Uluru is a cathedral and though the outside form is visible, the underlying spiritual concepts are not a matter of public record.

To its owners, this symbol of Australia is a living reminder of the Dreamtime struggles. Uluru was also an important source of food and water. The stories which relate to every aspect of its extraordinary form carry clear moral codes: good prevailing over evil, the spiritual over the physical, the importance of hospitality and the maintenance of the Law. Uluru still serves as a gathering point for ceremonial occasions which attract Pitjantjantjara people from a radius of 300 kilometres.

Far right *Making fire. Photo by Crooks, courtesy Macleay Museum.*
Right *Aranda people near Alice Springs, 1934. From the Ellison Collection, National Library of Australia.*
Below *Ceremonial decoration. Courtesy Macleay Museum.*

A classic portrait of the desert Aborigine. Reproduced from Paradis Primitif, *by Jacques Villeminot. Courtesy National Library of Australia.*

Below left *Skinning a snake. Courtesy Macleay Museum.*
Below *The goanna has always been a food source central to traditional lifestyles. Courtesy National Library of Australia.*

267

The author's favourite section of
Australian coast. Photo by
Carmen Ky.

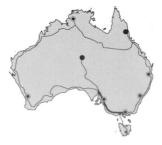

The Murray to Melbourne

THE sophistication of the Ngarrindjeri prepares us for their neighbours, whose traditional lands centred on the south-east corner of the continent, now the state of Victoria. As we travel east the breathtaking splendour of Victoria's south-west coast opens before us.

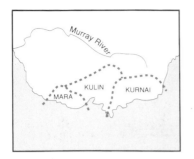

The area of Victoria had three distinct language groups, and some 37 major clans or groups.

Weaving baskets at Coranderrk. Courtesy Museum of Victoria.

These nations were able to sustain large and numerous clans, particularly along the volcanic coastal plains of south-west Victoria. Lying between the Grampians and the coast, these fertile plains enabled intensive hunting and gathering, and abundant coastal resources were readily accessible. The last volcanic activity in this area is recent enough to have been recorded in local tradition.

The modern mythology of Victoria (outside the state) would have it that it's always raining in Melbourne. And if it's not, just hang a round a minute. In traditional times the high rainfall — which ranges from 1400 millimetres in the humid Otway Ranges to around 500 on the driest parts of the plains — resulted in a bountiful lifestyle for many nations who found ample food resources in the swamps along the south-western coastline. These swamps were a result of the volcanic overflows, which had interrupted the natural flow of the rivers as they made their way to the coast. Here were found all the game and fish needed.

Language is the most effective way of grouping the complicated interlocked societies of modern Victoria. The area includes three basic languages or dialects — *Mara* (in the south-west), *Kulin* (in central Victoria), and *Kurnai* (from the Melbourne area, up the coast to the New South Wales border). Each of these groups had at least five clan dialects within it.

As in so many other areas, the Europeans found it hard to deal with the lack of obvious political authority within the groups. These were bound together by complex kinships and marriage rituals (a man often had more than one wife), and by trading relationships which shared resources between all the people. These bonds were structured through carefully conceived trading techniques, all designed to maintain continuity and prosperity in a sacred world, full of rich religion and strict discipline.

Our journey down the Princes Highway, south from Ngarrindjeri country — which extends well into modern Victoria — brings us first to the lands of the Mara (around Warrnambool), whose inventive culture can still be seen in the ruins of their stone villages. Contrary to the popular viewpoint (that *all* Aborigines were nomadic) the Mara had extensive villages. In one paddock

alone, at Condah Swamp, there were 146 separate houses and it has been estimated that a population of approximately 700 lived in this one village.

The houses were U-shaped or semi-circular with domed roofs, and were made of wood and clay built on stone foundations. Paths linked the dwellings in the village in arrangements established over many generations. These dwellings were not occupied all the year round but formed bases for the Mara as they conducted ceremonial gatherings, trade or harvest festivals.

The largest gatherings — always attended by thousands of people — were in autumn, when the eels and migratory fish were running, and in spring, when birds' eggs were plentiful. In autumn and winter whales could be taken. Great public hunts were held across the open plains with kangaroos, emus and other game as prey.

Noorat, a hill near Terang, was a favoured meeting place. Clans from near modern Geelong came to trade their stone (for implement making) and their much-prized gum (made from wattle) which had the reputation of being the toughest adhesive available. Around Noorat, the grassy plains and savannah woodlands meant that forest kangaroos were plentiful and their skins were considered the most superior for cloak making. So a regular pattern of resource-sharing was established .

These eastern Mara peoples had managed and traded their stone for as long as anyone could remember. After all, winters were cold and kangaroos on the plains were more plentiful and had better skins.

Other trade items were greenstone, from Spring Creek (near Goodwood), which was used for axes; sandstone from a salty creek near Lake Boloke, used for scraping and polishing wooden implements; saplings from the mallee scrub in the Wimmera, for spears; and wood and grass-tree stalks from Cape Otway for other types of spears. Marine shells and freshwater mussel shells were also traded, mainly by the Watharung from the Hopkins River area.

An important trade item was the red ochre, brought from the Cape Otway region. It was used mainly to decorate the body for major ceremonial performances, being mixed with water and painted on with a brush made from the banksia flower. Every clan had its speciality, and because of these clear differences they maintained healthy trading relationships.

The *murnong,* a small parsnip-like yam much prized for its sweetness, was a favourite vegetable. Long lines of women once stretched as far as the eye could see digging up the yams with specially made poles, before carrying their harvest back home in sturdy baskets.

In the villages, cooking was a collective exercise. Great stacks of *murnong* (in special reed baskets) would be ready to cook, for all the families which had contributed. *Murnong* was plentiful throughout the year, although other plants were used, including the roots of bracken which were pounded to extract the starch, made into flour and used to bake bread.

The rich countryside knew no real scarcity. Land and resource management helped to conserve the environment and enhance the production of plants earmarked for food. The harvesting methods for *murnong* also served to plough up the soil and encourage new growth. Firestick farming eliminated weed growth and encouraged the food staples.

A feature of Victorian traditional life was the social life which came with the good relationships and small distances between clans and nations. As well as the regular trading meetings, joint ceremonial occasions marked religious and festive events.

This co-operation also extended to hunting. Spokesmen for several neighbouring nations would meet to determine the location and time. Messages would be sent round to all the villages and camps and on the appointed day each nation's hunters would spread out in a long line as they united with other clans and form a circle up to 30 kilometres in diameter.

All the game would be driven to a central point, traditionally at Muston's Creek, about 5 kilometres from the junction of the River Hopkins. Then women, children and old people — more than a thousand people were often involved — joined in to work the game in to the centre so that the warriors could dispatch it with spear and club.

Woman with child. Courtesy Museum of Victoria.

The eel industry

In this area of Australia there was once a vigorous eel industry which operated along similar lines to modern eel industries in Europe and Asia. The most celebrated eeling ground was in the western districts, at Lake Bolac. All nations gathered here, sometimes in great numbers, to catch the eels and stage traditional festivals.

They used permanent stone and wood houses in a village nearby, but also camped in less permanent locations around the district, taking every opportunity to trade. At such times, the messengers ranged far and wide. All the main swamps were crowded with people, drawn from all points of the compass. All was done in accordance with tradition and each nation would be allotted a particular section of the river bank.

In the Lake Bolac area, no one would catch eels without permission from the owners, usually granted without question. If any attempt was made to trespass or poach, armed warriors would repel the intruders, and if the dispute was pressed it would be resolved in a ritual fight.

When the river was in flood, seemingly inexhaustible supplies of small eels were caught at night by the light of torches. In the Mount William region, a more sophisticated method was developed. At the foot of the Grampian Range, about 100 kilometres inland, there once existed a vast drainage system, designed and constructed just to catch eels.

At the fringes of the marshland, channels and banks were constructed and linked to a further network of channels covering an area of about 7 hectares. Given that it was all constructed with digging levers — sticks sharpened at one end to throw up clods of soil — then moved by hand to form the channel embankments, the achievement of such complex drainage works is remarkable.

So sophisticated was this system that early European visitors could not understand how they worked, although they noticed eel pots strategically placed at small apertures in the channels. All the water from the mountain streams was channelled into the system on the way to the marsh so that no fish could escape the system.

In the Toolondo district (at the foot of the Great Dividing Range) in the western districts, a drainage project involved 3.75 kilometres of channels, connecting the Budgeongutte and Clear Swamps. Three main channels, 2.5 metres wide and a metre deep, took runoff from the elevated swampy ground down to both swamps.

These conservation projects were designed to harvest eels, but they also provided a means of managing the swamplands, coping with excess water during the floods and retaining water in dry times. By providing a stable water supply they helped to regulate the size of the eel population.

These major public works involved a great deal of co-operation between the nations of the region. Hundreds of workers were needed for the ditch digging and embankment construction, but the incentive was an assured food supply. In the Mount William project, three nations came together for the construction and management: the Tjapwurong, Jaadwa and Watharung.

The society, technology and economy of the Mara peoples and their neighbours were far more ingenious than was acknowledged by the white invaders, despite the work of some who sought to understand those whom they had dispossessed.

As the wars of resistance prevailed, these great engineering achievements fell into disrepair.

Just north of the Princes Highway, Lake Condah (also known as Condah Swamp) is a fascinating area to visit, with some of the most sophisticated development of traditional Australia. The Lake Condah drainage system constructed by the nations of the region has been mapped and studied in detail by Victorian researchers. These canals were up to a metre in depth and 300 metres in length. Traps were built across the stone races and canals. Nets or eel pots were set in apertures in the stone walls, constructed from a local black volcanic rock. The eel pots were made from bark or rushes, with a willow hoop at the mouth, and the shape enabled the men standing behind the weirs to grab the eels as they emerged through the narrow end of the pot. They were killed with a single blow to the back of the head and threaded onto poles.

The traps operated to take advantage of both rising and falling water levels, and about twenty men would be involved in their operation on any working day. Whole villages were built both for the project workers and their families, and also for the fishermen, hunters and food-harvesting women.

The Lake Condah region was a centre for the Mara and was often the focal point for thousands of people, when smoked eel was the staple food at the regular festivals.

Opposite, top *Eeling was a sophisticated art and a variety of methods were used to catch them. Major engineering works were built to maximise the catch, but woven reed traps were widely employed. This example is from the Murray River, photo by Reg Morrison, courtesy Museum of Victoria.*
Opposite, below *Victorian swampland, a perfect habitat for the eels. Photo by AusChromes.*

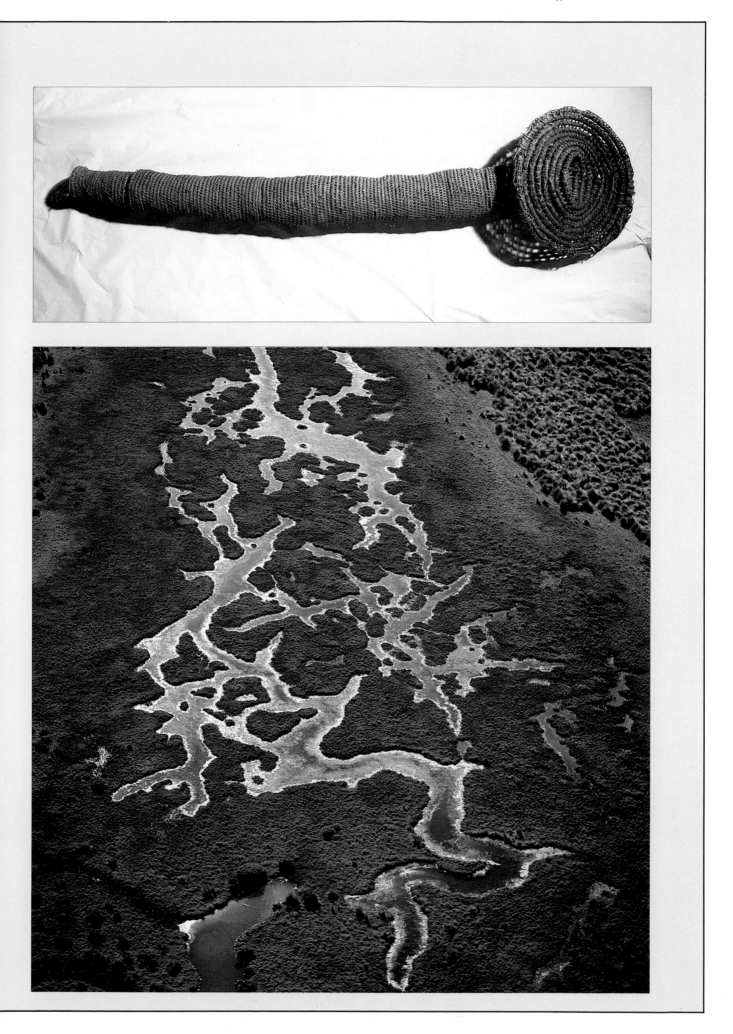

Framlingham

The Mara-speaking people formed a cultural bloc which occupied the coastal regions to beyond the South Australian border. They could have numbered as many as 10 000, and once the European occupation of this region began (in 1829) there was constant warfare along the coast. The colonial police defeated them in battle, then poisoned their flour and the water supplies. They also contributed to the decimation of these people with a range of deadly diseases.

So successful were they, that within 32 years there were only 505 survivors. Denied their land, they were left to starve or beg around the townships, where they were 'nuisances'. During the gold rush they were 'encouraged' to work for half the European wage. Many of their descendants, however, still live in their own lands.

The sheer brutality of genocide — practised through firepower, poison and disease — awoke the conscience of some of the British who helped the remaining Mara find a place of refuge at Framlingham, near Warrnambool. The decimated community — refugees in their own country after thousands of years of land ownership — developed friendly ties with the community at Lake Condah as they struggled to avoid extinction.

The Aborigines Protection Board of Victoria agreed to let Mara people stay on (in their own country, and only at an agreed area in Framlingham) just as long as it did not cost the Board more than a hundred pounds a year.

Five other 'stations' (for other clans of the Mara nation) were established, including Coranderrk, set up as a training centre for orphaned children. After twenty years of respite from war and pain of dispossession, the Victorian colonial government threatened further changes.

Money made by the community was seized and sent to the Treasury in Melbourne; any Mara man or woman who was believed to have European blood was seized by armed police and banished from their family areas. Children were taken from their families and 'given' to white families as domestic servants. Before long, greedy landowners sought even more of the land held by station refugees at Framlingham. First they wanted 800 hectares, and then the lot. The families were to be driven from the land and offered a hundred pounds compensation for their houses and improvements.

But the Mara people had more friends than they knew, including many white people from the area who knew and respected them. Even local members of Parliament protested against the 'ruthlessly cruel' proposal to leave them totally homeless. It was a turning point in black–white relations when more than 500 white residents of Warrnambool, Camperdown, Terang, Mortlake and the surrounding districts registered their protest against evicting 'the original possessors of the soil'.

This time the people won their battle for the remnants of their original lands and Melbourne public servants complained they had set up a 'free republic'. The real problem seemed to be their wish to be their own masters. For ten long years (until 1902) armed uniformed men, on the instructions of the Melbourne administration, raided homes and arrested men, women and children who showed any signs of European ancestry. They were collected and banished, their homes sold off.

Some fled into the bush and built little huts (out of sight) to keep in touch with family and friends on what remained of their 'station'. But the racist policies prevailed and marriage to a man or woman, who might have some European ancestry, was effectively discouraged. Those who defied the colonial authority and married nonetheless were forced to leave their families; if they returned home they were fined the equivalent of a year's wages for 'trespassing'.

The saviour of the people at Framlingham was John Murray, the local Member, who championed their cause in the first struggle. He became Chief Secretary and later Premier (in January 1909) and stood firm in his support, finally ordering an end to the iniquitous race rules governing marriage and the seizure of mixed-blood children.

After World War I (in which some Mara men fought), the entire Mara country was once more under threat with a proposal to complete the process of dispossession. Racism was rampant, both during and after the war, and police were categorising families as 'half-castes', 'quadroons' and 'octroons' as well as determining who should go and who should stay, purely on the basis of colour.

During the Depression years the battle to hold onto their lands continued and aid of all kinds was refused. Warrnambool Hospital turned away black patients. There was no work (or hope of work) and they were refused 'relief' (as the dole was called at that time) because it was reserved for whites.

By 1934 the race laws permitted only eight people to live on the now tiny reserve, while over a hundred relatives hid in tents and hovels in the surrounding bush. The school had been demolished in 1890 , but when a new school was started the people again found hope.

World War II came and went but the Framlingham people's struggle continued. Families were still ordered away on various pretexts, promises were never kept and, by 1947, seventy-three people lived in thirteen substandard cottages. When asked to comment about their plight, the so-called 'Protection' Board said it had nothing to do with them.

By 1950 the remaining Mara people, who had once been described by white Melbourne bureaucrats as wanting to establish a 'free republic', were now being accused of being communists. This new claim followed the Mara people's pointing out that the land belonged to their forefathers and had been seized without payment.

Pressure to effect a wholesale clearance was renewed and a former police magistrate was appointed to advise the government on what should be done with the Mara people (and other Victorian survivors). They had to 'assimilate', he reported, and another program got under way. This time the white spouses of any of the Mara people were ordered off the land. Following this inquiry, it was determined that these people should leave their land forever , to seek refuge in neighbouring towns.

In 1964 the Mara people had 'celebrated' a hundred years of struggle to retain a tiny toehold on their original land. Victory finally came in 1971 when 236 hectares (which was all that remained of the original 1788 hectares reserved in 1861) were transferred to the ownership of the Framlingham Lands Trust, made up of the remaining seventeen residents.

The Mara people became a part of Australian history with their land claim, but the people of the north made a different kind of history. The country of the Madimadi centred on Lake Wallace, site of the future Edenhope. Further north was the drier mallee country where the Wutjubalak controlled the Wimmera and Southern Mallee districts.

These three clans encompassed some 13 000 square kilometres, including today's towns of Hamilton, Casterton, Naracoorte (in South Australia),

Above *A coastline in retreat. The Twelve Apostles at Port Campbell are surviving remnants of much larger formations, weathered over millions of years by the powerful Southern Ocean swells. Slowly the ocean is claiming back a coastline created some 25 million years ago, when this section of coast was under water. Photo by Trevern Dawes.*

Opposite *Victoria's south-west coast receives an annual rainfall of some 1200 millimetres, creating verdant forests and majestic waterfalls. Photo by AusChromes.*

Kaniva and Horsham. The arrival of the white invaders at Lake Wallace in 1845 was marked by an immediate massacre, led by a man named Hamilton who gave his name to the town.

The highway takes us on to Geelong, set against the backdrop of the You-Yang peaks and the traditional lands of the Yawangi clan. Here, many camp sites have survived. One is located 5 kilometres from Flinders Peak and 1.5 kilometres north-north west of Wooloomanata home station. North-west of Wooloomanata are a series of hills which culminate in the Anakies (or Twin Hills), where there is a major camp site at the head of Howells Creek.

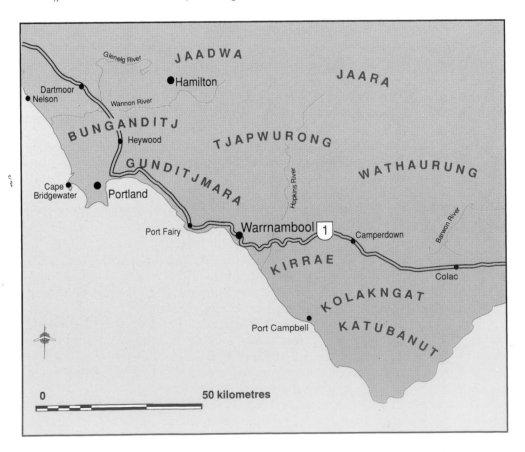

The area around Cape Ottway, showing traditional clan areas.

The cricketers

It was twenty years after the massacre of locals and the establishment of the township of Hamilton that Tom Hamilton (the brother of its founder) introduced Black Australians to the joys and mysteries of cricket. It was from here that the first Australian cricket team destined for international competition was drawn.

By 1865 cricket, played between the great station properties, became so popular that regular matches were held.

Hamilton's Aboriginal team first defeated Edenhope, then Hamilton, and went on to challenge Melbourne, on Boxing Day, 1866, when the team included such names as Officer, Sugar, Jellico, Cuzens, Neddy, Mullagh, Bullocky, Tarpot, Sundown and Peter.

Ten thousand roaring fans saw them beaten on that occasion but they remained popular and they went on to challenge New South Wales cricketers in a tour which saw them not only financially cheated but physically abused to such an extent that several team members died on tour.

Despite all this, the team was rebuilt and a touring party of fourteen arrived in England in May, 1868. All the team members had been born before the white invasion of their homeland and the team showed crowds their cricket prowess and their skill with a range of traditional weapons.

Their impact in England was summed up by the London *Daily Telegraph:* 'Nothing of interest comes from Australia except gold nuggets and black cricketers'. The team won fourteen matches and lost the same number.

The outstanding player was Unnarrimin, or Mullagh, who took 9 for 9 in one game and who is buried today at Harrow near Edenhope, where the sports ground (Mullagh Oval) and a pink granite obelisk commemorate his life and career. One of the other players, Zellanach, or Cuzens, was from Framlingham. His brother James Cuzens, or Mosquito, was a man of many talents: a skilled craftsman, he once wrote to the all-powerful Aborigines Protection Board pointing out that he had worked for six years as a carpenter and had been paid nothing. Other team members included Bullocky, Redcap, Twopenny, King Cole, Tiger, Dick-a-Dick and Jim Crow.

No black Australian cricketer gained national prominence again until the 1930s when Queensland's Eddie Gilbert established a reputation as the fastest bowler in the world. He once bowled Donald Bradman for a duck, who said he was the fastest bowler he ever faced.

The story of the Aboriginal cricketers was told by D. J. Mulvaney in *Cricket Walkabout.*

The Aboriginal cricket team that challenged Melbourne in 1866. Reproduced from Australian News, *courtesy National Library of Australia*

Many camp sites exist along Little River where abandoned artefacts are still being collected by enthusiasts. One camp was located on the high ground close to the school in Little River township.

An important centre was on ground overlooking the Leigh River, at Inverleigh. It was heavily populated with campsites stretching for nearly a kilometre above the swamps that provided a fertile reservoir of food and water.

Several campsites are to be found along Native Hut Creek between Inverleigh and Murgheboluc. The coastal camps of the Wothowurong people — such as at Corio Bay, Stingaree Bay and Point Henry — have long gone, and traces of the camp at Clifton Springs have now probably been destroyed by building construction.

To the south is Bellarine Peninsula, where John Batman, on his treaty-making expedition, came across a village of houses which he assumed were 'marine villas' because of the collection of shells and fish left behind.

One of the great survivors of the people from the area of Geelong was Beruke, named after a kangaroo rat which ran past his house when he was being born. He changed his name to Gellibrand after acting as guide to an expedition in search of two lost travellers, Gellibrand and Hesse. Later he travelled to Melbourne and joined the Native Police, a paramilitary unit stationed there.

The story of his wife, Eliza, is typical of how disputes were settled. Her people at Devils River had given her in marriage to a prominent warrior of the Goulburn River people. But Eliza preferred Gellibrand, to whom she had originally been promised. She ran off to join Gellibrand at every opportunity, defying her father and her husband.

A group of men from the Yarra region, photographed in 1858 with shields, spears, boomerangs and clubs. The men standing are wearing the traditional cloaks made from possum or kangaroo skins. Those sitting are wearing European blankets. From the La Trobe Collection, courtesy State Library of Victoria.

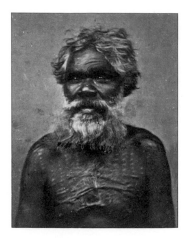

Gellibrand. Courtesy Museum of Victoria.

After two years of constant running away she was caught, tried and sentenced to a spear in one thigh, but she still sought to be with Gellibrand. Eventually it was agreed by the two peoples that a traditional joust should be held and the two contestants for the love of Eliza should fight it out in single combat. After a long and fierce encounter, Gellibrand was declared the winner and Eliza was finally allowed to join him.

Gellibrand subsequently served with the Native Police all over Victoria: he is buried near South Yarra Pound, but of his faithful wife, Eliza, we have no trace.

Among other survivors from this area include three who lie in adjoining graves in Western Cemetery. One of them was known as King Billy Gore, the son of Billy Wa-wa, a leader of the Barrabool clan. He was born on the shores of a lagoon which became the present service station in Jacobs Street, Geelong. His father was away at the time of his son's birth and said he had seen a bunyip: when told of the birth of his son he proudly named him 'Worm bunyip' to mark the occasion. The name appears on his grave.

William Buckley

It was on the Bellarine Peninsula that a white man, William Buckley, lived with the Watharung people for 32 years.

Much of this time he lived at Bream Creek, near Torquay, where there was a large village. Implements including axes, hammers, anvils and choppers have been discovered on the site. A network of fish traps operated and Buckley took his turn as a member of the working community.

Buckley was born in Cheshire, about 1780, and was transported to a new prison settlement at Port Phillip in 1803. A site named Sullivan Bay was selected by the English commander (David Collins) about 2 kilometres east of the present Sorrento pier, between two points now known as the Eastern and Western Sisters.

During the following weeks a dozen prisoners escaped, and two days after the Christmas of 1803, Buckley and two mates made a dash for freedom, planning to walk to Sydney. They hadn't gone far when his two companions turned back and were never heard of again. Buckley pushed on to the west

A selection of drawings by Victoria's most famous Aboriginal artist, Tommy MacCrae. From the La Trobe Collection, courtesy State Library of Victoria.

until he came to Mount Defiance, where he built a hut in a sheltered spot by a freshwater stream. Some months later three local hunters found him and they shared a meal, but when they suggested he join them he reacted aggressively and they left him. As soon as they had gone he regretted his hasty reaction and set out to find them in the Otway Forest. But he lost his way and only found his hut after days of wandering.

'The first settlers discover William Buckley', by F. Woodhouse. From the La Trobe Collection, courtesy State Library of Victoria.

Finally he decided to give himself up. The return journey to Sullivan Bay was a nightmare, the weather cold, food short, his clothes reduced to rags. He made a rough shelter to stay overnight at Spring Creek and tried to go on the next day, using a broken spear he had found on a mound as a crutch, but on the west side of the Barwon River he collapsed, exhausted.

Two local women, who had seen him stagger past, followed him and when they saw him fall they called the men who carried him back to their camp. Buckley awoke to find crowds of friendly excited people calling him *Murranguruk,* a famous warrior who had been killed shortly before.

The mound from which Buckley had taken the spear was, in fact, *his* grave and because he was white (and that was the colour of the dead), they simply assumed Murranguruk had returned.

So began an extraordinary new life for Buckley, now Murranguruk, whom they patiently taught to speak the language, and use the weapons and the utensils of daily living. He took part in the hunting expeditions and the contests between nations to resolve disputes which, he said, were almost all over women.

Buckley married twice. His second wife, Parrarmurnin Tallarwurnin, was fifteen at the time of their marriage and was a resident for a time at Framlingham Station. Buckley was perfectly content until two of his fellow warriors brought him news of John Batman's landing near Indented Head in 1835. The newcomers were kept under observation until it was decided that they would be attacked as they were trespassers.

Buckley found the call of his blood too strong and left his family and friends of half a lifetime, returning to Batman and company. What a sight he must have made as he marched into their camp — tall, bearded and proudly wearing his handsome kangaroo-skin cloak and carrying his spears, club and shield, as befitted a warrior.

Buckley was pardoned, and settled first at Port Phillip and then in Hobart Town where at the age of sixty he married once more, this time to an English woman. He died in 1856, aged 76.

Melbourne

Melbourne, capital of the modern state of Victoria, and Australia's second city, was always an important meeting place, where peoples of the region gathered to stage elaborate ceremonies associated with religious cycles, initiations and dispute settlements. It was also an important trading centre for the three main clans of the region — the Wurundjeri (whose country comprised the whole Yarra Valley), the Bunurong, who held the Mornington Peninsula and Western Port, and the Watharung, whose lands comprised the Bellarine Peninsula, the country along the Barwon River and the Werribee Plains. Their neighbours also joined them at times to form a loosely knit five-nation confederation, linked by the *Kulin* language.

According to local tradition, the Port Phillip region was the work of the great creative ancestor *Bunjil,* the wedge-tailed eagle, who still watches over the land. As Joan M. Kenny relates in *Aborigines Melbourne* (Nelson, 1985), he shaped all the natural features of the area, made the animals and plants and taught the people how to behave on Earth and conduct the ceremonies which would ensure the continuation of life. Bunjil was the creator of all the Kulin peoples. He had two wives, and a son whose name was *Binbeal,* the Rainbow; Binbeal's wife was the second bow of the colours in the rainbow. Bunjil employed six young men to carry his messenges to men and women all over Earth. They were *Djurt-djurt,* the nankeen kestrel; *Tharam,* the quail hawk; *Yukope,* the great parakeet; *Dantum,* the blue mountain parrot; *Tadjeri,* the brushtail possum and *Turnung,* the glider possum. All were capable of mighty deeds in the name of Bunjil.

After he had made the all the country and the living things in it, he taught men how to make and use weapons, and the rules of social behaviour.

Above *A man from the Yarra region. Courtesy Museum of Victoria.*
Opposite *Queen Rose, from Ballarat. Courtesy Museum of Victoria.*

283

When he had finished, Bunjil gathered his wives and sons together and told *Bellin-bellin*, the musk crow, who had charge of the winds, 'Open your bags and let out some wind'. Bellin-bellin opened a bag containing the whirl-winds, which let out a blast so great that big trees were thrown into the air, roots and all.

Bunjil wanted more wind, so Bellin-bellin opened all his bags and released a wind so strong that it carried Bunjil and all his people to the heavens, where they live in peace and plenty as stars. This story is complemented by the tale of the 'filling in' of Port Phillip, which was once dry land, where the Kulin hunted kangaroos and emus.

One day, when the men were away hunting and the women were harvesting yams, some small boys were playing in their camp, throwing toy spears at each other. One of the spears, however, upset a water container, which released a flood and threatened to drown the people. Bunjil felt sorry for them, so he placed a rock near where Mornington now is and told the water not to go any further. Then he made the heads of the bay with two other rocks and told the waters to run out between them into the ocean.

Another account of how Port Phillip was made is given in one of the versions of the creation of the Yarra River. Woiwurong (Wurundjeri) people only had access to a fairly restricted food gathering and hunting area because their lands were drowned by a great lake, called Moorool. Mo-yarra, a senior Woiwurong man with great powers, decided to set the waters free and to create new land. With stone axes he dug a channel south through the hills that surrounded the lake towards Western Port. He didn't succeed since only a little water flowed through his channel. Mo-yarra went to live on the swamps at Western Port and each winter he covers the hill-tops with white feather-down that he plucks from the swamp birds.

Bar-wool was another senior Woiwurong man. He too decided to use his powers to free the waters. He cut a circuitous channel around mountains north and west until he came to Warrandyte. There he met another Woi-wurong, Yan Yan, who was also busy channeling to drain the lake where he lived, Morang, into the Plenty River. At Mooroolbark they joined their channels and together they led the waters down to the Heidelberg–Templestowe Flats. Continuing on, they cut a twisting trail through hard ground until finally they reached Port Phillip. The waters rushed out to cover the flat plains and make the bay.

At the end of the time of creation, the ancestral heroes departed for their homes in the earth or the sky, leaving their symbols and part of themselves behind in the landscape. These are the sacred places , all over Australia, that the people were charged to protect. Part of this duty to the ancestral heroes are rituals which incorporate song, poetry, dance, mime, painting, music and re-enactment of the great Dreamtime sagas.

One feature of this area in traditional times was the existence of a 'confederacy' of nations; the three in the Melbourne region (the Wurundjeri, the Bunurong and the Watharung) had links with each other, and with peoples such as the Taungurong (or Goulburn people) and the Kurung (from the area of Geelong). These five nations used Melbourne as a centre for ceremonies, trading and intertribal gatherings.

In pre-invasion times food resources were extensive. At Bolin Swamp, on the Yarra about 20 kilometres north of Melbourne, there were enough eels to feed people for a month each year. Le Mans Swamp (in present-day Caulfield), Carrum Swamp and swampy areas near Mordialloc were all popular eel fishing locations.

The three nations sharing the Melbourne region created a network of paths connecting major camps throughout the entire area. One such ancient road followed the shoreline of Port Phillip around Beaumaris, where a well had been built to provide a constant supply of fresh water.

Fish in the bay, such as flounder and rays, were speared in shallow waters. Boats with fishing lights were used at night, the torches attracting the fish to the surface where they could be more easily caught. The fish in creeks and rivers were abundant and weirs were sometimes constructed to help harvest them. Shellfish, both marine and freshwater, were a popular addition to the diet. Kangaroo and possum were not only good eating but their skins were used to make garments, particularly long cloaks.

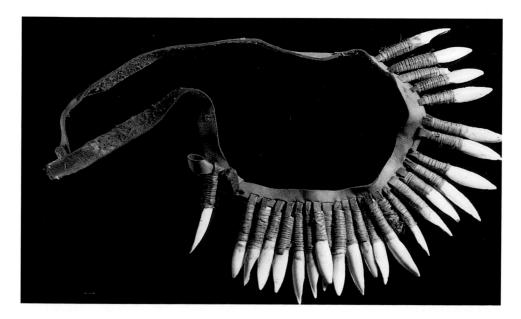

A necklace of wallaby teeth. Photo by Reg Morrison, courtesy Museum of Victoria.

A woman from the Yarra district. Courtesy Museum of Victoria.

Throughout what is now the concrete jungle of twentieth-century Melbourne, there was once abundant bird life, including emus, swans and bush turkeys. The numerous swamps and lagoons around the Melbourne area teemed with waterbirds as well as snipe, plovers, brolgas and quail. Lyre-birds, or *bullen-bullen*, were sought for their tail feathers and parties of up to forty hunters would go to the mountains on hunting trips.

These nations manufactured the usual range of weapons such as spears, clubs, shields and boomerangs, but they also constructed fish weirs, fishing spears, nets, carrying bags, water containers and canoes.

They were a handsome people who wove clothing from grasses and fibres and made cloaks of possum skins. Only one of the superb cloaks for which this region was famous survives in Victoria today and is displayed at the Museum of Victoria in the heart of Melbourne.

They used possum skins as rugs or mats, and fine shell tools were used to carve elaborate designs on the cloaks and mats. On festive occasions, feathers, bones, shells and kangaroo teeth were adapted into ornaments.

The arrival of Batman

One of the events that led to the demise of nations in the Melbourne area was the arrival of John Batman. A Parramatta-born son of an English prisoner, he came to Victoria from Van Diemen's Land (as Tasmania was known) in 1835, representing an association of sheep farmers, officials, merchants and professional men, for whom he was to purchase tracts of land from the local people.

Batman and his party (which included seven Eora people from Sydney) sailed into Port Phillip Bay. He explored as far as the You-Yangs and the Barrabool Hills, in the Geelong area. Then he anchored off Gellibrand's Point, the site of today's Williamstown, and set out on more exploration which took him up Saltwater River, now the Maribyrnong, to a few kilometres beyond Keilor, and finally to Merri Creek near Northcote.

The treaty which Batman had drawn up was 'signed' by the Jagajaga brothers (and five others) in 1835. It purported to give to Batman's syndicate all the land from Geelong Harbour to the head of Port Phillip, amounting to

The last of his people

In the last century, when it seemed that the original Australians would disappear from the planet, it was fashionable when an old man died to proclaim that he was the 'last of his clan'. One such veteran captured the imagination of the Europeans. He was Barak, of the Wurundjeri people, born near the present site of Yarra Glen and initiated into the crow division of his people.

Barak was said to have been present at the signing of the famous Batman Treaty, on the east bank of the Plenty River, north-west of Eltham, by which it was claimed that the original site of Melbourne was ceded to Batman. Barak attended the first school established at Langhorne Mission, now the Botanic Gardens.

He joined the Native Police Corps and married shortly after becoming spokesman and lawmaker of his people when his cousin, Wonga, died. He was also the traditional owner of the Mount William quarries, though they had long been abandoned with the decline in traditional crafts .

He married three times but all his wives died, as did his children. Lonely and failing in health, he finally died on 15 August 1903. Descendants of the Yarra people now live around Melbourne, and many of them come from those families that were settled at Coranderrk.

Opposite *King William. Courtesy Museum of Victoria.*

approximately 40 000 hectares. The price 'paid' for the land under this treaty was 20 pairs of blankets, 30 knives, 12 tomahawks, 10 mirrors, 12 scissors, 50 handkerchiefs, 12 red shirts, 4 flannel jackets, 4 suits of clothes and 50 pounds of flour. A second deed was negotiated, amounting to some 200 000 hectares.

The confusion at the treaty meetings must have been incredible. None of the Batman party, including the Eora men from Sydney spoke the Kulin language, and the completion of a treaty by sign language must have been an extraordinary ceremony.

The agreement was further complicated by the fact that no individual (or group of individuals) in traditional society had the authority to relinquish any land or resources, which had been eternally allocated. Nor did the British authorities acknowledge Batman's treaty. They said the British Crown had taken possession of *everything* and no one could own or negotiate anything without their permission. John Batman emerges, however, as the man with the vision to earmark the site of Melbourne as a 'place for a village'.

About 13 kilometres north of Melbourne is the city of Keilor and a further 1.5 kilometres to the north (near the junction of Dry Creek and Maribyrnong River) in October 1940, there was an accidental discovery which made world headlines. A quarry worker, James White, was digging in the silty soil at a depth of about 6 metres, when he found the skull of a man who lived 13 000 years ago. In August 1965, at Green Gully, south-west of Keilor (in the same strata as the Keilor skull), a complete skeleton — which turned out to 6460 years old — was unearthed: it presented a mystery not solved to this day.

The skeleton was an example of the Australian burial practice which, in many areas, specified that the dead be placed on a burial platform high in a tree for a year before the skeleton is removed for ceremonial burial. To the amazement of the researchers, the complete skeleton was made up of bones from a man *and* a woman without the duplication of one bone. Who and why did someone, thousands of years ago, painstakingly put together 236 bones to make one skeleton out of two? And what happened to the other bones? It is surely the most bizarre case of 'togetherness' in the history of Australia.

Opposite *A woven basket from Victoria. Photo by Reg Morrison, courtesy Museum of Victoria.* **Below** *'Batman signing the treaty with the aboriginals', by John Wesley Burtt. From the La Trobe Collection, courtesy State Library of Victoria.*

Winning hearts and minds

King David. From the La Trobe Collection, courtesy State Library of Victoria.

As a part of British attempts to pacify the local Victorian clans, an extended family of sixteen people was brought to Melbourne from Tasmania as an example to the local clans of how they, too, could survive if they did not resist the invasion. Two of them, given English names of 'Bob' and 'Jack', escaped and took to the bush with three Tasmanian women. One of these women was the famous Truganini, whose skeleton was subsequently kept on public display in Hobart for nearly a century as the so-called 'last of the Tasmanians', before a proper burial was organised by the author in 1968.

This party of five decided that they had lost the war in Tasmania, but that victory might still be possible in Victoria. So they began a guerilla campaign against white occupation which enjoyed brief but outstanding successes.

They successfully attacked seven stations established on black land — mainly in the area of Western Port — and inflicted half a dozen casualties on the invaders. But they were captured in a surprise dawn attack by the 28th Regiment and armed police, and put on trial before an exclusively English jury in a court presided over by a judge who was later banished for misconduct. No one spoke their language in court, no one translated, no one heard their replies and the jury were certainly not their 'peers', as was prescribed by English law. The three women were acquitted but the two men were found guilty and sentenced to public hanging.

In its early years, Melbourne was little more than a muddle of huts, open sewers and dusty streets, frequented by a handful of white people and many Aborigines. The British military quickly began establishing a colonial administration, which included a Supreme Court House in a little brick building on the south-west corner of King and Bourke Streets.

Melbourne's first judge was John Walpole Willis who gained fame as the only English judge to be twice removed from his own court and who attracted a record number of complaints for impropriety and misbehaviour. Among many infamous decisions was one which banned any Black Australian from giving evidence on his own behalf.

In cases of indiscriminate rapes and killings (which were numerous), the whites (if they were charged) were always released when the case came to court. Willis was such a disgrace to his profession that even New South Wales Governor George Gipps described him as an 'apologist of the cruellest practices by some of the least respectable settlers on the Aborigines'.

Against this background it will not come as any surprise that the first public hangings in Melbourne were of the two Black Tasmanian war leaders, survivors of the war which had already decimated the Tasmanians.

The site chosen for the hanging was a small rise to the north-west of Old Melbourne Gaol, in Russell Street. The scaffold was a narrow shaky platform, made from two heavy uprights sunk into the ground about 4 metres apart, with a cross beam nailed on top and a rope slung over it. Two metres above the ground, short planks supported the drop platform with one plank which could be pulled away so that the victims could drop to their deaths. If all went well, the offender would die quickly, with a broken neck. Two ladders, one at each side, enabled the platform to be mounted. Two English prisoners, neither of whom had any experience, were ordered to carry out this first hanging.

The appointed day was 18 January 1842 and 3000 people gathered in bright sunshine to watch the spectacle. Every vantage point was occupied. The two prisoners were taken by bullock cart from the gaol, along Collins, William, Lonsdale and Swanston Streets to Gallows Hill. The crowd was in great form, laughing and calling to the prison chaplain to cut short his twenty minutes of prayer. The two Aborigines, dressed in white for the occasion, knelt with the chaplain and, on rising, had their arms tied behind their backs. They looked from one face to another in the crowd for a sign of sympathy but found only excitement at their imminent demise.

They were then forced to climb the rickety ladders, arms tied behind them, trying to balance on each step. In the end, they were partly pushed and partly dragged onto the platform. The hangman fixed the ropes around their necks from behind, then he pulled white calico caps over their heads. The ladders were taken away and the two hangmen hauled on the rope. The trap opened only partially so they fell only about 60 centimetres where they twisted and writhed, the ropes slowly biting into their throats and strangling them.

Even the bloodthirsty crowd found the slow torture a bit much and one bystander knocked away the obstruction to their full fall. As they plunged down, one of them continued to be slowly strangled as the noose had become displaced. Eventually they were both dead and they were left swinging mutely for an hour before being carted off to the black cemetery now the site of Victoria Markets.

Throughout the 1840s the black war continued on various frontiers around Melbourne, with the European firepower (and the spread of their diseases) always ensuring their final victory. After each attack by the Aborigines, retaliation killings would follow, which were planned with military precision, though casual massacres were also common. In one documented incident, three local women, one of whom was pregnant, and a child were shot. The killer had held the gun against the stomach of the pregnant woman and pulled the trigger. Eventually, seven 'gentlemen' were charged with the killings but were acquitted in court.

Charles Walters, or King Billy.
Courtesy Museum of Victoria.

Tasmania's rugged coast and mountainous interior posed challenges to the hunter/gatherer lifestyle. Cradle Mountain National Park. Photo by AusChromes.

Tasmania

LTHOUGH our journey around Australia (on Highway One) does not take us through Tasmania, this island represents such a fascinating part of original Australia it cannot be passed without a visit.

Tasmania is an island of around 68 000 square kilometres; almost the same size as Sri Lanka and a touch smaller than Ireland. Despite their separation from the mainland (some 12 000 years ago) the original Tasmanians were a part of the *first* Australian explorers, who spread down through the continent from 40 000 years ago. We know they were living in Tasmania around 25 000 years ago, in the middle of the last Ice Age, when the high peaks were covered with glaciers and the oceans full of icebergs. Yet they chose to stay on, between 40 and 43.5 degrees south of the equator, probably the southern-most human habitation anywhere in the world at that time.

Many thousands of years passed until the end of the Ice Age and the melting of the ice flows caused the oceans to rise and Bass Strait to become a waterway — a significant barrier to contact with the mainland.

It is believed the island population was made up of some nine linguistic and cultural groupings, each comprising between five and fifteen bands, varying from the Worrady and Nuenonne of the south-east to the Noeteeler, Pallitore and Peeberranger of the north. Much of the knowledge is sketchy, however, due to the rapid decimation suffered by the Tasmanians at the hands of the settlers.

Much of what has been recorded comes from the observations of navigators and settlers. Among these, the English missionary George Augustus Robinson offers the only real insight into the people themselves. He travelled the island extensively and became close to two Tasmanians in particular: Truganini, a woman of the Lyluequonny people from Recherche Bay, and Worraddy, a Nuenonne, from Bruny Island.

The Tasmanians had some significant cultural differences from mainland Australians. At the time Europeans arrived they did not eat scaled fish, which had been dropped from their diet, for unknown reasons, some three to four thousand years ago. People of the same age *were* allowed to marry, although the partner still had to be from another band. There were also several clear physical differences which distinguished the Tasmanians from their mainland relations: in particular, their woolly hair and reddish-brown skin.

Traditional clan areas in Tasmania.

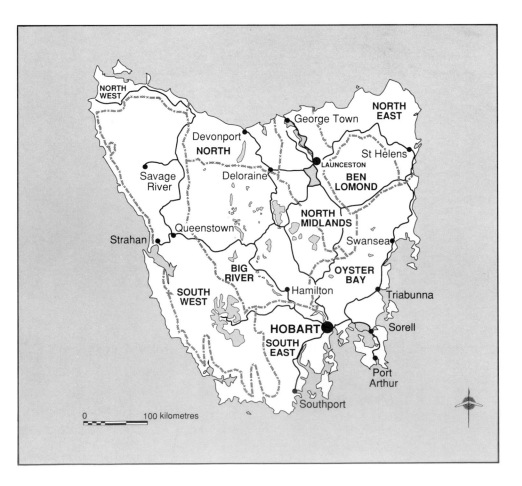

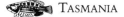

Truganini, Tasmania's best known Aborigine. Contrary to popular opinion, she was not the last Tasmanian. Truganini came from the Recherche Bay area and after the resistance had been suppressed she was relocated to an Aboriginal settlement at Oyster Bay, where she outlived everyone else at the settlement by 11 years. Despite begging for her body to be buried after she died, her bones were put on show in a museum showcase until 1976, when she was cremated in a special ceremony. Photo by J. W. Beattie, courtesy National Library of Australia.

Tasmania has very little land which lies close to sea level and lowland plains are limited to northern regions. In many areas the mountains adjoin the coast directly and rise sharply, forming some of the most spectacular mountain scenery in Australia. The island also has thousands of lakes — the north-east section of the central plateau alone has 4000 — which formed a significant resource, providing many thousands of kilometres of shoreline on which to hunt, fish and collect shellfish.

Some bands in the south-east travelled about the coastal areas together (their movements directed mainly by food resources), without venturing inland during the winter, as did bands from the Big River and Oyster Bay district in the north of the island. Differences can be seen between clans of the east and west coasts, mainly due to climatic variation and opportunity. The west coast is exposed to the prevailing winds (the roaring forties) and backed by a heavily forested hinterland which, unlike tropical forests, was relatively poor in resources. The oceans, however, provided a bountiful supply of shellfish and seasonal sources of fur seal and muttonbirds. These people regularly burnt the forest margins, to create an environment more suitable for game, especially wallabies, and for vegetables. They built semi-permanent dwellings and lived in bands of around fifty, sharing six to eight huts.

Shelter was less important on the east coast, which enjoyed the protection from the prevailing winds offered by the high inland regions. Their habitat had extensive woodlands and a wide distribution of food resources.

Several examples exist of fine stone engravings, which date back at least 20 000 years and feature patterns of lines, dots and circular motifs. Their meaning is not known.

Early observers thought that the people were rather less than average in height, though settlers noted individuals of 200 centimetres (6 feet 7 inches) or more. The Tasmanian men had hair more like that of the Melanesians, tightly curled, and they greased it with a mixture of oil and ochre, which accentuated the natural ringlets considerably. Women, on the other hand, wore their hair closely cropped, often with one ringlet of longer hair.

As on the mainland, women did most of the gathering, using digging sticks to extract roots and tubers, prise open oysters and other shellfish or break into muttonbird nests. Women made long grass ropes which they used to get possums out of trees.

Both men and women scarred their body by rubbing a mixture of powdered charcoal and red ochre, mixed with grease, into the wound. Their religion was thought to be based on celestial beings, which play out roles as good and bad spirits in a similar way to traditional mythology. The day was ruled by the good spirit *Noiheener* or *Parledee*, and the night by the bad spirit *Wrageowrapper*. Many other beings were involved in the creation of fire, rivers, lakes, mountains and animals, and the culture had many totems and taboos. Apart from the ban on scaled fish (they could hardly believe it when they saw Europeans eat these fish), and there strict rules on who could eat the male or female kangaroo or wallaby. To help them ward off bad spirits, they carried amulets made from bones of the dead.

Along the coasts, the bands were regularly spaced, each occupying some 25 to 30 kilometres of coastline, though the distances were shorter in the rich west and longer in the south-west where food resources were sparser. Often the bands came together, for seasonal missions in search of seals and muttonbirds, or at ochre mines (at Mount Housetop and Mount Vandyke) where they mined the body-painting materials so important to traditional life. Each band shared its natural resources with visiting bands. The band from the mountains would give permission for the ochre to be extracted and then would come to the coast in search of seals or to the lakes in search of ducks and eggs. Or perhaps to the plains for kangaroo hunting.

Lake Pedder, whose waters were raised during the 1970s for hydro-electric storage, now forms the centrepiece of the 440 000 hectare South West National Park. Photo by AusChromes.

Above *An early colour lithograph of some of the Tasmanian craft, which were more sophisticated than most found on the mainland. Courtesy Mitchell Library.*

Left *The Freycinet Peninsula, on Tasmania's east coast. Photo by Robbi Newman.*

Bottom left *Tasmania's rugged south-west coast. Photo by Steve Triance.*

Bottom right *The Tasmanian devil is a carnivorous marsupial now only found in Tasmania. where its numbers are actually increasing. Photo by Sean Davey.*

A group of Tasmanians, photographed at Oyster Cove in the 1860s. Photo by J. W. Beattie, courtesy National Library of Australia.

The nine clans or cultural alliances of the bands of Tasmania fall into three main groups: the eastern and northern groups occupying the Oyster Bay region and the eastern and northern shores; the midland group consisting of the bands from Big River, the north Midlands and Ben Lomond, occupying virtually no coastline; and the third group stretching from the north-west corner of the island down to the south-east, with extensive coastlines but limited hinterland. All three groups had access to each other's resources by agreement.

Most of the animals were marsupial, including several varieties of kangaroo, possums and bandicoots. Two other predators have gained considerable fame: the thylacine and Tasmanian devil. Neither has been found alive on the mainland in the two hundred years of European occupation and although the thylacine was observed by early settlers, no documented sightings have been made in the past fifty years.

Archaeologists have come up with a full range of views on the evolution of the Tasmanians. Some say there was a cultural decline created by separation from the mainland: 'a slow strangulation of the mind'. Those of this view cite the dropping of scaled fish from their diet about 4000 years ago as evidence of this argument. Others have argued that there are clear signs of adaption to the challenges and opportunities of the new environment, and that the Tasmanians were improving their lifestyle when the Europeans arrived in 1804. This view is supported by the development of sophisticated watercraft (in the south-east, south-west and north-west) over the last 2000 years.

The Tasmanian people were reduced from a population of around 1200 at the beginning of European settlement to fewer than 300 within 30 years. In 1828 efforts were made to round up the remnants and confine them to one area, but numbers had already been decimated and the 'Black Line' sweep of 1830 — when troops and armed volunteers formed separate fronts to drive the remaining Tasmanians onto Tasman Peninsula — netted one man and a boy, and the man escaped.

The brutality of the conflict in Tasmania received extensive coverage in England, at a time when sentiment over the anti-slavery crusade was at its

peak, and there was wide concern at the cost of colonising Tasmania. In just a few years the Europeans had lost around 200 men in conflicts with the Tasmanians. It is estimated some 800 Aborigines died over the same period. Governor Arthur, writing to the Colonial Office in 1834, noted that he had been 'reduced to the necessity of driving a simple but warlike, and, as it now appears, noble minded race, from their hunting grounds'.

Despite the 'boasts' of many white people that they 'solved' the Aboriginal 'problem' in Tasmania, there are currently more than 5000 Aboriginal people registered on electoral rolls throughout Tasmania. These people, who successfully negotiated 10 000 years of ice and 12 000 years of isolation from the mainland, survived the open genocide of the British invaders more effectively than many realise.

Study of a Tasmanian, by Robert Dowling. Courtesy National Library of Australia.

*Tooronga River, Gippsland,
Victoria. Photo by AusChromes.*

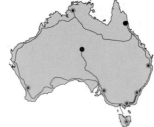

300

North to Sydney

EAVING modern-day Melbourne and the Kulin peoples behind, we begin the final leg in Highway One's circumnavigation of the continent. Around Morwell, we enter into the nation (and language area) of the Kurnai, whose clans occupied the east coast of Victoria.

Spearing swans, a drawing by Tommy MacCrae. From the La Trobe Collection, courtesy State Library of Victoria.

Below *King Billy at Lakes Entrance, 1916. Courtesy National Library of Australia.* **Below right** *The author's great great grandfather, Burnum Burnum, of the Wurundjeri people. Courtesy Museum of Victoria.*

The trip north from Melbourne is, for me, a very special part of our journey. The area is full of my matralineal affiliations, from Melbourne up to Batemans Bay, including Morwell, Wilsons Promontory, Bairnsdale, Buchan, Lake Tyers, Orbost, the Cann River, Eden and Bega.

All around Melbourne, the spirit of my great great grandmother is written on the landscape. When I drive through eastern Victoria I do so with a great sense of reverence; dreaming my way through the landscape of my ancestors and my birth I can feel the spirits of my ancestors in many places. In northern Victoria, it's the spirit of my great grandfather on my mother's side, Tommy MacCrae, a member of the Kwat Kwat people, whose territory included the Wahgunyah and Corowa districts. Having grown up in the traditional lifestyle of his ancestors, Tommy MacCrae did not see a white man until he was in his teens and watched the European penetration of his lands during his most impressionable years. Later he worked as a stockman on stations in the district, as well as returning to the traditional hunting and fishing patterns of his heritage. He was an old man before his artistic talent first came to light, as he drew with the help of a broken stick on the sunbaked surface of the Murray River flats. His talent became a source of considerable local interest and some prestige, before the then postmaster of Wahgunyah, R. Kilborn, gave Tommy a small pad, pen and ink, suggesting he make some drawings more permanent than those in the mud. This became the first of many such books he filled with his unforgettable images of the times.

His methods were quite extraordinary. Lying full length on the ground, propped on one elbow, he drew totally from memory, working methodically upwards from the bottom of the page, a process he never varied. His subject matter included the full range of native life and customs, though many of his sketches captured with haunting impact the incursion of the Europeans and Chinese on traditional lands. He remains Victoria's most famous Aboriginal artist and his work is held at the Victorian State Library.

The Princes Highway carries us east and then north, with Mount Baw Baw and the rugged southern fringe of the Great Dividing Range — snow-

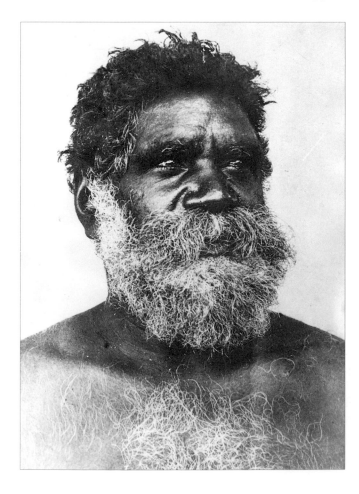

Left *The Bogong Mountains in Victoria drew people to the highlands every summer to feed on the bogong moths.*
Below *Around Lake Tyers stories have been retained telling of a great flood long ago when nearly all the people were drowned. Some turned into reptiles, birds and animals, others into dolphins. Photos by Robbi Newman.*

covered for most of the short winter — to the north. Further north, Bogong National Park is a reminder of the great tradition of bogong moth feasts in the peaks of the mountains during the warmer summer months, a ritual associated with great festivals and gatherings. The bogong moths — like the bunya nuts of Queensland — attracted people from many kilometres away. They would arrive in the mountains skinny, and leave, some months later, considerably fatter.

The pattern of dispossession following the establishment of Melbourne was the familiar one, remnant clans of the Kurnai struggling for their very existence. The invasion of East Gippsland began from the sea by the sealers and whalers who followed Bass from Sydney after 1798. They were fierce, 'primitive' (and often diseased) people, who set up outposts on all the Bass Strait islands and along the eastern coast. Relying on superior firepower, they simply took black women at will, and in numbers, for sex and as servants. The warriors who opposed the kidnapping of their women fought bravely, but their reward was usually a fatal encounter with muskets. On Phillip Island, the sealers managed to wipe out the seals almost as fast as they wiped out the local population.

Lake Tyers

The author at Lake Tyers, the birthplace of his mother. Photo by Carmen Ky.

The Kurnai-speaking clans occupied the whole east coast of Victoria, reaching as far south as Wilsons Promontory. Photo by AusChromes.

For most of the twentieth century Lake Tyers was the only remaining black Australian station in Victoria. (Framlingham, where the remnant Mara people lived, was fighting for its tiny toehold of land, and was not classified as a station.) In traditional times it was an important meeting place for surrounding nations and, in this century, has been a powerful symbol for the original Australians who in this and many other areas today call themselves the Koories.

Lake Tyers is also the location of the first formal government grant to an Aboriginal community in Victoria and the story of this area provides an insight to black–white relations in Australia following an end to the shooting. An Anglican mission from 1861 to 1908 (when the Victorian State Government ran the station), Lake Tyers was a repository for people transferred from Ramahyuck (in 1906), Lake Condah (in 1917) and from Coranderrk, in 1923. These survivors of various clans and nations had already been herded into stations once, then moved on again (as numbers dropped), so Lake Tyers continued to be a major refugee centre.

About 1940 there were around 300 people at Lake Tyers but the state government had decided on further dispersals. The struggle to keep control of their remaining lands continued through the 1950s and 1960s, until Lake Tyers (and Framlingham) were at last recognised as belonging to Aborigines.

In August 1968, the first Aboriginal town council in Australia came into being and Lake Tyers began to develop its own brick factory for the construction of several houses, a church and a school.

The clans of the Kurnai believed they were taught by a great Dreamtime ancestor, *Mungan-ngaur,* how to make implements, nets, canoes and weapons. He taught them all the skills of living and gave them the names they bear. It was Mungan-ngaur himself who instituted the *Jeraeil* (or initiation ceremony), and it was his son, *Tundun*, who sustained the music of the Kurnai.

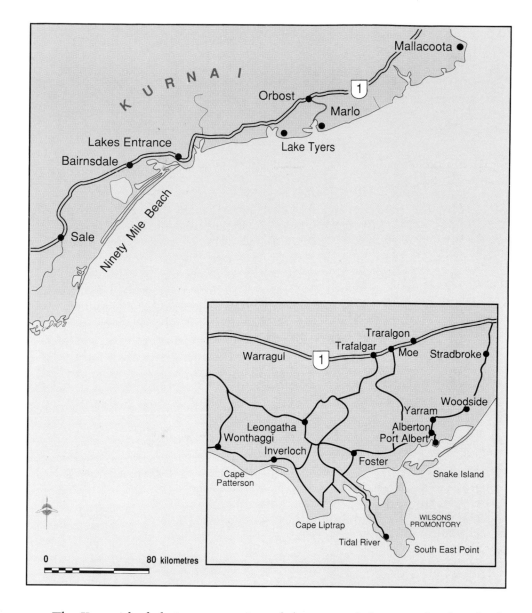

The Kurnai had their own version of the story of the great flood, which they believed was caused by the revelation of the nation's secrets to women. Mungan-ngaur punished them for their disobedience, sending fire to fill the space between earth and sky. According to Kym Thompson in *A History of Aboriginal People of East Gippsland*, 'men . . . went mad with fear' and killed each other; family fought family; husbands murdered wives and brothers each other. Then came the great flood and nearly all the people were drowned: some turned into animals, birds, reptiles and fishes. Mungan left the earth and ascended into the sky where he remains. Tundun and his wife became dolphins. From that time on knowledge of the sacred mysteries has been handed down from father to son, and there are heavy penalties for revealing them to women. Central to the Jeraeil ceremonies is the *tundun,* or bull-roarer, which bears the name of the son of the Great Creator.

On the eastern shore of the Nowa Nowa Arm of Lake Tyers, there are two special locations — the Devil's Hole and Nargun's Cave — which are closely connected with the Dreamtime hero *Nargun*.

Lake Tyers is the adopted homeland of the living members of the Wurundjeri, many of whom have filtered back home to the Melbourne region. The Aboriginal reserve at Lake Tyers also became home to displaced peoples from all over Victoria. It is also the birthplace of my mother, Lily McRae. Her brother, Sydney McRae, who I knew as Uncle Poona, was an accomplished artist in his early years who depicted events of his day, though he was most famous for the distance he could swim underwater on a single breath. Twice he escaped from the prison on French Island, near Melbourne, by swimming underwater for great distances, through shark-infested waters.

The bogong moth

In a ritual repeated every year as far back as anyone can remember, people would gather in the mountain ranges of the southern alps each summer to feast on the bogong moth (*Agrotis infusa*). The Bogong Mountains, the Brindabella and Tinderry Ranges as well as the Kosciusko region were all areas to which the moths migrate during summer, where they aestivate (the summer equivalent of hibernate) from October till March.

The moths come from their breeding grounds on the western slopes and plains of New South Wales and southern Queensland, feeding on the nectar of eucapyptus trees and other flowers along the way. They instinctively find their way to the same habitats their species have occupied for at least a thousand years.

Around December each year, people would arrive from far afield to feast on the moths, aestivating in the cool granite caves and crevices of the highlands. It was a time of feast and festival, with the protein-rich moths available in their millions, as well as moth-fattened crows, currawongs and other birds.

The moths were lightly roasted over ashes, and great care was taken not to scorch them. The people often stayed in the highlands for months, feasting, trading, conducting ceremonies and occasionally fighting. The main items of trade were spears, wooden artefacts, axes, ochres and possum skin rugs, which often involved as many as eighty skins sewn together with kangaroo tail sinew.

Left *The highlands of Victoria and southern New South Wales offer an ideal summer climate for the moths. Photo by Philip Quirk/Wildlight.*
Below left *The moths feed on nectar during their annual migration to the highlands. Photo by Densey Clyne/Mantis Wildlife.*
Below *The moths aestivate on the cool granite faces of caves and crevices. Photo by Glen Carruthers/Mantis Wildlife.*

Kurnai lifestyles

The Kurnai are described by Kym Thompson as a highly organised and sophisticated people, with clans associated in a complex system of kinship and family obligations. A family would normally live within the husband's father's territory, but if a man was born outside the territories of both his parents he might also claim association with the territory in which he was born. Kinship relationships and obligations were most obvious in the distribution of food: fish and vegetable foods were eaten within the immediate family but meat had to be distributed under strict guidelines.

A medium or large animal was divided first between the hunters, who would eat some of the entrails while out hunting. The hunter who actually killed the animal would be given certain portions, such as the legs or tail. On returning home, the best parts of the animal (or the bigger part of any small animal) would be given by the hunter's wife to her parents, who would then give some to all the father's children. The hunter would give the remaining meat to his immediate family. The following day, his wife's parents might return uneaten meat. The whole procedure was based on the principle of sharing and maintaining the closely interwoven relationships on which their intricate society was built.

Like customs practised all over Australia for the settling of disputes, Kurnai law provided for ritual punishments. Those found, after a trial, to be offended could throw spears and boomerangs at the offender, who faced his accusers alone, with only a shield to defend himself. Watercolour by Joseph Lycett, courtesy National Library of Australia.

Lake Tyers people, photographed on the lake in traditional bark canoes, 1886. From the Riley Collection, courtesy National Library of Australia.

Initiation ceremonies for young men attracted all the clans of the nation, and the ceremony would go on for several days.

Courtship and marriage among the Kurnai was a complicated affair — as it was throughout Australia. A man would usually marry a woman from another group, whose brother or cousin would, in turn, marry a sister or cousin of her husband. Most marriages were arranged by the elders and designed not only to create new bonds between the couple and their immediate group but also between divisions of society. Marriages within the same division were prohibited. These customs began to break down after the European invasion. More couples eloped and brides were often kidnapped: the white conquerors simply took whatever women they wanted, at the point of a gun.

Under Kurnai law there was a formal arrangement for the settlement of disputes, involving a ritual trial and punishment. The offended group threw boomerangs and spears at the offender, who would have to face them alone, with a shield. The law provided that he was permitted to parry and dodge but not to fight back. Once he sustained a wound, the punishment was complete.

Traditional medicine

In all traditional Aboriginal society the doctor or healer held great power because he was also an intermediary between the physical and spiritual worlds.

As a result of their visits to the 'Land Beyond the Sky', traditional doctors were believed to hold the power of life and death. The secrets lay in special incantations which gave them power over the elements (rain, tempest, and so on), as well as over the spirits of the living and dead. They were believed to be able to see movements of enemies and sources of food.

In most clans there would be two or three young mean serving as apprentices. The knowledge and power passed on included the widely known practice of 'pointing of the bone', an expression which has passed into modern Australian language. The bone used was a *yulo*, usually made from the fibula of a man. A twisted cord of kangaroo sinew or fibre was attached to the blunt end, which was used to swing the yulo around the head of the seated 'victim' and throw it towards him, inducing an immediate trance. The doctor would carry his body to a secluded spot and perform a small but effective operation, removing kidney fat. Afterwards the skin around the incision was joined together in such a way that no wound could be detected. The doctor then sang a song, at which the victim would rise, stand on one leg and then the other before returning home to die.

But the main role of the clan doctor was to cure. Credited with being able to fly, he was often summoned great distances to effect cures, which varied from incantations, applications and massage to herbal medicines. Sometimes, stones, crystals or pieces of bone were removed from the sick as a part of the cure.

The doctor was sometimes a woman: one was known as the 'White Lady' and the symbol of her authority was a long staff — sometimes adorned with white cockatoo feathers — which was carried for her by a strong man.

The doctors of the Kurnai were divided into *birraarks* and *mullamulluns*. The birraarks were 'seers who dealt in magic, and claimed to be able to visit the spirits in the Land Beyond the Sky', and to be able to fly and to talk to the spirits of the dead. The mullamulluns knew the power of faith, hot applications, massage, sucking and all the properties of herbal medicines. The birraarks were subject to many restrictions: they were not allowed to kill or take people up to the sky and they were not permitted ever to laugh, nor could they eat or handle any part of a kangaroo with blood on it. If they were hunting, others had to carry the dead animal and organise the cooking for them.

The doctor would assemble the people in a suitably secluded place where he would conduct seances, to put people in touch with the spirits of the dead. It was claimed that he would disappear completely to fetch the spirit, then a noise would be heard in the treetops, followed by the sound of visiting spirits jumping from the trees. The voices of the doctor and the spirits would be heard in conversation with each other, as well as answering inquiries from the assembled people about the health and welfare of dead friends and relatives. There might also be questions about the movements and welfare of living friends and the location of any white invaders in the vicinity. The seance would end when the voice of the spirits declared that they must go (or else be blown into the sea by by the wind).

Mullamulluns had the power to kill at a distance by sorcery. They could throw a stick or point the bone. One of the procedures (called *barn*) involved a young he-oak, branches lopped, stem cut to a point. A clearing was made around it and the figure of a man carved in the earth so it looked as if the he-oak was growing out of his chest. A circle was drawn around the figure and the victim was 'sung' into the circle. As he entered it, small spindle-shaped pieces of he-oak were thrown at him and he then would fall to the ground in a trance and his tongue would be pulled out its full length and the sides cut free. He would return to camp not knowing what happened and simply die.

A curious cure for a headache was practised by doctors of the neighbouring Murray people to the north. A clump of grass was pulled out and the patient's head placed in the hole. Then the sod would be replaced (over the patient's head) and the doctor would sit on the sod. Shortly, the headache would go.

A drawing by Tommy MacCrae. From the La Trobe Collection, courtesy State Library of Victoria.

To the Kurnai people a red sunset was an indication of warmer weather, especially when eagles were seen soaring high. Photo by Robbi Newman.

Koalas were seen as friends and givers of good advice, but they were also considered good eating. Photo by AusChromes.

A world of symbolism

Certain signs were recognised as indicators of change in the weather. For the Kurnai, black cockatoos screeching was a sign of rain as were noisy frogs and black jays. For the Mara people, a red sunrise, or a halo around an old crescent moon, a rainbow in the evening, or noisy frogs, crickets, black jays and magpie larks all meant rain. (Remember the Mara lived on the south-west coast of Victoria, where it rains a lot.)

A halo around the sun meant fine weather, as did a bright sunrise or moon. A red sunset forecast heat, and eagles soaring high and descending vertically was an indication of warmer weather.

Animals, birds and reptiles in the Dreamtime stories of the creation often appear as individuals. The bat is often seen as a kind man, rendering help to human beings. The mopoke always seems to be in trouble and usually comes off second best. The emu is another 'loser' in the mythology, always getting speared and losing her eggs.

To the Kurnai, an eclipse of the sun signified that a man had been caught by a *mullamullun* (and his kidney fat removed), while an eclipse of the moon told them that someone known to them had been killed. A red moon also signified a death: the red was clearly the blood of the victim. The moon was the home of a spirit and moon rays were considered dangerous. A falling star also indicated a death (in the direction shown by the falling star) and was a portent of evil.

An echidna or dead mouse close to camp, or a pigeon cooing at night, were other signs of someone dying. Koalas were seen as friends and givers of good advice, although they were also recognised as good eating. An eagle hawk perched on a tree close to a man or a wagtail coming close and not flying off were other signs of danger.

Some people would never point at a rainbow with a straight finger, in case it became crooked. The Mara believed that if someone saw Venus set twice in one night that person would die before morning.

Lightning was seen by many as a bad spirit, throwing fire to burn the country, shatter the trees and sometimes kill people. The Murray people thought there was a link between lightning and the river turtles, because, after a bolt had struck the ground, there was a smell like the river turtles.

The Kurnai believed that if the ground crackled under the head of a sleeping person it was a warning of danger, while a loud hissing from damp wood on the campfire foretold the coming of friends. To some nations, spitting in the fire was an insult to the person you were with when you did it. An itchy nose was a sign of good news or the arrival of a friend, while it was believed that pierced noses helped the youngsters to grow tall.

Owls were thought to be watch birds for bad spirits, hooting to warn them of man's approach, and often brought a message of death. The blood-curdling screeching of the winking or powerful owls as the 'death birds' was a warning of violent death.

At Lake Tyers, the mail bird is still believed to foretell the arrival of the mail while the mopoke was almost universally thought of as an evil omen, warning of a coming enemy raid with its call *boron-bon*. Pelicans at Lake Tyers are welcomed as heralding the arrival of a baby; the white cockatoo the arrival of friends; the black cockatoo and jay the arrival of rain. Crows bring warnings of dangers and should not be killed in case they call up a storm.

The Kurnai believed that if kangaroos formed a circle around a person in a dream it would be a sign that some magic was being practised. Dreaming of an agitated dog meant that kangaroos would be hunted successfully next day, and if a man ever heard a dog talk he would be turned into stone.

If a man beat his wife, he could be sentenced to cure her (and be punished) by having his arms tightly bound above the elbow, and his veins opened at the wrists. His blood would be allowed to pour over the injured woman until he repented.

During menstruation, women were under strict taboos since they were believed to pollute whatever they touched. In some nations, this meant a woman retired a little way from the home dwelling; in others, they were not allowed near the men, or the paths to and from home. If they wanted to cross a creek near their camp, they would go downstream so they would not pollute the water. Menstruating women were not allowed to touch any food or water, or to go food gathering. They were not even allowed to stoke the fires. Mothers-in-law were not allowed any contact with sons-in-law but they were under an obligation to make gifts of food to their fathers-in-law.

Among the Mara people native turkey tails were reserved for the old men and if a young man disobeyed the law and ate them, his hair would go grey. Black duck and turtles were also reserved for the old men.

An unusual cure for snakebite from the Mara people involved looking at the sun. If the image of an emu appeared you would die; if not you would recover. The Kurnai believed if a snake was encountered and it looked steadily at the person, it was a warning; but if it followed him home then it was a bad spirit, out to do him harm.

All the nations used charms, some made from locks of hair cut from the head or beard of a dead man, which were tightly bound with possum-fur string and painted with red ochre. Others were bones, and sometimes mothers carried the umbilical cord of their babies.

If an echidna was seen close to the camp at night it was seen by the Kurnai as a sign that someone was dying. Photo by Lee Pearce.

Unusually coloured or shaped pebbles, such as quartz crystals or banded jasper, stones, glass marbles, australites and possum fur were used as charms, sometimes worn, sometimes carried in small possum -skin bags.

The area around Marlo township (14 kilometres south of Orbost) is important in the traditional history of the district. It was the site of an important quarry, the ancient source of white pipeclay called *marlo,* which was used for ceremonial body-painting.

The white invaders brought many evils but two smallpox epidemics, in 1789 and 1829, killed off half the population of south-east Australia. Only the more isolated clans escaped decimation. It was in the late 1830s that the full tide of European settlement reached Gippsland. They came overland from New South Wales, driven by drought. The Kurnai clans began to fight back in earnest, earning praise from many as the best guerilla fighters in Victoria.

Two of the early invasion forces were turned back, but by the 1840s European firepower was beginning to overwhelm the Kurnai. Using the rescue of a party of shipwrecked white women as an excuse, a killing party from Melbourne surprised a group of Kurnai (on the eve of Christmas 1846) on the Brodribb River, upstream from its junction with the Snowy and killed them all.

A second expedition resulted in more killings (and yet another in 1851 came to the same locality at the mouth of Milly Creek where 20 men were shot). This killing party broke the back of Kurnai resistance and, aided by epidemics, the result was never in any doubt.

About two hundred Koories live in East Gippsland today, the majority at Orbost, the rest at Cann River. A co-operative has been developed (which generates a million dollar turnover), with its headquarters at Bairnsdale. Here they have established a medical clinic, day care and alcohol rehabilitation centres, a secondary school, student hostel, cultural, children's and housing programs.

Just north of the New South Wales–Victoria border, Block Head in the Nadjee Native Reserve. Photo by Colin Totterdell.

*The entrance to Cloggs Cave.
Photo by Josephine Flood,
courtesy Australian Institute of
Aboriginal Studies.*

Cloggs Cave

An important testimony to traditional Australia is to be found at Cloggs Cave, on the Buchan-to-Orbost Road, which was inhabited during the Ice Age. The cave, which lies at the foot of the Victorian Alps, 76 metres above sea level and 37 kilometres inland from the present coast, was discovered and explored by archaeologist Josephine Flood in the early 1970s. In her book, *Archaeology of the Dreamtime*, she describes her first impressions:

Outside the cave entrance was a rockshelter with the roof blackened from the smoke of many campfires. A short, rocky passage led into a dimly lit inner cavern, with a high cathedral-like roof . . . The back of the cave is higher than the entrance which means cold air drains out but warm air remains inside, simply rising to the back of the cavewhere there is a narrow passage but no exit. In fact, in every way it was a perfect . . . residence. Even had there been no traces of prehistoric occupation, I would have done a test excavation, but there was some small artefacts and mussel shells on the surface of the rockshelter floor.

More than a thousand years ago, this was a tool manufacturing area and thousands of small stone chips and flakes have collected from those operations over the years. In the inner chamber a series of 8000-year-old fireplaces have been discovered, together with ground ovens made from heated stones on which food was placed for cooking, and covered with bark and green bushes then hot ashes.

Around this time the diet included possums, koalas, bandicoots, kangaroos, rock and swamp wallabies, wombats and a wide range of birds. Digging further into the past of 20 000 years ago, the cave was the lair at times of the Thylacine and the Tasmanian devil (and the giant kangaroos which became extinct). Then, about 17 000 years ago the Kurnai began their tool manufacturing there, sharing the cave (at that time) with the owls.

As the Ice Age receded, more and more use was made of the cave and, between 13 000 and 9 000 years ago, the Kurnai were using it as a lookout over the valley, expanding their tool making and developing their fireplaces and ground ovens. They also used the cave for the treatment of hides and the making of cloaks and other items of clothing. Around 8500 years ago the weather became so warm that the inner cave (with its fireplaces) was vacated. The rockshelter was used from time to time during the past thousand years and tool making continued. Europeans invaded the Buchan Valley in the 1830s and within thirty years war and disease had taken such a toll that the cave was left to the bats.

The cave was used only by bushwalkers and cave explorers until its antiquity was established and today it is on the Register of the National Estate by the Australian Heritage Commission.

Wallaga Lake, with Mumbulla Mountain in the distance. Photo by Carmen Ky.

 # Across the border

Crossing the contemporary state border into New South Wales, we enter the lands of the Yuin people, who arrived on this coast about 20 000 years ago. The ancient centre of the people is Wallaga Lake, between two sacred mountains, Mumbulla and Goolaga, where the external spirits of the Dreamtime still live. This is the land of the five great forests — Bermagui, Murrah, Mumbulla, Tanja and Tanja West — all state forests today, that stretch from Wallaga Lake to Bega.

The Wallaga Lake region is my father's homeland and and the land of my birth. It was in 1931 that my father, Charles Penrith, walked all the way from Wallaga Lake to Lake Tyers, a distance of more than 300 kilometres, where he met my mother, who was then a young girl. They subsequently eloped, returning to Wallaga Lake, where she gave birth to four children before she died at the age of 21.

The Wallaga Lake area is rich in heritage and history and archaeologists have confirmed a continuous occupation of the area by my father's ancestors for around 20 000 years. For me the area is bountiful in heritage and tradition; I think of my grandfather, Bert Penrith, my great uncle, Percy Mumbulla and my father's spirit, now safe among the tall eucalypts and burrawang palms of the Murramurang National Park.

From a resource-rich ocean shore to forested hinterland, we had access to all the riches we could wish. Coastal peoples ventured inland for canoe bark and vines for fishing lines and we ate vast quantities of burrawang (*Macrozamia*) nuts, prepared by roasting then pounding the nuts and washing away the dangerous chemicals present in the raw plant.

The people of the Murray River area who resisted the overrunning of their traditional lands met a similar fate to others. A watercolour painting of a battle on the Murray River, courtesy Mitchell Library.

An epidemic of smallpox in 1789 preceded the physical appearance of Europeans, and a second epidemic — some thirty years later — decimated the Aborginal population. Venereal diseases — brought in by the whalers at Eden — contributed to the decline in population. Within fifty years of the arrival of Arthur Phillip and the colony in Sydney, the population of the Yuin people around Bega had dropped from many thousands to just 308 (in 1847).

The surviving few, herded up into reserves, fed tinned food, alcohol, tobacco, white sugar and flour, were destined to spend the next five generations on the dole. Despite the growing agony of dispossession from their lands, the people kept the traditional stories alive in song and legend, which were passed on to the younger generations. All the landforms of the area, from Mumbulla Mountain to Merrimen Island, in the centre of Wallaga Lake, are explained in the legends, and the stories have been retained by the elders of the people who now proudly proclaim their heritage. Over the years the people have ventured beyond the confines of the reserves and into the great forests where they were able hunt their traditional food. As a result of this supplementing of government handouts with bush tucker, these people survived the Great Depession of 1930s more effectively than many whites.

My great grandfather on my father's side, Biamanga, was of the Umbarra, or black duck dynasty. My uncle, Ted 'Gubboo' Thomas, is a widely travelled and respected spokesman for us, and has helped document our traditions and build a new future for my people. Bert Penrith (my grandfather), was a harpooner in the whaling days at Eden, working with his 'brother' killer whale to round up migrating sperm whales in much the same way a farmer uses his sheep dog. He was a giant of a man who, at the age of 80, could lift 2 bags of cement under each arm, from a crouching position. He lived until he was 107 and his voice, even in his later years, was so booming that he could be heard in a normal conversation, over a kilometre away.

The real centre of our universe is Mumbulla Mountain, and resting place (a sanctuary to my people) is Umbara Island (also known as Merrimen Island), in the middle of Wallaga Lake. In 1978 Gubboo mounted a successful campaign to stop the New South Wales Forestry Commission from logging on Mumbulla Mountain (named after Biamanga). The government accepted that this mountain was indeed a sacred shrine of our people and in 1980, 7508 hectares — centred on Mumbulla Mountain — was declared an Aboriginal Place under the National Parks and Wildlife Act.

The precise location of the sacred sites is not shown on any map, nor can it be revealed here. Most of the sites are on areas of flat ground along the tops of ridges, walked by my ancestors for thousands of years. Management of Biamanga Aboriginal Place rests between the Yuin Tribal Council, the National Parks and Wildlife Service and the Forestry Commission.

Our local creation mythology gives meaning to the landscape, including Biamanga and Goolaga (Mount Dromedary), and goes back far enough to

The quiet waters of Twofold Bay, Eden, which was the scene of an extraordinary relationship between local people and the mammals of the sea. Photo by Carmen Ky.

The author at the place of his birth, Mosquito Point, Wallaga Lake. Photo by Carmen Ky.

include the rising of the waters at the end of the last Ice Age. The legend was last recited at the burial of my grandfather, Bert Penrith:

Long ago, Daramulun lived on the earth with his mother Ngalbal. Originally the earth was bare and like the sky, as hard as a stone, and the land extended far out where the sea is now. There were no men or women but only animals, birds and reptiles. He placed trees on the earth. After Kaboka, the thrush, had caused a great flood on the earth, which covered all of the east coast country, there were no people left, except some who had crawled out of the water onto Mount Dromedary. Then Daramulun went up into the sky, where he lived and watched the actions of men . . .

The sacred mountains were the centre of a series of religious events staged throughout the area. Bora rings have been found in valleys nearby, which served as the sites for initiation ceremonies. The *dulagar* track, a route taken by one of the mythic beings from the mountains to the coast, is still known by some of the people at Wallaga Lake.

One of the most famous places on the South Coast is Tilba Tilba where lived, according to the legends of the Yuin people, the *wathagundarls* (small people who were believed to frequent the mountainous country). According to the story, the little people lived in rocks and caves and they were too dangerous to be trifled with. The wathagundarls were very strong and powerful; if upset, they would knock you down with a stick, tear your clothes off and drag you over to a bulldog ants' nest. The irate little people would hold you over the nest, and sit on you until the ants bit you to death. The bulldog ants would not hurt the little people because they were their *mudjinjarls* or spirits that could be called upon to do their bidding.

The little people of the Yuin story were always naked. They used bows and arrows and lived only on birds, eating their food raw and never making a fire. They came out in the evening just about dark, never left one another and had no language but only grunted.

Ben Boyd National Park, south of Eden, retains much of the original feeling of the south coast. Below, the Quoraburagun Pinnacles. Below right, Bittangabee Bay. Photos by Philip Green (below), and Colin Beard.

Today, the Yuin people on the south coast of New South Wales are rediscovering the culture which has enabled them to survive war, defeat and repeated epidemics.

Cattle stations were established around Batemans Bay, Bega and Twofold Bay in the late 1820s and early 1830s; a whaling station was established at Twofold Bay in 1828. By the mid 1830s the advancing invasion had reached the border of East Gippsland with a number of stations established around Genoa.

The two mountains, Goolaga and Mumbulla, in Mumbulla State Forest in the Eden district, are examples of sacred sites which have survived the last two centuries. Yuin elder, Guboo Ted Thomas, has described Mumbulla Mountain as of vital importance to the culture and dignity of the 3500 Aborigines living on the South Coast today.

The mountain, about 30 kilometres south-west of Wallaga Lake (and not far from Bega), is indeed a sacred mountain. Guboo Ted Thomas has pointed out that in the sacred groves of the mountain the initiation ceremonies of young men were carried out and the law was handed down to the people.

The Yuin people can still feel the spiritual power in the sacred places of the mountain and for them it is their cathedral. For thousands of years, young Yuin went up the mountain as boys and came back as men. Painted with red ochre, they would leave the bora ring to follow the Dreaming track from one sacred place to another, which were all visited in the proper order.

Spotted gums and macrozamia palms are found together in many places on the New South Wales south coast. Photo by Colin Totterdell.

A canoe tree at Broulee. Photo by Colin Totterdell.

At each place there were special ceremonies with singing and dancing to tell the story of creation in the Dreamtime. There were special tests, too, of hardship and endurance to prove that they were worthy of becoming men. The law was explained to them, they learned about Darama, the Creator, who gave the law to the people. It tells of the people's links with the land, our mother, from whom we are born and to whom we return.

The mountain represents the school where young men were taught discipline, respect for elders, and about food and plants, herbs and medicines, hunting, tracking and survival.

This process teaches respect for the land, and all its plants and animals. All things are bound together and all are part of the Dreaming, where unity and harmony must be respected. They learn about the Yuin people, about their totem, Umbarra, the black duck.

After the initiation is over, young men are led to the sacred pool where they wash away the red ochre of their initiation. This is the end of the Dreaming track and they then return to their families as men. Now they can live and hunt with men, as a part of the process by which elders guard and hand on the law. The law from the mountain guards the people.

Twenty thousand years ago, when it is believed the Yuin came to the South Coast, the sea level was some hundred metres lower and the shore 13 to 16 kilometres further out to sea. Ancient campsites have been found at Durras North, Burrill Lake and at Currajong (on the coast some 56 kilometres north of Burrill Lake). Rockshelters have also been found which testify to the lifestyle of the people over thousands of years.

The Eden whalers

Eden, on the New South Wales south coast, was, for over a hundred years, the setting of some extraordinary examples of interspecies co-operation which sustained a local whaling industry.

Local people had evolved an instinctive communication with a pack of killer whales (orca), which arrived in Twofold Bay each July and worked with them (and later the white whalers) to hunt and kill the baleen and humpback whales which passed close to the coast around Eden on their winter migrations. The killer whales, whom the people believed to be their long departed ancestors, would split into groups to hunt down the passing whales, before driving them in close to the shore where they could be harpooned by the whalers. When the migrating whales passed at night, the killer whales would attract the attention of the whalers in town by striking the surface of the water with their flukes.

Driven inshore, the whale was then easily harpooned and once the harpoon was secured the killer whales would hold the rope in their teeth (to slow down the whale) and leap across the blowhole as it surfaced to prevent it from breathing.

The dead whale was normally left to the orcas overnight — when they would take it to the bottom and eat the lips, tongue and fluke — before gasses inside the whale brought it back to the surface for the whalers to collect the following day. This co-operation — from the killer whales towards the Aborigines, and on to the whalers — has never been documented anywhere else in the world and gives Eden its own unique place in history.

My grandfather, Bert Penrith, was a harpooner at Eden for thirty years and I remember him telling me, as a child, of one time when his longboat was sunk by a huge whale 25 kilometres out to sea. But his brother, the killer whale, rescued all the men from the boat by allowing them to hold on to his dorsal fin while swimming gently back to coast, where he deposited them safely on dry land.

Apart from fish (with snapper, bream, parrot fish and groper predominant), there was also a range of game in the Yuin diet, including wallabies, potoroos, dingos, fur seals and possum. One campsite at Bomaderry Creek (a few hundred metres upstream from its junction with the Shoalhaven River at Nowra) is remarkable because the people ignored the good fishing and concentrated exclusively on game.

In contrast, a site 1.6 kilometres north of Curracurrang (in a small cove at Wattamolla) shows the people ignored the game and concentrated on fish such as snapper, groper and leatherjacket. Fish hooks and multipronged spears for fishing were used up the coast to Botany Bay .

The Yuin people escaped European domination only briefly. Even before the first official English exploration party reached Jervis Bay in 1791, guns and epidemics had already had effect and by the time Alexander Berry settled on the banks of the Shoalhaven River 31 years later with the blessing of the colonial authorities, the bloody years had taken their toll.

The Berry Estates at Coolangatta, Greenwell Point and Jervis Bay were the main centres for the Yuin people after the shooting had stopped. By 1900, two centres had been established in the Shoalhaven area — at Roseby Park, at the mouth of the Crookhaven River and, on Jervis Bay, near Huskisson — but the invaders kept squeezing at their lands and, eventually, the only communities which survived were at Roseby Park and Wreck Bay. Both have defied years of war and dispossession; today they look forward to a chance to build a new future.

The nation on the coastal region north of Shoalhaven was the Wodiwodi, their southern neighbours were the Wandandian. It was from a rock on the eastern slope of Coolangatta (NSW) that the dead, after burial in the sands of the shore, arose in spirit and departed for the afterworld. Grooves in the rock marked where they had slid down to catch a tall cabbage tree, visible only to the spirits of the dead, along which they would walk.

If they had not behaved well during life, a barrier of flames would block their path to after-life. Treading the fiery path they were further tested as the crow spirits threw spears and lizards threatened them. When they arrived in the paradise of plentiful game, if they were marked by a spear or fire, they could not stay. If they emerged from the ordeal unscathed, they were decorated and welcomed by a traditional corroboree.

Two bora grounds, located on ridges overlooking Wreck Bay, were used for initiation ceremonies, and for occasions of joy and celebration, as well as the religious ceremonies dedicated to the Dreamtime creators and givers of the law. Each young initiate had a front tooth knocked out to mark graduation. Governor Arthur Phillip had the same front tooth missing, which helped to make him welcome— before the war broke out.

The Bherwherre Peninsula and the surrounding area included two freshwater lagoons where bird life was abundant. The fertility of the countryside was promoted by firestick farming, and it yielded many vegetables. The fruits of the plum pine, lilly pilly, bush cherry, quandong, ground berry,

Above *The rugged coastline near Kiama.*
Above left *The tall, straight splendour of a blue gum forest on the south coast. Photos by Trevern Dawes.*

Mickey Johnson, of the Illawarra district. Courtesy Wollongong Historical Society, and the National Library of Australia.

geebung and native currant were all popular. New fern shoots were gathered and roasted and the large macrozamia nut was soaked in water to leach out the poisonous substances, then crushed and used to bake nutritious cakes. Honey was collected and a wide range of game, as well as pipis, oysters and cockles from the along the shoreline, completed a varied diet.

After the shooting stopped and the epidemics had taken their toll, the people who survived quickly adopted European maritime technology and became net fishermen capable of making their own gear and even pursuing large whales.

Wreck Bay led the way and Aboriginal fishermen suddenly found themselves citizens of the Australian Capital Territory. They had built their own homes, modest as they were, and fished (using nets), for mullet, blackfish, jewfish, kingfish, whiting and bream. The Wreck Bay fishermen would row more than 13 kilometres down the coast in search of a good catch.

Fish were freighted up from the beach by flying fox in one location, then loaded onto a Cobb & Co. coach (operated by local white people) or taken by rough road to the railhead at Bomaderry.

The community weathered the depression and its aftermath and in the 1970s the old spirit reasserted itself with the forming of the Wreck Bay Co-operative. A new spirit of independence now seeks to preserve the ancient settlement and its modern achievements.

The other capital of the South Coast, Wallaga Lake, remains as land belonging to the people. The last of the traditional initiation ceremonies was held in 1918 but the Yuin people today are developing new ceremonies to honour the creation heroes of the Dreamtime and the law itself.

Among the old sagas still told is the story of the *maleemas,* or beautiful women, who lived in the big caves near Nowra on the Shoalhaven River. They would 'sing' to a man they wanted to capture and perhaps keep him for six months.

Daruma of the Great Spirit still lives in the land. The hidden paths to the sacred sites lead to his presence and Guboo Ted Thomas explained: 'I go to the sacred places today. I wear the red head band as a mark of respect. I feel the power of the spirit which is always with us'.

A kangaroo hunt. Watercolour by Joseph Lycett, courtesy National Library of Australia.

The last stage of our great continental journey brings us back to the lands of the Eora around Botany Bay and Sydney Harbour. In fact, Kurnell Peninsula was one of the main centres of life in the area. The coming of the Europeans left relics in the form of bottle glass, clay pipes and musket balls.

Many believe that when Captain James Cook first visited Kurnell in 1770, there was a bloody clash with the Eora which was never recorded, but which was reflected in their attitudes 18 years later when the First Fleet arrived from England.

The Eora relied on fish as a staple and enjoyed oysters, cockles, whelks and abalone. Limpets and winkles were also popular. Their fish include snapper, bream, catfish, flathead and groper. Dolphins and seals were hunted and, inland, tiger cats, kangaroos, wallabies, possums, bandicoots and potoroos, snakes and lizards. Freshwater turtles were prized.

Tool-making stones were imported from other people for hammers and grindstones and they made use of nets, fish hooks and spears. Every day about fifty canoes would be dotted across Botany Bay, which was also an important meeting place for the coastal nations, the Eora clans and the Dharuk people of the Hawkesbury.

Portrait of a New South Wales Aborigine by Henry King, courtesy The Australian Museum.

Our arrival back at Botany Bay brings us to an end of our journey, which has covered the territories of hundreds of nations and a time span of 40 000 years. We have returned to the place which marked the arrival of the ships of the great European empires, and with them the beginning of a new era for the earth's oldest continent, Australia.

Botany Bay is also a reminder that it was here that 40 000 years of heritage turned a tragic corner in its destiny. In our journey around Australia we have observed many cultures, with different languages, lifestyles and customs. We've seen a vision of Australia as it was in the Dreaming on this, the greatest island on earth: every mountain, river, headland and plain having an explanation and clear traditional ownership. Yet all this land was declared to be owned by the British Crown on the basis that there was no-one living here, the infamous *terra nullius* policy.

This policy had arisen in part from the reports of James Cook and Sir Joseph Banks that the 'natives' were few in number and limited to coastal areas. Under British law, the only basis on which a claim could be made on 'undiscovered' lands was that such lands were 'desert and uninhabited' and the rights of nomadic peoples to land they visited irregularly was acknowledged. Arthur Phillip corrected this view in his earliest reports, reporting the 'natives' to be far more numerous than anyone had expected. And yet the British never changed the *terra nullius* policy, despite emerging evidence that the land was indeed populated.

The second governor of South Australia, George Gawler, understood the problem of granting land rights to the traditional owners when he observed that 'if the claims of the natives are not void before all, they are preliminary to all. They cannot occupy a middle station'.

Professor Henry Reynolds, in his book *The Law of the Land,* summarises the situation this way:

The official view has always been that Aboriginal claims were always void before all. The intellectual and moral gymnastics required to sustain that position have been quite extraordinary. Before the settlers arrived in Australia there was some reason to suppose that the continent was to some extent uninhabited and that the Europeans would actually be the first occupants. But that idea was known to be erroneous within a few years of arrival of the First Fleet and certainly by 1800 . . .

Outwardly a majority of white Australians has rejected the claims of historic injustice. But there has always been a sense of uneasiness, a lurking shadow of guilt, a 'whisper in the heart' which encouraged a tendency to explain the problem away by blaming the Aborigines themselves and to argue that they lost their land because they were too primitive, or too passive or too savage or too unproductive. It eased the conscience but did nothing for the moral health of the nation.

I hope this book has helped in a perception of Australia's real heritage. Only with such an awareness can the 'whisper in the heart' be answered.

Bibliography

Anderson, Lois P. 'The Role of Aboriginal and Asian Labour in the Origin and the Pearling Industry, Broome, Western Australia, 1862-1940'. BA (Hons), Murdoch University, 1978.

Barwick, Diane 'Equity for Aborigines? The Framlingham Case' pp. 173-218 in Patrick N. Troy *A Just Society? Essays on Equity in Australia* Sydney, Allen & Unwin, 1981.

Bennell, Eddie and Thomas, Anne *Aboriginal Legends from the Bibulmun Tribe*, Adelaide, Rigby, 1981.

Berndt, Ronald M 'Aborigines of the South-West' pp. 81-89 in R.M. & C.H. Berndt (eds) *Aborigines of the West: Their Past and Their Present*. Nedlands, WA, University of WA Press, 1979.

Bondler, Sandra 'Aboriginal Sites on the Crown-timber Lands of New South Wales: a Report' (Sydney) Forestry Commission of NSW, 1983.

Bonwick, James *John Batman: the Founder of Victoria*. Edited by C. E. Sayers, Melbourne, Wren, 1973.

Crawford, I.M. *The Art of the Wandjina: Aboriginal Cave Paintings in Kimberley WA*. Melbourne, Oxford University Press, 1968.

Dickson, F.P. 'Aboriginal prehistory of Botany Bay' pp. 44-50 in D J Anderson (ed) 'The Botany Bay Project: a Handbook of the Botany Bay Region'. Sydney, The Botany Bay Project Committee.

Dixon, Bob 'Words of Juluji's world', pp 147-165 in D.J.Mulvaney and J.Peter White (eds) *Australians to 1788*. Sydney, Fairfax, Syme & Weldon, 1987.

Dortch, Charles *Devil's Lair, a Study in Prehistory*. Perth, Western Australian Museum, 1984.

Draper, Neale 'Food resources of the Moreton Bay Aborigines', pp 124-127 in *Occasional Papers in Anthropology No 10*, 1980.

Egloff, Brian J. *Wreck Bay: an Aboriginal Fishing Community*, Canberra, AIAS, 1981.

Ferguson, W.C. 'Mokare's domain' pp. 121-145 in D. J. Mulvaney and P J White (eds) *Australians to 1788*. Sydney, Fairfax, Syme and Weldon, 1987.

Flood, Josephine *Archaeology of the Dreamtime*. Sydney, Collins, 1983.

Grassby Al & Hill, Marji. *Six Australian Battlefields*. Sydney, Angus & Robertson, 1988.

Gray, Dennis 'Traditional medicine on the Carnavon Aboriginal reserve' pp. 169-183 in R. M. & C. H. Berndt (eds) *Aborigines of the West*. Nedlands, WA. University of Western Australia Press, 1979.

Green, Neville *Broken Spears: Aborigines and Europeans in the Southwest of Australia*. Perth, Focus Education Services, 1984.

Green, Neville, (ed) *Nyungar:the People: Aboriginal Customs in the Southwest of Australia*. Perth, Creative Research/Mt Lawley College of Advanced Education, 1979.

Haigh, Christine & Goldstein, Wendy. *The Aborigines of New South Wales*. Sydney, National Parks & Wildlife Service.

Harney, W.E. & Elkin, A.P. *Songs of the Songmen: Aboriginal Myths Retold*. Melbourne, Cheshire, 1949.

Hill, Marji & McLeod, Neil *From the ochres of Mungo: Aboriginal Art Today*. Melbourne, Dorr-McLeod, 1984.

Howard, Michael C 'Aboriginal society in south-western Australia' pp. 90-99 in R.M. & C H Berndt (eds) *Aborigines of the West: Their Past and Their Present*. Nedlands, WA., University of WA Press, 1979.

Kenny, Joan M *Aborigines Melbourne*, Nelson, 1985. (The Port Phillip Project).

Kohen, J.L. and Lampert, Ronald 'Hunters and fishers in the Sydney region' pp. 343-365 in D. J. Mulvaney and J. Peter White (eds) *Australians to 1788*. Sydney, Fairfax, Syme & Weldon, 1987.

Lampert, R.J. 'Coastal Aborigines of Southeastern Australia' pp. 114-132 in D J Mulvaney and J Peter White (eds) *Australians to 1788*. Sydney, Fairfax, Syme & Weldon, 1987.

Lauer, Peter K. "Report of a preliminary ethnohistorical and archaeological survey on Fraser Island' pp1-38 in *Occasional Papers in Anthropology No 8*, 1977.

Lourandos, Harry 'Swamp manager of Southwestern Victoria' pp. 293-307 in D. J. Mulvaney and J Peter White (ed) *Australians to 1788*. Sydney, Fairfax, Syme & Weldon, 1987.

Macfarlane, Ian, comp. '1842 the Public Executioners at Melbourne', Melbourne, Public Record Office of Victoria, 1984.

Massola, Aldo *Bunjil's Cave: Myths, Legends and Superstitions of the Aborigines of South-East Australia*. Melbourne, Lansdowne Press, 1968.

Massola, Aldo *Journey to Aboriginal Victoria*. Adelaide, Rigby, 1969.

Maynard, L 'Aboriginal Rock Carvings in the Sydney Area', in *The Aborigines of New South Wales*. Sydney, Sydney University Press.

McBryde, Isabel *Aboriginal Prehistory in New England: an Archaeological survey of Northeastern New South Wales*. Sydney, Sydney University Press, 1974.

McDonald, Lorna *Rockhampton: a History of City and District*. St Lucia, Queensland, University of Queensland Press, 1981.

Meagher, Sara J and Ride, W.D.L. 'Use of natural resources by the Aborigines of South-Western Austrlia' pp. 66-80 in R.M. & C. H. Berndt (eds) *Aborigines of the West: Their Past and Their Present* . Nedlands, WA., University of WA Press, 1979.

Merlan, F. & Rumsey, A. 'The Jawoyn (Katherine area) Land Claim: Claim Book'. Darwin, Northern Land Council, 1982.

Mulvaney, D.J. *Cricket Walkabout: the Australian Aboriginal Cricketers on Tour 1867-8*. London, Melbourne University Press, 1967.

Nind, Scott. 'Description of the natives of King George's Sound (Swan River Colony) and adjoining country' pp. 15-51 in Neville Green (ed) *Nyungar: the People: Aboriginal Customs in the Southwest of Australia*. Perth, 1979.

Nugent, Ann *The Story of Fishing at Wreck Bay as told by the people*. Canberra, Schools Commission, 1980.

Petrie, Tom *Reminiscences of Early Queensland*. Recorded by his daughter Constance Cambpell Petrie. Hawthorn, Victoria, Lloyd O'Neil, 1795. First published 1904.

Posonov, V.V. *Results of an Archaeological Survey of the Southern Region of Moreton Bay and of Moreton Island (1963-64)*. St Lucia, Queensland, Department of Psychology, University of Queensland.

Quinlan, M 'Bellbrook: my father's country' in *Aboriginal Child at School, 1983, 11 (4)*, 19-20.

Reynold, Barrie 'Challenge and response in the Rainforest', pp 167-173 in D.J.Mulvaney and J.Peter White (eds) *Australians to 1788*. Sydney, Fairfax, Syme & Weldn, 1987.

Robinson, Roland *The Man Who Sold His Dreaming*. Sydney, Currawong, 1965.

Roth, W. E. *The Queensland Aborigines*. Vol. 1. Facsimile ed. Carlise, WA, Hesperian Press, 1984.

Roth, W. E. *The Queensland Aborigines*. Vol. 1. Facsimile ed. Carlise, WA, Hesperian Press, 1984.

Salvado, Dom Rosendo. *The Salvado Memoires: Historical Memoirs of Australia and particularly of the Benedictine Mission of New Norcia*. Translated and edited by E. J. Storman. Nedlands, WA, University of Western Australia Press, 1977.

Sherwood, John, ed. *Aboriginal Education: Issues & Innovations*. Perth, Creative Research, 1982.

Steele, J.G. *Aboriginal Pathways in Southeast Queensland and the Richmond River*. St Lucia, Queesland, University of Queensland Press, 1983.

Stuart, Donald. *Broome: Landscapes and People*. Photographs by Roger Garwood. Fremantle, WA, Fremantle Arts Centre Press, 1983.

Thompson, Kym 'A History of the Aboriginal People of East Gippsland: a Report'. Land Conservation Council, 1985.

Visions of Mowanjum: Aboriginal writings from the Kimberley. Adelaide, Rigby, 1980.

Index

To Lily

The production of a book of this scale requires the help of many people, to whom I will always be indebted. Their dedication over many years to help me complete this project has been a personal inspiration.

Of many people who helped with research and preparation of the material through resources at the Australian Institute of Aboriginal Studies, Marji Hill, Alex Barlow and Al Grassby all made significant contributions.

One of the most daunting tasks in compiling a book such as this is access to archival material and I believe the photos of the original Australians in this book — most of which have never been seen before — will help to build an important new perception. In this regard I want to thank all the libraries and museums who helped find and print this material, in particular the National Library of Australia, The Australian Museum, The Battye Library, The Library Board of Western Australia, The South Australian Museum, the State Library of Victoria, the Museum of Victoria, the National Museum of Australia, the Mitchell Library and the Macleay Museum.

I also wish to pay a particular tribute to the photographers and photographic agencies whose help was invaluable in depicting the Australian landscape and whose contribution, I hope, is clearly apparent. In particular I would like to thank Carmen Ky, Philip Green, Colin Totterdell, Bill Bachman, Grenville Turner, Oliver Strewe, Densey Clyne, Jim Frazier, Colin Beard and Peter Walton. Agencies such as AusChromes, Wildlight, Mantis Wildlife and Weldon Trannies have all been most supportive.

On a personal level, my sister Jan Palmer has always been dedicated to my succcess and well-being and my manager, Faith Martin has supported my endeavours and aspirations with unfailing loyalty.

And finally I'd like to state my gratitude to David Stewart, who supported the concept of the project when I first put it to him more than eight years ago. His belief in me and his untiring work to see this book come to fruition represent the difference between just 'another good idea' and the book you see before you.